ANTIPHONIES

ANTIPHONIES

❦

Essays on Women's Experimental
Poetries in Canada

The Gig

TORONTO, ONTARIO

For Tom & Marla,
& for Nancy Shaw

Antiphonies:
Essays on Women's Experimental
Poetries in Canada

Editing and typesetting: Nate Dorward
Printed in Canada.

ISBN 978-0-9735875-4-8

Cover design:
Gnocchi (www.mygraphicfriend.com)

Cover images from musical scores
by Catriona Strang and François Houle

THE GIG
109 Hounslow Avenue
Willowdale, ON M2N 2B1
Canada
ndorward@ndorward.com

web: ndorward.com/poetry/

CONTENTS

THE WOMEN (FIRST REEL): ON SUSAN CLARK

Edward Byrne

WRITING / CLASS

The publisher of *Writing Class: The Kootenay School of Writing Anthology* is rumoured to have said that his intention in publishing the book was to "finish off" the KSW. The introduction to *Writing Class* was first presented at a conference on "foundational narrative."[1] If the function of a foundational narrative is to sustain resistance in a moment of struggle, then the tale offered in the introduction is really more of an origin myth, the function of which is to sustain an institution once it's established, to buttress an entity whose completion already threatens dissolution or change. And doesn't the creation of an anthology *per se* serve such a function, even while quietly announcing, or prefiguring, a death? The use of an origin myth to frame this anthology is paradoxical – or, perhaps (giving the benefit), parodical – because institutionalization *is* death in the ethos of the KSW, and the introduction to *Writing Class* is highly conscious of this.

The anthology covers the years 1984 to 1994. It was precisely at the end of this period that an infamous and sensible proposal to restructure the collective was put forward at the Annual General Meeting. This was a moment in which the institution – for, in spite of its self-description, it always exists as an institution by dint of available grant capital – was up for grabs. There had already been a couple of silent bids – from the cultural studies contingent, from the feminist contingent. This particular bid – which actually took the form of a written, and therefore not silent, proposal, and was brought, at the AGM, to that unthinkable gesture in a culture of consensus and coercion, a vote – came from the direction of an older, patriarchal avant-garde, from the age of giants, itself prior to the heroic age. The women organized the resistance. Tears were shed, and in some quarters those tears, not the extraordinary turn-out or the impassioned speeches, were erroneously blamed for the defeat.

The KSW then fell into a period of desuetude. This period has been referred to, by some who still hold to the myth of a heroic era, as the "caretaker regime." If such a regime actually existed – and if the measure is attendance, at readings, at meetings, it did – there is room for some debate about its duration. Certainly by the time the KSW lost its grant from the city of Vancouver, probably for being "idiots" (see below, p. 15), the collective was back in fighting form. Beyond that arousal, however, the most dramatic regrouping was the soft, deep entry of a post-situationist contingent from the Friends of Runcible Mountain.

Having so far avoided the naming of names, I'm now reluctant to nominate an agent of change that led the school away from, in particular, instruction, which is to say the institutionalization of pedagogy as paid instruction – away from the notion, not that writing can be taught (of course it can be taught) but that it should be taught. It is necessary to name Aaron Vidaver, however, because one of his undertakings serves my narrative in a very specific manner. It was he who curated the series Anomalous Parlance. How he traversed the ground from Anomalous Parlance, which persisted in the fetishization of writing, to the anarchist political practice that produced the astonishing collective work *Woodsquat*,[2] is another story. For the moment, I'm interested only in the story (the reading) of Anomalous Parlance as redress.

Anomalous Parlance was a series of readings and talks that included Susan Clark, Lisa Robertson, Nancy Shaw, Catriona Strang, Christine Stewart, and Lissa Wolsak. In this essay, I will only be dealing with the work of Susan Clark, but I want to first situate the work of these women in the context of that now distant event.

Writing Class was marked by exclusions. Its editors cannily incorporate these exclusions into their narrative. Deanna Ferguson is treated, in the introduction, as if she were included. In fact, she is marked as included by her own act of self-exclusion.[3] Exclusion was her choice and, in the interpretation of the editors, an act of "cultural defiance" and "refusal" emanating from her own "obvious sense of exclusion" (42). Their comments on Deanna Ferguson lead directly into another, more ambitious tactical movement of incorporation, this time the incorporation of the women they describe as "Giantesses" or the "Barscheit Nation," confounding two or three far less than programmatic ventures. A reading of the "Barscheit Nation" manifesto as a subversion of futurism, seen as the prototype of a masculinist power discourse *in extremis*, is super-imposed on a group identity fabricated by the editors of *Writing Class* and called "the Giantess collective." Thereby "a contingent coalition working within the KSW" forwards their narrative, cor-recting a possible imbalance – a tendency to "subordinate gender issues to those of class" – by elaborating a language practice that foregrounds "other significant political issues besides those usually associated with capital and class relations" – i.e. feminism (42–43).

Catriona Strang, one of the so-called Giantesses, is also excluded from the anthology, again by her own choice, although this is not mentioned. A trace of this exclusion persists. She's the only author, besides Deanna Ferguson, who's listed in the bibliography but not actually included in the collection. I want to imagine, for the pur-poses of my narrative, that Catriona Strang excluded herself because of another, and this time not self-inflicted, exclusion – that of Susan Clark and Christine Stewart, who both figure in the recounted episode of the "Giantesses."[4] It's this exclusion that I wish to con-sider. And I'm not arguing, in any sense, that these writers should have been included, any more than, say, Tom Wayman or Colin Browne (founding fathers both) should have been included. The anthology is a retrospective polemic, a construction, an origin myth. It has a logic, an argument, which only a full analysis of its intro-duction and contents could unpack.

In brief, the anthologists argue for a writing practice which is, in itself, an opposition to capital and its relations of production and of class. What this means, however, is not a discursive practice which, through metaphorical illustration (Wayman's "hammer" [28–29]) or declarative command (Stanley's "explicit social com-mentary" [32]), interpellates a class-conscious subject and calls for political action, however vague that call may be, but rather a writing practice which reorganizes ("at the point of production") the lan-guage act itself, quite consciously and through the operation of a number of formal devices that can be, and are, in the manner of the Language School essay (polemic followed by close reading), readily identified.

I'm not convinced that this distinction is as distinctive as it's made to appear, or that the writers treated actually exemplify the latter practice rather than the former. In other words, I'm not con-vinced that the metonymical devices enumerated operate that differently from the metaphorical and iconic devices spurned. What is certain, however, is that the writers included in the anthology write, quite deliberately, from a class-conscious subject-position resulting from their own class origins, class situation or formation. The real antagonist is not Wayman or Stanley – allegorical propaganda or social realism – but what is characterized as "an aesthetic celebration of individual creativity," or romantic individualism, identified with the work of Robin Blaser and Brian Fawcett. In this respect, the authors, recognizing that they are not dealing here with the bourgeoisie, but only with bourgeois consciousness as they conceive it, assert that marginality, social exclusion (read homosexuality) or political disenfranchisement are not guarantors of an "objective perspective on social matters" (33). The KSW, suspicious of an individualism that speaks from this office, and far from being a "visionary organization" itself, addresses a much narrower and more manageable question: whether language can displace capitalism.

This would seem quixotic, except for the choice of verb. Isn't capitalism, as a set of cultural relations, or even property relations if these are understood only as counters, continually "displaced" by the heterogeneous social justice struggles we engage in, and by the antagonisms endlessly expressed within the poetries we propagate? Didn't Blaser put his queer discursive shoulder to the wheel with "Even on Sunday"? Don't Lisa Robertson and Dorothy Trujillo Lusk both construct texts that, within a rhetoric of address, "displace" the dominant relations of power, within and without the language they employ? Don't we live in the hope that all these minor acts of defiance, however they may be accommodated and recuperated, lead beyond a neverending displacement of capital, to its dismantling?

When I say that neither Susan Clark nor Christine Stewart belongs in this anthology,[5] I mean to judge them by the criteria the anthology itself establishes. I think that their work, like the work of others captured by Anomalous Parlance, *is* post-romantic. It's delirious not realist, excessive not minimal, dialectical not analytical, philosophical not sociological, argumentative, but within a rhetoric of figures, not Aristotelian. Its argumentation is constative and accumulative. It confronts the literary with its own decrepit image. Its retention of a disturbing kernel of the beyond is always utopian, not paradisal.

BELIEVING IN THE WORD

Susan Clark's *Believing in the World* (1989) is "a reference work," part of "an encyclopaedia project" (*The Round*). It is a dictionary, treating of words, but as if they had no boundaries. It is not phenomenological, in spite of a superficial resemblance to Ponge ("Fire enjoys reaching up," "Dust has no ambition"). It has no desire to break down the barrier between word and thing. In fact, it redefines words, puts them to other uses, develops them as terms of art, more in keeping with philosophical than with poetic practice, more like Levinas than Ponge. The "grass": "multitude" and "neighbourhood."

Where does this particular notion of the reference work, of the encyclopaedia, come from? The encyclopaedic impulse is there in modernism, but more as a need to write the world, its totality. Here, as in the work of Christine Stewart (*Taxonomy*) and Lisa Robertson (*The Apothecary*), among others, it obeys more of an avant-garde (surrealist *and* feminist) impulse to subvert the authority of the reference work by adopting and then mocking its form, its reach.

Their encyclopaedic work is ludic, festive, disruptive. The encyclopaedia is an impossibility, like the dictionary or the index – like empire (the apotheosis of patriarchy, which in itself, as a micropolitic, is not impossible at all). It is the impossibility of the encyclopaedia that fascinates, precisely because it prefigures a rupture within the order that requires it. These works despise authority. It is the authority displayed in rhetoric, in the structure of language, in grammar, syntax, that is attacked. "We are Flaubert," says Debbie. "Think hard; when we speak of style, we speak of desires. They vex a prick's ubiquity," says "The Barscheit Horse."[6]

"Believing in the World" sounds like the title of a self-help book, or an immense, naïve reaching toward faith in a wonder-working immanence. And this book, or pamphlet, carries remnants of a literary style that will be stripped away as Clark's work progresses towards a grand subversion of the book, of literature, of rhetoric (argumentation), away from an approach based on overarching devices – literary or surrealist games – like the mock dictionary, or even the encyclopaedia.[7] However, the title is immediately undercut by its subtitle. "Believing in the World: a reference work" is an excellent joke because, of course, a reference work both cannot be, by definition, and always is, in its usage, a matter of belief. Belief in the world, like belief in any totality, like belief, is something we fall into, endlessly. It is at once the motor and the horizon of all our acts. "Believing in the World," of course, can also be read as an act – believing, as an act that takes place in the world, has no exterior locus or destination. The problem of belief stands at the outset of this book, and weaves its way through it like a delicate and debilitating fabric.

Believing in the World begins with "Fire." "Fire" is perhaps the most Pongean of these texts and here, at the outset, marks an enduring aspect of this body of work, a certain overdetermined relation to words. That they are abyssal, and dear. It is finally only the thing, or the word as thing, that can be grasped, like a newel post, to conquer vertigo. But the thing is not the referent, it is the whole material world into which the word sinks, by which the word is distended.

Stuck here, a complaint took the form of an appeal, and I was advised to reread the first section of Levinas' *Totality and Infinity*. After that rereading, I can't help but invest this text with meta-physical desire. "Fire enjoys reaching up," toward the most-high. "And its reach means forever." There is no destination for such desire, no totality into which it can be absorbed. "Fire is the riot of one being." There is no transcendent other, no absolute other. "If I say we, you infer love." The only other is the other person (*l'autrui*). "Fire can remember nothing." But this other is, precisely, abso-lutely other.

"Grass" ("infinitely underfoot") speaks of the "multitude, neigh-bourhood" in which "each human [is] a single event." "Train" speaks of the "hair's breadth, earshot" which separates us, of the "subtle pow pow pow of our selves colliding." "Love" describes us as "arched each over the pitch of so great a distance to fall and wait and wait til we *can* fall." "A bridge which collapses leaves two shores. Or is all this impossible. In which we both wake and sleep." The acts which move against this binding (*religio*), which "distend" us (Levinas, or Clark), "the way out of what you are," "are neither consumption, nor caress, nor lethargy" (Levinas). "It is impossible to ask this much" (Clark).

It is tempting to continue thus, to read Levinas into the "face to face" in "Age." But I begin to feel a distortion, and a nostalgia for the other (*l'Autre*) finds its way back into the text. In the "face to face" with death, age "gives over, bit by bit" to its "next being."

But what is death but the absolutely other, and the other a reminder of our (eventual) not being? "Next being" then = proximal
being.

With "Dust" I completely lose the thread of this imposed reading
(not a close reading, but a forced reading, admitting its violence).
Reading "Dust" I wish I had commenced this exercise with Kristeva
rather than Levinas. Dust "by smutting wishes to illume." There
is another, persistent, thread here, in the abject, the most-low.

Anyway, the point is not that *Believing in the World* is a gloss of
Levinas – it isn't. It is, however, a poetry that accumulates into an
argument, as do the philosopher's vertiginous but agglomerative
sentences. It is, ultimately, reaching, tentative, essaying, but thetic.
However, the thesis will remain always just beyond grasping, an
"apparatus of impossibility." In this its poetry outstrips its thesis
and always will.

There are other characteristics of this first book that persist: a
black humour, born of fear ("Husband in a brittle bed: snuff!
sparito"); the unbounded aphorism ("A woman is better than sol-
diers"); the apparent puzzle ("This cups hands around something
just in front of the spine . . ."); the dire/comic apothegm ("If
something is deadly poison, someone must've died"[8]); a classifying
mania, which here is contained within the apparent larger structure of a reference work, but later becomes pandemic; an erosion
from within the structure of the book (unanchored footnotes and
cross-references); the hysterical, the phobic, the abject ("In their
house everything is normal but the smell," "The fresh green of
vegetation in the water makes us queasy"); the disastrous, the
irreparable, as in Dickinson (see "Love": the collapsing bridge, the
flood, choking, gynocide).

And the lyrical. The lyric is a miniature of the encyclopaedia. A
small, contracting, but always complete universe. In this body of
work, the lyrical is a rupturing, intrusive, echoic impulse, an
interruption, like the lyrical in Braxton's compositions – not an
appeasement, not a demonstration, not nostalgic, but an homage
to the impossible, past and future.[9]

The last piece, "Rain," takes the form of lyric – or at least some
of its sections have line breaks, caesurae (hardly any enjambment),
and some of its lines make conscious use of number. Opening the
book with Ponge, closing with Dickinson, one could speak of a
lyric mastery binding the work. To give an example:

7.

I did not kiss but drank kisses
The sky lies over so

Spent, given
Any one word is too large

As you are minutes are gone from the world
The buildup consists of deaths

And my house is of paper
The rain smells of the other

Repeat, repeat
Exhausted, choose

Surprise gathers, wept

And yet, the lyricism is overwhelmed by other cares. And still, reading "Rain," I want to cling to the Levinasian vocabulary – the "voluptuous," "'Is' copulates among us amock," "The rain smells of the other." And yet we are not compelled to the Levinasian conclusion of hospitality.[10] I think we will not arrive there, in spite of an increasingly ethical textual comportment.

In a sense *Believing in the World: a reference work* stands in a symmetrical relation to *as lit x: the syntax of adoration*. If one wished to tease out a larger structure, with these two pamphlets introducing and closing the body of this work, one would then have to contend with what lies between, the ruin of the book, its debris.

(THE TEXT'S NIGHTMARE OF THE BOOK, BURIED ALIVE)

structure

I thought this was the completion of my book, forthcoming, ever forthcoming, called *Suck Glow*. It seems to be turning into a book of its own. I thought it was going to be more in the vein of encyclopaedia and it seems to be turning into a play of some kind. This was going to be an article – so called – called "Topics of Mental Life," with many sub-heads. It now seems to be something called "Theatre of the New World of the Time" with many "Characters" or "Situations."

> – Susan Clark, introductory remarks to a reading
> at the Kootenay School of Writing, June 1993

I'm going to read from a manuscript called "Tied to a Post," which is in a state of wildness. "Tied to a Post" is subtitled "essay in abstraction." It's the first part of yet another book. Actually, there may just be tiered books. It's part one of *Idiot Fit . . .* Idiot fit, in other words the idiot made, not born. And the idiot is from the Greek *idion*, which is the origin of our word "idiot." The *idion* is a citizen who does not partake in the functions of the polis, does not fulfill the duties of a citizen.

> – Susan Clark, introductory remarks to a reading
> at Robson Central, October 1998

A section from book two of *The Round* appeared in the first issue of *West Coast Line* (another, earlier KSW anthology),[11] where it was announced that a further installment would appear in *Motel*. This work, however, bears a closer resemblance, at least structurally, to subsequent writing than to *Believing in the World*. Perhaps *The Round* is morphing into *Suck Glow*, the first appearance of which occurs the same year in *Motel*. In particular, this "new" work mounts a more direct attack on the structure of the book. "Pages" become numbered units detached from the pages they necessarily inhabit. "Pages" are noted as "following" other sections of text in a very unpagelike manner. The text itself takes up a critique of the book:

I fall upon a book: it's flat, hard, only opens; is as though only one could feel.

This sense of the world as already articulate: past tense. Reality being not "the vain sexual ecstasy of an object," but a book exploded to fill the shelf.

Every memory so quickly losing our feet,
vs.
the immense vertical concrete contemplation of the whole book, closed.

The books with which I say I have "a romantic and sexual rapport" sit on the shelf.

And yet the book always remains the intended, if impossible, armature of these writings. Books are announced, tables of contents are provided along with bewilderingly small and partial selections in numerous journals. At readings, everything is put in the context of its, supposedly, larger structures. *The Round. Suck Glow. Theatre of the New World of the Time. Bad Infinity.* The latter is shown as fragments of sections: "Tied to a Post," "the Agglomerative," which may themselves be imagined as books.[12]

These "books" seem to overlap, flow into each other structurally ("there may just be tiered books"). *Suck Glow* becomes, perhaps, *Theatre of the New World of the Time.* And the sections often break down into smaller embedded structures. "Gether" is published as "from 'the Agglomerative'" which is described as "a classifying section of *Bad Infinity.*" But "Gether" consists of various "sections" ("Sticky, 0 / [the ontological section]," and so on) within which are small lyrical stanzas resembling the "pages" seen elsewhere in *Bad Infinity,* and similarly titled: "ontos I.. i.," "ontos I.. ii.," for example.

All of this amounts to a delirium of classification, a parody of structure. But in a certain sense it continues the careful de-structuring of the rational that began with the encyclopaedia work. The encyclopaedia is at once a dream – on the cusp of modernity – of containment, of an interwoven, bound whole, a totality, which reaches its apex in Hegel, and an utter impossibility, the fulfillment of which would embrace infinity. This is what the "structures" of Clark's work tell us. These are "apparatuses of impossibility."

syntax, or debris

Proposal: Language contains many apparatuses of impossibility. It has to. Or, it just does.
> – Susan Clark, "Notes towards a discussion of the Poetics of Impossibility" (Dec. 5, 2000, for a KSW seminar)

A primitive, super-sophisticated artificial intelligence: syntax.
> – "Notes towards a discussion of the Poetics of Impossibility"

The writing takes the form of a series of propositions. Often syntactically peculiar, seemingly incomplete, undecidable. There are lyric elements, lyric shapes, but overall one is drawn to puzzle not to sing. However, *no amount of reasoning will untie these knots.* There is almost more delirium in the texts than in their structure, or

their delirium is also structural – "a delirium of syntactic destabi-
lization."[13] One is endlessly stopping over phrases. As if they would
yield to a prolonged gaze. But, impossibility's darlings, they won't.
And it's really their *way* of not yielding that is interesting.

The subtitle of Clark's thesis on Emily Dickinson refers to
"syntactic and epistemological aporia as radical poetic apparatus."
She speaks there, and elsewhere, of "apparatuses of impossibility"
and posits a poetic operation that attempts "what neither language
nor the wind can attain." This is not an uncommon approach to
poetics, particularly after Mallarmé. One is tempted, immediately,
to make reference to hermeticism, or back to the "romantic individualism" thesis of Barnholden and Klobucar.[14] However, there is
no gesture toward "the rosy world" of the sublime, the ineffable,
but rather an embrasure, a distention, within the wholly other,
infinity, the abject, death, the impossible. The interesting thing
to me, in this context, is the cohabitation of a heightened and
omnipresent use of address, and a simultaneous opacity of discourse. The hospitable and the inhospitable.

"These poems," she says of Dickinson's work, "are not riddles
with known answers, they are not the treasures of any system's
sales pitch" (7). Puzzles are a form of address, inhospitable to the
extent that the puzzle-maker holds or withholds the answer. Does
the unanswerable puzzle result from the madness of the questioner,
the inhospitable Mad Hatter, or from an unbounded hospitality, a
gift of diminished reference?

There is a sense in which this writing – what I'm calling the
debris of the book, between *Believing in the World* and *as lit x* –
constitutes a form of "phobic speech," of language as the construction of a counterphobic object, "emptied of meaning, tearing at
high speed over an abyss, untouched and untouchable" (Kristeva,
52–53).[15] This work, as it progresses, carries forward the contest
with structure,[16] but more and more at the level of syntax, the
structural apparatus becoming a joke that is no longer, in itself,
puzzling.[17] That is, most often the line, or the sentence, gives the
appearance of a thetic proposition, but its syntax breaks apart any
such possibility. It is not a surrealist sentence, undoing itself through
the marvellous, but a fractured sentence broken by its own lack of
limitation. One has an overwhelming sense of being addressed,
and of questions being addressed, but feels oneself, and the questions, endlessly displaced. One does not want to think this hard
and come up empty-handed again and again. But it's impossible

to leave it alone, to stop picking away at it, because it never offers itself as a simple pleasure, like tautology. This is not a generous discourse. No sufficient reward in image, music, thought – only failed intellection. Or is that a free lesson?

didactics

– the encyclopaedia is secretly modelled – like language – on the religio-romantic concept of Devotion which makes it all better by proposing then necessitating an infinitely postponed salvation to clean up the mess.

– Susan Clark, "Gether"

Belief, she says somewhere, throws us beyond knowing. "So, if adoration's mind only wishes to drive our mind beyond itself, its best hope is this syntax – a machine only the mind obeys, and exquisitely, to death" (*as lit x*, 19). Belief. Adoration. Devotion. A delirium. Hysteria ("bursts along the stream of Blank's [Blanche Wittman's] memory banks" ["Gether"]).

But, Susan, belief *is* the structure of much of our knowing. Hence believing, adoration, devotion become cynical acts of knowing. No amount of reasoning . . .

Oh, I know that that "beyond itself" doesn't exist. How many times have you told me? . . . (*as lit x*, 20)

Not a utopia, a dystopia. Here. No amount of reasoning . . .

Reasoning brings us only to a series of short cul de sacs. See, for instance, "wont I.. iii. Where stolen heat . . . wells . . . the things then . . ." ("Gether"):

> Poor mine dug, she's in my hands
> and hands don't see the apples out of reach

Sometimes it's as if the word is the unit of composition, displayed so that they, the words, cannot accumulate into phrases. "Poor mine dug . . . ." One wants to put them together. Mines are dug. The mine may be what this writing is after. The impossible, abject in its presence, poor. But golden. "Mine" is also the interior. "Dug" also the exterior, the breast. My (mine) breast. Apples also breasts, also golden, out of reach. But one is left finally with a cluster of words: poor, mine, dug, and the pleasure of the unsayable, accented, heated (she does have an ear).[18]

> But a yellow it
> flicking 'round and 'round
> its green button – oh darling
> oh – suddenly – o'clock –

The "a," *l' objet petit "a,"* is, of course, absent, silent.[19] The hands
(of a clock) flicking round its button. Orgasm. (This is the "love"
section of "Gether," where the "to" is noticeably more absent.)

> where lauded and harping
> the little arms junct
> any self in their midst
> a mere and
> (I'm / we're)
> dissolute from study

And one wants to say "Masturbation!" or "Time!" as if responding
to a riddle, like those poems from *The Exeter Book of Riddles* she
appends to the Dickinson thesis, where, for example, the answer is
obviously "penis" but really "onion." (See the next poem in this
sequence, "wont I.. iii / But [*that is*, aubade].")

And you wonder, "Where do these poems come from, Susan?"

And she says, at the bottom of the page, "And of course these
come / out of nowhere and I say / nothing every time has occurred /
hotly. . . ."

After the "Anomalous Parlance" reading of *as lit x* someone told
me that they found the performance unsettling. For that spectator
it was like watching something unpleasant, involving another's
pain, an accident scene. The writing somehow anticipates this reception in its own phobic repetitions. There are, for example, the
accident scenes (not always accidental). A woman struggling,
trapped in a submerged car ("Gether"). A woman plunging from a
rooftop ("Theatre"). "Like a person might blow up of their own
accord, hmmmm?" ("Theatre"). The bus bombing in the [blown]
"Beyond recognition" section of *Bad Infinity*.

But for me this perception of the performance was simply a
confounding of the writer and the text, an assumed specificity of
addresser and addressee ("I was fucked by you recently"), a perception of the writing, the performance, as symptom. I remember
feeling defensive and referring to Artaud: "To have done with the
judgment of god." But this, upon reflection, is an inept comparison.
Artaud demonstrates that there is no dividing line between madness
and reason, except the intensity of pain. One *must* not separate his

madness from his writing and observe it. But Artaud is hurling himself, from an interior pain, from his flesh, against a totality that is external and prevents his access to infinity,[20] against a totality such as nascent postwar American imperialism.[21] Whereas Clark throws herself (images of being thrown, stumbling, falling, occur frequently) outside herself and toward an infinite, an unknown, which is not on the other side of an oppressive totality, but right there in the other, the reader, the auditor. She displays a vulnerability, but also a pride that she is not pleading. Deaf ears hear.

She stood in that room and tossed a rope "across open water in high seas from boat to boat" – footnoted as "or this little gap between us, three feet of linoleum."

I remember another occasion, a seminar announced as "The Poetics of Impossibility," perhaps an attempt to open a conversation on the heels of *as lit x*. She offered questions in a long announcement. "Is abjection an infinity device?" "Is the transcendent a place of abjection?" "To ooze between subject and object in a place language has no name for?" "Are waste and the irrational . . . value?" An enormous reading list we were invited to add to. A *nota bene*: "This [the KSW] is a poetry environment (favours the additional), not an academic one (rhetoric as device)." This time, a long seminar table rather than the open space of a room. A large turnout. Her refusal to respond to inquiry, to instruct. I have a poor memory of the occasion. I remember that we talked, questioned. She abdicated responsibility to us. Or could not see any difference instituted by her place at the head of the table. An unwillingness to submit to interrogation, as if she were after a model of the seminar that did not yet exist – the seminar as psychoanalysis. A technique like that of the woman who falls into psychoanalytic practice in Chantal Akerman's *A Couch in New York* – an empty affirmation that facilitates the cure, "Yes, yes, mm-hmm."

The aim is not to answer questions, it's to get out, to get out of it. Many people think that it is only by going back over the question that it's possible to get out of it . . . It's very trying. They won't stop returning to the question in order to get out of it. But getting out never happens like that. (Deleuze, 1)

AS LIT X

As lit x is a pamphlet, an "essay," a performance. It is a gloss of *Bad Infinity* perhaps. Or it's a part of *Bad Infinity*, very likely.

"Bad infinity" is a Hegelian concept. In translations of Hegel I find "spurious infinity," "wrong infinity" and "negative infinity." I find "bad infinity" in Marcuse. It's probably in Althusser too. And in Lenin (perhaps the source of this translation), "Schlechte Unendlichkeit" is translated as "bad infinity" and glossed as "infinity qualitatively counterposed to finitude, not connected with it, separated from it, as if the finite were *Diesseits* [on this side], and the infinite *Jenseits* [on that side], as if the infinite stood *above* the finite, *outside* it. . . . In fact, however, *sind sie* [they are] (the finite and the infinite) *untrennbar* [inseparable]. They *are a unity*" (112).[22]

In Hegel bad infinity is endless repetition of the same – infinity is merely the other of finitude and hence itself finite. "Something becomes an other: this other is itself some[thing]: therefore it likewise becomes an other, and so on *ad infinitum*" (94). He also refers to this as "the infinity of reflection." Or the infinity of understanding. "Good" infinity (true, genuine infinity) finds, in the fact of the other being determined by the same, a limit of a different sort. In this fact of sameness, something becomes other but in becoming other remains itself, an unbounded infinity. Levinas would see Hegel's good infinity as, in fact, a totality, a false infinity. Hence one could say that Levinas (Clark) opts for the bad infinity in which the other is truly other, infinitely other, and our salvation, our humanity, can only be in this recognition, in the face of the other.

> I was fucked by you recently.
>
> It made me think about modes of pronominal address. (1)

This, as a beginning, in that small room, was felt as imprecation, implication. You damaged me, threw a spanner in the works, or, *not* taken metaphorically, his "engine" in her "furnace mouth" ("from *Suck Glow*"). One wanted to look around ("Who, me?"). But didn't. "You" was us. Which she makes clear on the next page. "I wish you all lose yourselves [in sex]." And then we are, perhaps, cursing her: "Fuck you, Susan." Which she glosses as "forget you." An intricate dialectic of forgetting. Forgetting where we are. Forgetting ourselves. And "she" is standing in front of "us." "We" are sitting before

"her." "I" wants to forget "you." Momentarily. And then, adoration. Fucking as adoration. But this is immediately abjected, falls
into the gruesome, the impossibly other, which is beyond before.
A *summa poetica*: "Impossibility is that which is adored: the delicate machine which is meaning but can't produce it" (*as lit x*, 5).

This notion of adoration, this reaching after, which is a reaching
toward the infinite, within a kind of abasement, makes my skin
itch. There's a Christianity internal to this discourse which, for
me, is allergenic. When Levinas says that his philosophy can be
summed up in the expression "Après vous," I immediately imagine
two such acts of generosity before the other (*l'autrui*). "After you."
"No, after you." Then a *really* bad infinity ensues, à la Groucho
Marx. Or: pursue a singular, relentless submission and you will
get fucked (over) anyway. And perhaps want to. "It is use of the
other as annihilation of the self" (*as lit x*, 11).

But then, again and again, I realize that this is a practice that
sees its own foolishness, is self-annihilating.

Is there nothing unimportant on which I can wipe my hand? ("Not Not")

It was so beautiful I fell over / and from where I lay could not remember why
("Theatre of the New World of the Time")

Shot by self after argument. ("Not Not")

"As lit x," the phrase, compresses, condenses this complex – but
indeterminately, or interminably, somewhat like the "winging girls"
she tries to unpack for us in *Bad Infinity*, becoming herself a bewil-
dered reader ("from *Bad Infinity*," 20). *As lit x*:

> As lit annihilates. . . .
>
> *[tu] as lit x,* you have bed x, or *[tu] as lit x,* you've read x (*as lit x*, 8)

And one could extend this paronomastic exercise, supported by
the text:

> as (if)
> a slit
> lit(erature) [*lits et ratures*]
> lighted
> landed upon
> x [*sous ra(p)ture*]
> ex (over*ex*cited, in*ex*haustible, self-refl*ex*ive)
> times
> X [*crucified*]

And so on, or, disseminated, as paragram, as virus:

> *as talk, it's*
> *as essay, it's . . . itself*
> false alterity
> as a *writing* practice after Levinas
> Levinas says language itself
> Absolute waiting
> Lit which knows what's here, it
> as *it* slows its content
> *all, that's it*
> As lit the nomad

"'my encyclopaedia' . . . *look* at this mess! / . . . Achiastics, wrecked, ma" (12).

And all this pandemonium in the hands, in the grasp, in the embrace, of the idiot (one who loses rights), the "immigrant" (one who has no rights), of the nomad (20).

It is in this debilitation of the totality, of the encyclopaedia, that I am with her still. It is, yes, a "self-destroying [Tinguely] machine" called "my encyclopaedia" (12). But, in its endlessly coming apart it continues to work away at the given, at the structure of the whole, with a "delicate" wrench.

And its syntax must forever and forever be a syntax of adoration which throws itself and goes nowhere – passive, hopeless, overexcited, inexhaustible, self-reflexive and useless, of course – like the finest poem in Creation. (12)

Stumbling here, once more, I feel momentarily – perhaps it's the phrase "finest poem in Creation" that raises a welt – an enemy of this writing. As I feel an enemy, over and over, of so many poetic texts – and of poetry, which I nevertheless can't escape.[23] And then she addresses me, again, in this very predicament.

Oh, I know that that "beyond itself" doesn't exist. How many times have you told me? . . . And isn't the State – some dyad, a kind of mirror stage, made explicit, then denied – a model, too, of our amorous inauthentic indistinction, a place where 'beyond' doesn't exist? [This, literally.] The polis had one word for it: *not*. I'm learning. (20)

A response to the obvious, "political" critique – "romantic individualism." The "state," constituted in ideology ("a kind of mirror stage") is figured as a "model" of good infinity, "a place where 'beyond' doesn't exist." That is, being outside the state is non-being, the *idion*, the idiot. As language, "our language" comes to us as law, "from us to us" (p. 20). We are, then, within it, as lit, standing here on the spot marked "x," instituted. . . .

Notes

1. See *Foundational Narratives: Proceedings from the Foundational Narratives Interdisciplinary Graduate Student Conference*, ed. Stephen Collis and Sharon Alker (Burnaby, BC: Simon Fraser Student Society, 1998), where an earlier version of the introduction appears as "The Wobbly Roots of the KSW" by Michael Barnholden, Andrew Klobucar and Dorothy Trujillo Lusk.

2. *Woodsquat*, ed. Aaron Vidaver (*West Coast Line*, Fall/Winter 2003–4).

3. She also chose not to participate in Anomalous Parlance.

4. I have no way of knowing this, being too lazy or dishonest to ask. The so-called "Giantesses" are left to be represented by Lisa Robertson and Nancy Shaw.

5. Obviously – I repeat – I'm being unfair to the anthologists by making all sorts of assumptions that may be unfounded. But I don't care. Don't anthologists set themselves up for this kind of treatment? Besides, I think it would be insulting to the editors of *Writing Class* to assume that their choices merely resulted from taste or other contingencies, particularly when they've written a fifty-page introduction for which the poems then become exempla.

6. Lisa Robertson, *Debbie: An Epic* (footnote to line 388); Lisa Robertson, Christine Stewart, and Catriona Strang, "The Barscheit Horse."

7. "The encyclopaedia at first suggests embrasure then palls . . . (see also: 'plute')" (Clark, "Not not").

8. Compare this with Levinas' "The doctor is an a priori principle of human mortality" (234), although don't ask me why.

9. This procedure is reversed in his "standards." That is, the standard form gives an appearance of completion, stability, but is interrupted by moments – techniques, devices – drawn from the outside.

10. Or is this really Derrida's term? "Bien que le mot n'y soit ni fréquent ni souligné, *Totalité et Infini* nous lègue un immense traité de l'hospitalité" (Derrida, *Adieu à Emmanuel Levinas*).

11. *West Coast Line* (Spring 1990), ed. Larry Bremner, Miriam Nichols and Lisa Robertson. *Raddle Moon* 17, "some Vancouver writers," is also a KSW anthology, and a response to *Writing Class*.

12. It is suggested, in *as lit x*, that the book is really called *Pandemonium* (13).

13. The phrase is from Christine Stewart's "This Then Would Be the Conversation"; it's attributed there to Clark, though it doesn't quite appear in this form in *as lit x*.

14. *Writing Class*, 20–21. A more cogent critique than escapism – and one which I feel breathing down my neck at the moment – would be based on the figure of "impossibility" itself, and its manifestation in language as tautology.

In *as lit x* Clark defines tautology as "pure meaning" (27). But see Tzvetan Todorov on Blanchot, for a critique of this strategy: "Blanchot's writing itself confirms at each moment this desire to liberate 'thought' from all reference to values and truth; from all thought, one might say. It's often been said of him that his 'je parle' is a way of rejecting all 'je pense.' His favourite stylistic figure is oxymoron, the simultaneous affirmation of something and of its opposite. . . . But simultaneously to affirm A and non-A is to put the assertive dimension of language into question and, effectively, take discourse beyond truth and falsehood, good and evil" (72, my translation). I think that Clark feels herself on the horns of this dilemma when she responds, *"Tautologous but ardent!"* (*as lit x*, 27).

15. See also David Marriott, "Signs Taken for Signifiers: Language Writing, Fetishism and Disavowal," in *Assembling Alternatives,* ed. Romana Huk. I am also indebted to Jeff Derksen and Lisa Robertson's essays which frame that collection.

16. The encyclopaedia – Diderot and Alembert's – is at once a manifestation of the state, a contest with the state, an impossibility, and a structure of patriarchy.

17. "The faux-rigorous, relentless, structuring devices – nesting, indices, supplements, footnotes, tables of contents, cross-reference – are to counter the fact that every successful page or poem self-annihilates. They're the corpse of it. And I'm sorry but I think that all the earnest *apparatus* – is just funny and a bit frightening. Like someone else's sex toys. Evolution?" (*as lit x*, 37).

18. One definition of "agglomerate": "clustered or growing together but not coherent" (*Webster's*).

19. The repetitions across the time of the work are astonishing: "The moment round and *a*round / . . . 'a' instead of 'I'" ("Not not"). One could cite endless instances of unmarked cross-reference which reinforce the impression of one large structure (the book).

20. "C'est un mot / dont nous nous servons / pour indiquer / l'ouverture de notre conscience [le néant] / vers la possibilité / démesurée, / inlassable et démesurée" (Artaud, 48). That is, the impossible.

21. ". . . ils veulent à toute force et par tous les moyens possibles faire et fabriquer des soldats / en vue de toutes les guerres planétaires qui pouvaient ultérieurement avoir lieu, / et qui seraient destinées a démontrer par les vertus écrasante de la force / la surexcellence des produits américains. . . ." (26).

22. "Everything (human) passes beyond its bounds (*Trieb, Schmerz*, etc.), but *Reason*, if you please, 'cannot pass beyond its bounds'!" (111). Lenin reading the greater *Logik* – this is how he spent his time in September 1914!

23. "The hatred of poetry is the proper material of poetry" (Phillipe Beck).

Works Cited

Artaud, Antonin. *Pour en finir avec le jugement de dieu.* Paris: Gallimard, 2003.

Beck, Phillipe. *Crude Marivaux.* Trans. Kevin Nolan. Cambridge, UK: C.C.C.P., 2001.

Clark, Susan. *as lit x: the syntax of adoration.* Vancouver: Friends of Runcible Mountain, 2001.

———. "from *Bad Infinity.*" *W* 3 (2000): 46–55.

———. "from 'Not not.'" *West Coast Line* 24:1 (Spring 1990): 76–81.

———. "from *Suck Glow.*" *Motel* 3, 1990.

———. "from *Theatre of the New World of the Time.*" *Avec* 7 (1994): 94–99.

———. "Gether." *The Gig* 3 (July 1999): 30–37.

———. "Impossibility – Exhilarates – Who tastes it: syntactic and epistemological aporia as radical poetic apparatus in Emily Dickinson's poetry." M.A. diss., Simon Fraser University, 1995.

Clark, Susan (as Susan Yarrow). *Believing in the World: A Reference Work.* Vancouver: Tsunami Editions, 1989.

Robertson, Lisa, Christine Stewart and Catriona Strang. "The Barscheit Horse." In *Exact Change Yearbook*, ed. Peter Gizzi, 123. Boston and Manchester: Exact Change and Carcanet, 1995.

Deleuze, Gilles and Claire Parnet. *Dialogues II.* Trans. Hugh Tomlinson, Barbara Habberjam and Eliot Ross Albert. 1977. New York: Columbia Unversity Press, 2002.

Derrida, Jacques. *Adieu à Emmanuel Levinas.* Paris: Galilée, 1997.

Hegel, G. W. F. *The Logic of Hegel.* Trans. William Wallace. 1892. 2nd ed. London: Oxford University Press, 1968.

Huk, Romana, ed. *Assembling Alternatives: Reading Postmodern Poetries Transnationally.* Middletown, CT: Wesleyan University Press, 2003.

Klobucar, Andrew and Michael Barnholden, eds. *Writing Class: The Kootenay School of Writing Anthology.* Vancouver: New Star Books, 1999.

Kristeva, Julia. *Pouvoirs de l'horreur: essai sur l'abjection.* Paris: Éditions du Seuil, 1980.

Lenin, V. I. *Collected Works*, vol. 38. Moscow: Foreign Languages Publishing House, 1961.

Levinas, Emmanuel. *Totality and Infinity: An Essay on Exteriority.* Trans. Alphonso Lingis. Pittsburgh: Duquesne University Press, 1969.

Stewart, Christine. "This Then Would Be the Conversation." See pp. 107–24 of this book.

Todorov, Tzvetan. *Critique de la critique: un roman d'apprentissage.* Paris: Éditions du Seuil, 1984.

FROM BAD INFINITY

Susan Clark

page 1 .. A clock

a clock is birds or no birds

birds are a clock or are no clock

> mother peer suck me
> wipe your face off on my sleeve
> such slack municipality
> this taken place

page 2 .. The taken place

a thing falls out
of a tree and lies
on the ground

> that nothing who's we bartered gave
> in the buckets of time we have

meaning to stand for unfallen the

> poor baby who could
> be dead and still not be clean
> you
> who
> could be dead and still not be clean

page 24 .. The army

"Revolutionary superperformance is a routine payoff
of advanced ideological dedication" – Mark Elvin

page 24 .. The army

The army would not speak of its warmth
– crowded nothing –
a small racket near sight
added an infant which is hearing
his big hands lit
then nothing
which is the army

page 24 .. The army

Like its might like
steps up which bore me
no resemblance
though it so much tends to make us by removing punctuation
think we are its
like

page 24 .. The army

Its might like steps up which bore me no resemblance
though it so much tends to make us by removing punctuation
think we were its
fell

behind and beneath us
– drawn –

as if its

page 24 .. The army
(start over:)

or
he was that man
drawn into the pasture
where someone identical with himself already was
unrecognizable

page 24 .. The army

as if
        held

to
what is standing
as if

this side
of the glass

        held
to the brink of the
screen / – 'home' –

like looking deeply into the eyes of a cow

page 24 .. The army

and
when you fall you fall
like a bag of shit
or

page 24 .. The army

. . . or, it might just be
a rejection of formal likeness

page 98 .. Disinterested ownership

The tail wags the monkey's vulva
Centre part these
Sovereign waters

Be careful, it loves "everything"
A, the

page 98 .. Disinterested ownership

Plaque, parcel, pork, plot
A, the.

The *beloved* this that has no name   *Capitalized* like the President's
body, undone   And the pieces in space, projected there
A, the.

The *woman* penis and yet it's
in rags

A "savage joy, mixed with shame, . . . Of belonging to someone,
and feeling oneself freed from liberty"

page 98 .. Disinterested ownership

My devotion wags the/his excess flesh
whose *head* cracked a nectar stream it   like
Is she loves "nothing" as
can't
its copulative trigger aches

page 98 .. Disinterested ownership

Cut the penis away and let him be used as a woman, say
like
a the
woman, or swept
along by the force of dependence

sit

page 98 .. Disinterested ownership

each to hang for damage to a machine (1812)

January 10, 2004: His answer was a little slow because he was
playing the arcade game and talking to me at the same time

page 98 .. Disinterested ownership

my heart swims in blood[1]

in deep space[2]

lain

1. Bach
2. Hubbell, photographs

LISA ROBERTSON:
HOW PASTORAL IS MORE
AND MORE POSSIBLE

Peter Larkin

Frank O'Hara throws in a towel of sorts in his "A Pastoral
Dialogue," given that "My hands beneath your skirt don't find
weathers" (60). O'Hara is a declared ancestor for Lisa Robertson's
own re-skirting (as non-avoidance) of pastoral desire, which attains
a virtual culmination in *The Weather*, a text which offers desire
a restituted pastoral domain rather than simply libidinizing a
cast-off genre as a counter-measure to roving hands. O'Hara's
"Oranges: 12 Pastorals" includes a usable affirmation: "This is the
miracle: that our elegant invention the natural world redeems by
filth" (9). At such a moment the male poet seems to abut
Robertson's own play with a self-transforming of desire so that
porn can be relegated to the commonality of a broader loam of
wish. Her "Roaring Boys" in *XEclogue*, though "vicious as a burnt
lip tongued," are nonetheless "sulking as a flicked skirt, cradled
in the precise euphoria of a method held in reserve – Dirty
per se" (Eclogue 8). We find ourselves reading "as a" where we
might have expected "at a." Is the "method held in reserve" here
something of pastoral's own resource of *otium* modifying a floating
libidinous euphoria, so that the "Dirty" is also what "breeds sentiment but what else is there to walk on. . . . The cushioning ground
urges us to remeasure our impatience" (Eclogue 9)? Much of
Robertson's work prior to *The Weather* makes no bones about its
preference for an apparently superseded pastoral which aims to
re-site or shelter in gender terms a tactile suburban theatre of soft
pleasures in the teeth of how the actual grounds may have been
laid out by a supervening cultural power. My own rather sketchy
and collagist reading of her work will aim to identify within it
traces also of a more reparative pastoral which remains protective

32

of the over-againstness of the natural. It is one which can offer an extra-urban or "provincial" (to borrow Robert Pogue Harrison's term)[1] horizon, just where the urban clearing actively forgets or surpasses nature from within the city's capacity to legislate nature within green, emparked spaces prematurely cleared of the non-human.

This tension between a divergently sybaritic or a re-versionary ecological pastoral remains apparent (it's an indication of Robertson's strength that it's allowed to be so) right through a project which Tanya Brolanski dubs a "pastoral of poetic bodies." As "How Pastoral" phrases it, "The trees leaned masochistically into my absence of satisfaction. They were trying to fulfil a space I thought of as my body" (21). While the space "thought of as my body" alludes to a collusion between trees and male landed property (simultaneously male desire), it is a domain which interrogates genuine differences in how a space is fulfilled in relation to how the human appropriates it, appropriations not themselves realized until they are *themselves* leaned into. This idea gets elaborated in another place as "The world was leaning on us, leaning and budding and scraping, as if it too was subjected to strange rules never made explicit" (*Occasional Work*, 250). One of the virtues of renewing pastoral may be to articulate what strange rules still lie out in a world which *can* be patiently distinguished from its oppressive or pseudo-naturalistic acceptations.

In her manifesto "How Pastoral" Robertson confronts the question of how to negotiate with a complicitous but would-be disingenuous genre head-on: "I wanted a form as obsolete yet necessary as the weather. I begin with the premise that pastoral, as a literary genre, is obsolete – originally obsolete" (22). That the weather can be timed out by the urban is both a pathos, an irony and a lived cultural actuality, but new necessities immediately flood in to fill that space of cultural self-arbitration which is so persistently less than autonomous (i.e., culture, which gives frame and history to human judgment, cannot "re-give" what is provided *to* it, which is what also posits horizons which cannot be so contained). Robertson can claim with justification that the pastoral genre is obsolete *ab origo*, though that gives little indication of what to do with its traces and residues, or with what might be read as "anoriginal" (i.e., primordially plural) or as rediscoverable and still-to-be-encountered horizons of the "provincial." Eighteenth-century aesthetics would never decide whether pastoral bore a legitimate

trace of the Golden Age or was meretricious urban nostalgia
(Rosenmeyer, 222).

It seems more natural to us that the birth of pastoral coincided
with the decline of the Greek polis and the appearance of the quasi-
modern metropolis that was ancient Alexandria (Poggioli, 3).
Medieval pastoral, which had been little more than an interlude
within epic action (the notorious pick-up point for a passing knight
within the subgenre of pastourelle) itself slipped towards a Renaissance reappropriation of Virgilian pastoral (which could include
both misfortune and prophecy); Christian pastoral elegy is itself a
steep shift, for ancient pastoral had been commemorative of death
but not included mourning as such. Virgilian pastoral lends itself
quite happily to postmodern reappropriations of the genre, as the
themes of imperial displacement are there for the taking, but Virgil
had been able to include these threads precisely as they wandered
into song. A more strenuously naturalistic pastoral of knowing
about and working with the land he had relegated to georgic.

Milton's intensification of pastoral elegy to break-point in *Lycidas*
is usually seen as having exploded the genre for subsequent writers,
for whom pastoral in any way faithful to shepherd song had gone
irremediably soft. It is at this cultural juncture that Robertson
makes her appropriating move, and the way is open to recuperate
a pastoral whose own cultural inertia is a useful tool for redressing
other forms of cultural marginalia anything but soft. Lady Mary
Wortley Montagu wrote a knowing set of "town eclogues" much
admired by Pope and transcribed by him, inevitably to be thought
of as good enough to be *by* him. But these eclogues prolong as well
as transpose the genre, not simply because a disabused woman of
the town retreats to "some deserted Place," but because in such a
spot "no false Freind" will "mourn my Ruin with a Joyfull Heart"
(Wortley Montagu, 50). How do "Gentle streams" "weep," and
how does their beatitude differ from *schadenfreude*? It's clear pastoral
is a slippery convention adept at turning to sharp complaint, and
Paul Alpers sees satire as at times the prevailing mood of pastoral
(Alpers, 30); pastoral can also add further reference points, those
residual contextualizations of paradise which never quite disap-
pear over the horizon. Rather, they are the horizon, a reminder
that surfaces curve and recess (i.e., deepen) as well as undergo
layout.[2]

If "skirt" indicates a switch towards the politics of pastoral girls
in Robertson's poetics, her initial skirting over the equally prob-

lematic area of Romantic naturalism (with its close links to the emergence of ecology) confirms her in a particular moment of pastoral, rather than an appropriation of the genre/anti-genre as a whole:

A system is ecological when it consumes its own waste products. But within the capitalist narrative the utopia of the new asserts itself as the only productive teleology. Therefore I find it preferable to choose the dystopia of the obsolete. (*HP*, 25)

Non-progressive pastoral may be more *counter*-utopian than dystopian. Are ecosystems simply consumers of waste in this context, or is waste not also retrievable as a sedimentation of fertile contour, which as such can be fruitfully overdetermined (made various or "re-various") along one direction, just as it remains underdeterminable or persistently obsolete in another. Alpers describes how the "soft" pastoral of antiquity and beyond eventually gave way to a hard pastoral of the mind at serious work in the later eighteenth century (263). Romantic naturalism's own appropriation of the genre is scarcely less radical than Robertson's, opening the way to a mutual interference of genres (and so indirectly some revitalization) rather than a strategic intervention beyond the point of generic exhaustion. Wordsworth's *The Prelude* reworks and "weakens" epic modes so that pastoral *otium* in its turn can mutate towards his own brand of visionary (i.e., heroic) mildness. Robertson's declaration in her manifesto that "[o]ntology is the luxury of the landed" is arresting polemic but simplistic cultural history (*HP*, 21). It can be argued how, even in the case of the picturesque, rewriting the landscape as ideal view was increasingly the work of the landless itinerant tourist (Gilpin published his work to raise money for a Poor School) and coincided with the rise of the middle-class professional writer (Michasiw, 94–95). Rachel Crawford has charted the mutation of the sublime of landed expansionist landscape prospect towards a frequently female intensification and domestic intimacy within the space of the suburbanized cottage or kitchen garden in the early nineteenth century (Crawford, 178ff).[3] By the 1790s it is the romantic pedestrian who is, if anyone, supplying an emergent ontology of landscape as distinct from either parliamentary enclosure or enclosed parkland. Anne Wallace has examined Wordsworth's own perambulations as a version of cultural labour which negotiates, out of a newly critical regionalism, both the landless poor and the landed mighty, together with the fraught status of the cottagers, the latter being Wordsworth's own ideal of independence without accumulation or of common, self-sufficient memory (Wallace, 61ff).

It's more difficult, in the light of this heritage, to maintain that pastoral is too generically introverted to be concerned with the natural world, or to perpetuate pastoral solely in the form of anti-pastoral. Robertson's reversion to a pre-Romantic, formally antiquarian pastoral re-incurs for her own purposes the decadence of the genre, but she never treats its residual seductiveness superficially and doesn't wrap it up within a self-destruct version of itself. She accents traces which still seem like their own defence. Robertson doesn't block, where it happens in a desultory way, the intermingling of the dream of a liberated sensuality with another equally marginal fantasy, the relation between tactile surface and a pristine openness to the givenness of the world. It is there Robertson verges on that moment in pastoral which Ann Vickery (writing on Barbara Guest) characterizes as "a perceived distance between the epistemic and the natural [that] is being undone" (253).

XEclogue, though apparently less concerned with this pastoral reserve than *The Weather* will prove to be, allows, nonetheless, its strategic vigilance to lie down with bedfellows not wholly oppositional. Trees suck-in oblique allusion and complicity like spongy moss but they are less than agents *per se*, and their ways of being about the city outskirts are both tugging and untagged.

> We felt this as the cabinet swung open
> We felt a strong burst of vitality ("Epilogue")

This closing tribute to the "green cabinet" tradition has after *XEclogue*'s ten sections earned some respect for vitality whether roaring (as in the "Roaring Boys") or not, so that unbounded vitality acknowledges a pastorally ownerless *otium* (you can't "dispossess" without vigilance: you can't unburden merely through vigilance). Lady M pronounces: "My back's to the wall. How can such slim felicity so bruise the trees?" (Eclogue 1). The trees strikingly bruise as totems of the male landed, but again might themselves be harmed if a backs-to-the-wall eroticism or a felicity reducible to self-advertising slimness continues the game of human monospeciesism, gingering up on gender issues but reducing trees to an indifferently libidinous backdrop. Robertson's whimsical poetic is open to such a further reading and repeats its possibility, even within a paradise which, at first touch, possesses a harmony "leather-like in unreality" (Eclogue 1). Green leaves go leathery by mid-summer too (spelling the death of the pastoral moment), but erotic desire seeks its own springtime when the libidinous is no longer wall-to-wall but open to how trees install an outplacing of this desire not simply the displacement of internally political intensifications of desire. The "coniferous movement of air" (Eclogue 5) (presumably flaunting the erotic gymnosperm) is felt on the skin but competes (at the last) with all the other surfaces of transgressive desire and utopian rehabilitation. "The woods are retrospective; they shelter biographies, histories and criticisms" (Eclogue 6). Rather a lot is being pasted up on those "walls," but what would a history or criticism make of being sheltered and how transformative would that be? Are such things always already overseen by a tree which then gradually seeps in (weakly enough) as a mutant amid all the other terms of that strategic catalogue of human configurations? So to hurl oneself at the past, however, is to use a language which "plantlike, anticipates its own destruction. Yet my negation caresses" (Eclogue 6). Plants put in for a stronger *destruktion* and, within negation, human caresses cancel out their own preferential species-specificity.

We're outside the garden. A perspective extends like a green aperture through which we view another world. For a moment, all the figures have been replaced by foliage. There is almost a fusion of what is nebulous reverie with the dark wood of ragged allegory. (Eclogue 10)

We may be outside the garden, but not as exiles, if in front of a Switzer-like perspective onto landskip, along an allee which is indeed a "green aperture." That world in view would be one of ownership and progressive agricultural production, but rather than hold an avenue of trees to figuring an economized plan, Robertson plays-in another world able to be replaced *by* foliage. A way seems open towards the more exactingly nebulous patterns of *The Weather*, though *XEclogue* does not itself choose between a more straitened ecology and the "dark wood of ragged allegory," a Dantesque realm where natural forms remain burdened by human inter-gender struggle/compensation not yet calibrated in terms of what might translate them on still further. Readers sense that the gender polemic persists as the most urgent horizon, actively reinscribing the natural onto a human scenery, but that also there may be other horizons of the natural which need to be precisely that –

unburdenable even while in the midst of the interminable teasing out of human self-violence and self-making within a world which might yet exceed any pure domain of the constructible. "The private earth dissolves, blooms, contemplates its horizon" (Eclogue 10). Does Robertson leave us the hint that the earth is too intimate to be *merely* the scene of our collective privatizations? "When I say 'life beside power' I mean destruct the formal destinies . . . unlock that paradise I mentioned earlier and give them back a renovated flower" (Eclogue 3). How to come to a "renovated flower" beyond the decor of reappropriation unless this means pastoral's dream of a gift *to* human culture, or pastoral's obstinate remainder-reminder that the human home is provincial to our own urban centring, the actual lay-out of our life?

What is the role of a male voice in this? Must it remain oppressively normative, however restitutive, when arguing for a natural horizon ushering in a more seemly self-dedicatory "death" of the human, but at the price of restoring the living death of a gender hierarchy? What work for male genius? Can it earn any grounds for its own initiative, or must it concede the absolute priority of the female symbolic, in which it can of course share, especially where that symbolic opens to the destiny of the couple, which would be Luce Irigaray's transcendently gendered horizon (a horizon at which she can be surprised by the male)? Or is the male voice now so radically nomadic by way of self-reaction that it inhibits new female localities or any specific gender-regional configuration?

Something has to go soft if it is to crouch or lie down on immediately overlooked surfaces. "For the politics of girls cannot refuse nostalgia," one of the *XEclogue* voices insists (Eclogue 6), and Robertson elsewhere notes that "[n]ostalgia, like hysteria, once commonly treated as a feminine pathology, must now be claimed as a method of reading or critiquing history. . . . Nostalgia will locate precisely these gaps or absences in a system which we may now redefine as openings, freshly turned plots" (*HP*, 25). Some postmodern sociology would agree: the sense of nostalgia is not ahistoric but particular to certain places at certain times. To be homesick demands a knowledge of being without a home and as such may operate as a hermetic justification of the modern which posits a comforting past as that which can be no more. But this is not incompatible with a capacity to transcend prevailing forms of the modern, a transcendence within which nostalgia may make the struggle against reification more absolute. Though within one sort of postmodernism nostalgia itself may be no more than a style or revocable aesthetic choice (Tester, 64–78). In Robertson's work we are never very far from the revocable, and if this suggests a lightweight appropriation of pastoral in her work, that would be to overlook the more strenuous aspect of her feminism, however much it invokes/revokes a sort of touchy-feely gorgeousness. "The additional complication of ecofeminism remains determining," Benjamin Friedlander judges, and Robertson's swerve to a city pastoral neatly chimes with Frank O'Hara's view: "a woman stepping on a bus may afford a greater insight into nature than the hills outside Rome" (quoted in Vickery, 249), where we can assume that this is anything but woman as naturalized object (such a figure would be "stepping off" not "stepping on"). If urban pastoral seems like a counter-naturalization of what surrounds (nature) by what is surrounded (the city), as well as a reversion to the megalopolitan origins of the genre, Friedlander is quite right to emphasize the "eco" attachment to Robertson's feminism. This might seem less of an issue in *XEclogue* or *Debbie* (there are clues) but it can hardly be avoided in *The Weather*. At such a moment it does become possible to ask: how does gender garden the wild? To what extent is gender a culturally admissible alibi for wanting to regress somewhere else when it comes to lying out on the grass? Given the need for an alibi to get to grass, and pastoral's docile obsolescence keen to be so reappropriated, does pastoral still come freighted with implications of desire which themselves test the limits of feminism for the female voice? How do the horizons of pastoral and feminism intersect if neither chooses to be the exclusive tool or identity of the other? The resulting hybid, eco-feminism, may simplify/amplify horizons every bit as much as it complicates terrains.

In Luce Irigaray's work horizons of gender reinstate the question of structure, as indeterminacy may not be so straightforwardly liberating for a female construction of personality after all (Lorraine, 220). Irigaray reserves the right to argue that some forms of identity are more empowering than others, and that stratification is endemic to living. Deleuze and Guattari themselves acknowledge that smooth space never exhaustively surpasses the stratified variety. An embodied subjectivity specific to time or place draws on a configuration which is less than every possibility, or involves a capacity to turn as well as drift or flow: "Disjuncts must be chosen in which incompossibles are ruled out" (Lorraine, 235). This renewed

understanding of the re-sourcing and stabilization of female personality has some rapport with the ancient vow of "stability," the
self-promising to be faithful to a place (as being open to everywhere by being able to posit itself as less than everywhere). Nostalgia in this context may be a some kind of fixing agent for the
sort of difference which makes marks. A classic view of nostalgia is
that it erases the gap between nature and culture, so a strategic
role for pastoral would be its tendency to cling to a nature prior to
or suppressed by human culture (Crawford, 60). As such pastoral
fits exactly the ubiquitous arbitrations of culture itself (the genre
could not be a more artificial inscriptional essay, with its "esse"
opening out the decorums of the political) while retaining for itself
the "leisure" to recall that culture's own insufficiency and non-
autonomy (culture is always underlain or overshot by something
somewhere else). Culture depends, it hangs upon a subversive but
re-versionary *otium*.

> In the upper
> left corner improbable clouds grouped
> and regrouped the syntax of polit
> esse: The feminist sky split open (*D*, lines 138–41)

Such a cloud syntax (ecologically exacting, atmospherically precise
as well as descriptively problematic and open to an idling conde-
scension) is already homing on *The Weather*. As such it is possible
for the feminist sky to open productively: beginning from a cleftness
of restitutive claim (or feminist masque caught in the paradoxes of
the sensible transcendent), but going on to open to its own self-
othering, whereby the female sky has an immediacy of desiring
atmosphere no longer that of a feminized sky.

> Do you remember the day we wanted
> to describe everything? We saw a
> euphoria of trees. This was the middle
> ground. (lines 25–28)

"Euphoria of trees" is shockingly exact, as well as a shock idling.
From Geoffrey Hartman we learn that pastoral, a last-ditch stand
against any totality of demystification, is itself implicated in a
euphemism or "euphemia" of language, a speaking well of the world,
or a speaking wellness from a "weak" middle position between
ecstasy and trauma (*Easy Pieces*, 148ff). Until now the trauma of
gender-deformation has tended to seek redress within some form

of counter-ecstasy in Robertson's work, though remaining pastoral enough to be softened up for a site, never quite free-floating. The "day we wanted / to describe everything" is a day with clouds overhead, those exact indicators of weather which frustrate static description. If *XEclogue* and *Debbie* work out from the ethos of radicalized Renaissance and Early Modern eclogues, *The Weather* locates itself more in view of the prosier (but never quite discursive) textures of Romantic naturalism.

Jen Hofer's spicily atmospheric review of *The Weather* shows how the poem gives us experience filtered through meteorology, the weather as "a window through which to read experience. As readers of the weather we are caught in the syntax of broken cloud movement, in the desire for accuracy of description, emotion, perception, belief, in the space outside our bodies, within which our bodies occupy an inquisitive niche." We can afford to ask: how exactly do clouds break, and how would their syntax break into a self-consciously "language" poem without there also being some mutation in the way nebulous things break? How easy is it to characterize the "niche" which our bodies occupy, or is pastoral more active here, its claustral speculations good for reworking such confined spaces (of exposure) so that the inquisitive doesn't just reticulate or comb but contemplates?

Clouds were slow to close with any history of their own. For a long time painters could only represent them in highly conventional and weatherless ways, even at a period when the terrestrial landscape was coming to the fore. It wasn't even possible to name clouds until Luke Howard (a contemporary of Wordsworth and Constable) devised a system (based on altitude rather than shape) which won acceptance. Celestial decor came to be seen as the most precise of weather indicators. Ruskin's treatment of cloudscapes in *Modern Painters* aimed to show how a virtuoso particularism would finally see off any lingering traces of the picturesque. Clouds were now nothing if not visible but also implicated in the problematic overflowing of the descriptive line. Was this purely a question of imagery, or was it part of an esoteric syntax more like sky-writing? Constable's cloud-studies were forms of natural transition, and as such he didn't look for randomness in their variability but towards the expression of complex dynamic principles. More recently Michel Serres has suggested that any exact knowledge of clouds would require an infinite amount of negentropy, and any economy of description that wanted to convert cloud to schema would cost the entire future. Order is itself a margin or exception to a more primordial cloudiness (Serres, 32–37). This itself may be verging on an overreading of clouds. Clouds may be better at lessening into marginal relations but remaining relational for all that, neither proposing ongoing randomness nor demanding an expenditure of mastery. These lesser defined waifs and wreaths of the atmosphere attract if anything a cultural over-representation while persisting as underformed "objects." As Arden Reed notes, one predicament which characterizes Romantic writing is the need to create images of a material which comprises no objects properly speaking (Reed, 13). How smoothly does the language of clouds run with the "improperer" speaking of language poetry? Robertson's pastoral mode insists that her weather stays out of doors, where clouds as the underformed can subsist as the undeformed, or the most natural of recourses for what is unnatural in the image. Clouds no longer conventional must go on attracting assimilable invention, whether broken or not. But a pastoral unfazed by this insight re-naturalizes convention as "convenio," the coming together of humans in the outside, which is what Robertson as sensuously calls the "social."

The Weather is more attentive to the "language" mode of fissured, paratactic declamation than are Robertson's earlier texts, where a svelte elegance had more wrap-around effect on syntax. *The Weather* is multifarious in texture (with the use of a litany-like segue) but the voice is tentatively lyrical or less apparently distributed across overt dramatization or eclogic dialogue. The high syntactic frontal flow (or cloud-floe) arranges the voice across both private and choral. As such, usable quotations from this text deter exemplary targets and leave an impression of severed gobbets, which accords with the overall compositional texture in any case. There may be few actual rents in the diurnal fabric of the writing (each main prose section is named after a day of the week, beginning with Sunday), but the micro-separations around each declamatory pulse both lean into self-quotation and partly withdraw from an overall logic of interpretation. That's probably as it should be. Everything else that matters continues. My impressionist sampling of *The Weather* would feel itself pulverized and sucked back by the entirety of the text, were it not that the figure of weather implies a survivable ratio (and relation) between the onflow of text and the micro-cells of its patient texture (see Larkin, 125–26).

The shades of Nancy or Lady M from *XEclogue* can be sensed

among the boscage but this is speech siting itself rather than cutie-parading in landscape:

> Skirt stretched
> taut between new knees, head turned back, I
> hold down a branch (*W*, 7)

Fashion-innovation is irreverently displaced onto knees themselves whether draped or nude, and knees might get renewed by walking outdoors. If so, does this imply a skewed, almost embarrassed shift from amorous decor towards naturalist sentiment? Is the branch held down for support, to look at the view, or to look up at what the weather may be doing to the sky on a day when a branch is sufficiently unchafed for it to be able to engage the human hand? "[O]ur expression of atmosphere has carnal intentions. We also do decay" (30). The cycle of death reinforces the self-sufficiency of the libidinous, but we trip at the thought the carnal might also express atmosphere. It's a fleecy jolt which moves death as sensuous reinforcement towards an outranging of the rage of desire itself. "[T]he description itself must offer shelter" (30), i.e., an account as weathered as this is sheltered not by being timed out by death (and so reverting to the erotic screen of the species), but by "timing out(side)" amid the days of the week, the basic framework for *The Weather*'s series of prose-poems. This is a timing which indicates where it is by means of the local configurations of circumambient, driven spaces. "[T]his weather is the vestibule to something fountaining newly and crucially and yet indiscernibly beyond." So opines the sky-blue, looseleaf "Introduction" (reprinted in *OW*, 63–69); in terms of its own rhetoric, which forthrightly shows forth and delectably argues, "indiscernibly" is a shock. "Indiscernibly" linked to its "and yet" can't simply talk up the new and the crucial, and the whole process of *The Weather* seems more to do with a *discernible* eco-social beyond, i.e., no horizons without the weather for it. Is this then Robertson's own *via crucis*, the appearance (in disappearance) of quite another mode of desire which comes to meet bodily desire but which greets it indiscernibly? A moment where Robertson's project of being urbanely embodied amid the weather is exceeded by the atmosphere's own capacity to launch the body along (rather than through) a further outness, so that the body remains on the earth's surface but makes room for its less than discernible earthly horizons?

"But the history of the atmosphere is recklessly slow" (*OW*, 68) can be read as a distinctive and errant delay behind the self-fleeting of the erotic. If its sluggishness is neither monumental nor cumulative, streets of cumulus may not be street-wise either but more like Wordsworth's cloud "mov[ing] all together, if it moves at all." The *reck* is lessened into a different care or desire so as to be no longer simultaneous with what is projected onto it, instead rerunning such a surface by under-taking it (moving slower than it), and the resulting slurring is one way in which the atmosphere is at the back of the human. "The sky is complicated and flawed and we're up there in it . . ." (*W*, 10). True too that the floor of the sky is not down here with us, but as we're not solely with ourselves we can be "there in it" if we accept just such a variable schedule of translations.

The phrase "A slight cloud drifts contrary to the / planet" (24), which crops up in the intervening verse between "Tuesday" and "Wednesday," also repeats itself within the prose fabric of the latter, where it attracts the adjunct "the day might be used formally to contain a record of idleness" (28). Idleness fills in the journal record and also recapitulates an entire history of pastoral *otium*. This formality is also how a "slight cloud" (i.e., less than absent) can drift contrary to a planet as part of a ritual of independent horizon reintroduced through a cruising rite of genre.

The weather as figure of process and temporal embodiment articulates a ground-as-displacement which performs a moving-through better than a moving-across-to. But such a slow rebounding atmosphere goes in for little symmetrical opposition, and the indiscretion of a whole sky to play with doesn't so much make desire unrecognizable to itself as draw desire out along its *present* lines of flight (where outdraw is more radical than blockage or subversion): "Every surface is ambitious; we excavate a non-existent era of the human. Everything is being lifted into place" (30). If this is utopian archaeology it is not inert once a "non-existent era of the human" is taken to be reaching out towards the atmospherics of what is sheerly given (a gift universally figured as goldenly past in pastoral). A state of giftedness cannot experience the timing of plenitude except as already over from within reception; desire to re-experience gift is not lack but an active suing for a sense of the given to remain present at the scarce (i.e., given non-totally *to* difference) horizons of actuality, where it can be glimpsed as not waiting to be made. Where it can become an "everything" once more through the voice of dedication. That is if we can take the ultimate polemic of pastoral to be a plenitude of gift flung in the face of utopia's more calculated totality of construction: "I celebrate the death of method: the flirting woods call it, the glittering rocks call it – utopia is dead" (*XE*, Eclogue 3). Pastoral involves a re-distribution of urban recognitions in order to fold out towards a horizon for the given.[4]

Weather figures ceaseless, swirling, frameless process, but it also reserves to itself a habit of the frontal, one which turns ascendant in the turning-with: "We flood upwards into the referent. . . . It is clothed in such a mild, quiet light; we intrude on the phenom-enology" (*W*, 31). Clothing is Robertson's plea for an inhabitably desirable surface, and "mild" is Wordsworth's strategic word of gentling *par excellence*, sharing the nature of timely "outerance" and converting sensation to decentred reflection, as in his "a gentle shock of mild surprise," where shock reverberates with something more than a sum of impact. This tissue of mildness can address threads like "Now look; we embed ourselves in immateriality" (35) and "This is a cloudburst; no-one's turn is dwelling" (40). An embedding which is not a stacked materiality is the equivalent to layering the weather with niches which aren't demarcations, and though "no-one's turn is dwelling" acknowledges an initial swipe at Heidegger's famous *kehre* or turn in favour of dwelling, the reading goes on echoing so that "no-one" attracts a Rilkean or Celanian resonance of the marginalized soul, until there can be secondary irony which is nested in affirmation.

Pastoral survives as a continued negotiation with persona, or with what is taken up to let go as non-abandonment. The follow-ing passage either addresses a transgendered, acculturated writing self, or an acquisitive reader of the pastoral convention:

You're really this classical man hearing a poem, this long voice reeling through chic traditions of green. But you flaunt privacies that split their sheaths. (34–35)

The "long voice" is presumably the male voice of received cultural memory, against whom the traditions turn excessive with freighted surfaces and all the unfinished business of counter-restitution. We have been here before in Robertson's work, but it is less clear, now we are no longer within eclogue, who the "you" is. Is it a subversive female persona resting on the sort of surfaces which risk "unneces-sary" adornments? Or is it the voice of the weather/cloud itself, in which case "privacies" must be taken as configurations which read tradition out to the vagaries of sky? – this gives us something like a hermaphodite language where the femaleness of flaunting privacies commingles with the maleness of splitting sheaths but without any hierarchy of agency. And not so much a merging as a broad sustaining of a ranging shape which moves all together like a cloud but isn't bonded or cross-woven; rather, simply rests within indeterminate *discernibility* which the possibility of a weathering process provides:

We are almost transparent. We rest on the rhetorical face. Body of cloud through the night. Now we will be persons. Body of cloud by the fibres collapsing. (56–57)

There is no weather outside address and a certain ascension of voice. This poetry is no longer an obvious pleading for a knowing or predatory acculturation, and it knows that any calculus of imagery is also to be borne up by the weather the image is already a component of: "Body of cloud personified. If we abandon a pronoun an argument is lost" (57). This comes close to a horizon of dedication indeed, where the libidinous is bleeding into an "I and Thou" numinousness: "We rest on the tiny-leafed material and resist. Body of cloud of the conventional pieties. Not for whom do we speak but in whom" (58).

> I enjoy
> as I renounce the chic glint
> which politics give to style (70)

The "chic glint" makes its renunciation duplicitous enough if all rest becomes resistance, unless we overread to prise out the material relation, so that we see that "resist" is a composite of "rest" and "is." Resistance already is (less than a utopian forced expectation) derived from the ontological rest of pastoral.

Robertson offers the last nine pages of *The Weather* as a sort of envoi, but calls it "porchverse," a place of parting, but also, no doubt, a point of invitation back into the project. Here her lyricism seems to come clean, to be scarified and minimal, though at the same time raising the question of reading in acute form:

> The porch unclasps each word
> of what I say: are these words
> perhaps nothing in July? (75)

A text with micro-fronts and subsystems places itself at another margin, but "porch" is also a ritual space of welcoming and letting go. The initial impression of "unclasps each word / of what I say" suggests vigilant, not to say defensive auto-deconstruction, but "unclasps" also reads as a letting go after intimate clasping. The words' own capacity to signify now has to think through its own seasonality, so as to be perhaps a nothing during the virtually cloudless month of July. Or is this the pastoral reviewing its own status before an enframing power, July the month of Julius? Or the language may not need to have any particular status in July simply because that month is a sufficient particular (rather like T. S. Eliot's justification of his quasi-symbolic autumn in "Little Gidding" "only because it *was* autumn weather" [Gardner, 184]). Robertson's poetry plays with a gap between linguistic arbitrariness and worldly sufficiency across which writers and readers are already paid up on both sides. She concretizes that space, together with echoes of Milton's own valedictory descent from pastoral to elegy in his *Lycidas*, two pages away from her collection's close:

> It is time to paw the
> landscape once more as radically
> as hard green berries
> replace the red and once more

> It is too late to be simple. (76)

After July's forestalling of the poem's language, that language has reverted to setting up its own moments of remonstrance or exhortation. And now it seems aggressively counter-seasonal. How do "hard green berries" (there may be a further allusion to Gary Snyder's "Manzanita" here) succeed red and presumably luscious ones? This is some sort of proof-text lying in wait for its own marginal glosses as so much glossolalia. Pastoral inexperience substituting for summer ripeness? Green ecology taking on urban-based left politics? And "pawing" a landscape suggests impatience rather than sheer brutality, however much the figure-play seems to want soft to be hard and the pristine to supervene on the mature. That paw may also echo the "unclasping" of "porchverse" as a whole. "It is too late to be simple" may be believable enough, and the only thing possible for Robertson to believe, but has the text itself come away so cleanly on the negative? I don't believe it is calling for the flat naïveté which takes primordial innocence to be conclusively demystified. Robertson spins a wide gap between her second "once more" and that final negative or elegaic statement, a gap as weighty perhaps as the gap between life and death in Geoffrey Hartman's reading of the stanza break in Wordsworth's two-stanza poem "A Slumber Did My Spirit Seal" (*Wordsworth's Poetry*, xx). "It is too late to be simple" is so placed that the "hard green berries" of bitterly aspiring pastoral will always have to be redenied in their again and again, for the innocency of desire capably resurfaces minimally refreshed. Innocence is the stronger other of a naïveté of received disillusionment. "I've never done anything / but begin" (78) is how *The Weather* actually closes. Of course, this poetry has done nothing else throughout, but has known how to begin amid a strongly implied "anything *else*" which becomes the recuperative weather-attachments of pastoral possibility. Language begins: horizon (as non-demarcatory but receptive interruption) expends desire over a con-summary weather which is the climate of a pristine beginning's continuation.

Notes

1. For Robert Pogue Harrison, the "provincial" is the horizon in which the bonds between nature and history find their most primitive tension: "To justify this tension is the task of the artist. . . . That is why 'staying in the provinces' entails . . . a returning along the tortured paths of metaphysics to the central vicinity of our mortal humanity" (321). This notion of provincialization chimes with Robertson's witty sketch of the relation of scaffolding to architecture, and she enacts a scenario which echoes Harrison's idea of the city's forgetful overcoming of its erstwhile forest margins: "men should arrange themselves on the scaffold as in a frieze . . . with the hacked forest behind them or the bare place that will become the city" (*OW*, 162–63). For Harrison, the site of the city might be "bare" because it has abstracted from its own space the fringes of the forest, though this doesn't reduce the city to pure imposition, nor does it mean that those fringes are primordially concrete. The "provincial" is where human self-abstraction from the world remains still bound to that from which it was drawn away. Along this margin is gathered radius as well as periphery, a bond which holds in tension the unfolding of historic time and the earth's (mortal) transcending of that periodization/spatialization.

2. Robertson can be doctrinaire in reducing surface to depthlessness: "The city is a florescence of surface. Under the pavement, pavement" (*OW*, 15). If we suppose one surface to be beneath another, we are not left with a repetition of surfaces, but two non-identical surfaces separated in depth, and involved in what can overlay or underlie, or in what might intervene between layers. My own reading of her work assumes that material surfaces give on to horizons.

Edward S. Casey argues that horizon "affords" depth as the outermost, circumambient edge of any givenness. Depth is mediated between the self-apprehended body on the one hand and the visual horizon on the other. Surfaces "loom" or exude an irreducible voluminousness. In relation to thinking about Robertson's *The Weather* it's interesting to note that Casey regards depth as not "the kind of thing that yields to measurement, it is like an aura or atmosphere that resists precise specification" (10).

3. A more nuanced account of the expanses and containments of British garden history can be found in Robertson's "Arts and Crafts in Burnaby: A Congenial Soil" (*OW*, 83–115).

4. It's awkward to reduce weather to a play of (utopian) surfaces: it is as much to do with a three- (or four-) dimensional process of volumes and masses, not to say structures. That is why *The Weather* interestingly tests out Robertson's otherwise prevailing postmodernism. As an essayist Robertson can be (however irreverently) prescriptive: "We believe that structure or fundament itself, in its inert eternity, has already been adequately documented – the same skeleton repeating itself continuously. . . . But the chaos of surfaces compels us towards new states of happiness" (*OW*, 128). With the atmosphere it makes little sense to separate out an "inert eternity," but we are not left to a world of pure surface, as what gives the weather its being can be turbulent but not reducible to novelty. Unbuilt structures (whose singularity might well involve an enigmatic "inertness") can be numinous as well as ruinous.

Works Cited

Alpers, Paul. *What Is Pastoral?* Chicago and London: University of Chicago Press, 1996.

Brolanski, Tanya. "Lisa Robertson: *The Weather.*" http://www.sptraffic.org/html/book_reviews/robertson.html (no longer online).

Casey, Edward S. "'The Element of Voluminousness': Depth and Place Re-examined." In *Merleau-Ponty Vivant*, ed. M. C. Dillon, 1–29. Albany, NY: State University of New York Press, 1991.

Crawford, Rachel. *Poetry, Enclosure and the Vernacular Landscape, 1700–1830.* Cambridge: Cambridge University Press, 2002.

Friedlander, Benjamin. "Nature and Culture: On Lisa Robertson's *XEclogue.*" 1995. http://home.jps.net/~nada/xlogue.htm.

Gardner, Helen. *The Composition of Four Quartets.* London: Faber, 1978.

Harrison, Robert Pogue. "The Provincial Center." *Triquarterly* 116 (Summer 2003): 315–22.

Hartman, Geoffrey H. *Easy Pieces.* New York: Columbia University Press, 1985.

——. *Wordsworth's Poetry, 1787–1814.* Exp. ed. New Haven: Yale University Press, 1971.

Hofer, Jen. Review of *The Weather*, by Lisa Robertson. *Rain Taxi,* Fall 2001. http://www.raintaxi.com/online/2001fall/robertson.shtml.

Larkin, Peter. "Wordsworth's Cloud of Texture." *The Wordsworth Circle* 18, no. 3 (Summer 1987): 121–26.

Lorraine, Tamsin E. *Irigaray and Deleuze: Experiments in Visceral Philosophy.* Ithaca, NY: Cornell University Press, 1999.

Michasiw, Kim Ian. "Nine Revisionist Theses on the Picturesque." *Representations* 38 (Spring 1992): 76–100.

Montagu, Lady Mary Wortley. *Court Eclogs, Written in the Year, 1716.* Ed. Robert Halsband. New York: New York Public Library, 1977.

O'Hara, Frank. *The Collected Poems of Frank O'Hara.* Ed. Donald Allen. New York: Knopf, 1972.

Poggioli, Renato. *The Oaten Flute: Essays on Pastoral Poetry and the Pastoral Ideal.* Cambridge, MA: Harvard University Press, 1975.

Reed, Arden. *Romantic Weather: The Climates of Coleridge and Baudelaire.* Hanover, NH and London: printed for Brown University Press by University Press of New England, 1983.

Robertson, Lisa. *Debbie: An Epic.* London: Reality Street Editions, 1997. (Cited as *D*.)

———. "How Pastoral: a Manifesto." In *Telling It Slant: Avant-Garde Poetics of the 1990s,* ed. Mark Wallace and Stephen Marks, 21–26. Tuscaloosa: University of Alabama Press, 2002. (Cited as *HP*.)

———. *Occasional Work and Seven Walks from the Office for Soft Architecture.* Astoria, OR: Clear Cut Press, 2003. (Cited as *OW*.)

———. *The Weather.* London: Reality Street Editions, 2001. (Cited as *W*.)

———. *XEclogue.* Vancouver: Tsunami Editions, 1993. (Cited as *XE*.)

Rosenmeyer, Thomas G. *The Green Cabinet: Theocritus and the European Pastoral Lyric.* Berkeley and Los Angeles: University of California Press, 1969.

Serres, Michel. *Hermes IV: La Distribution.* Paris: Editions de Minuit, 1977.

Tester, Keith. *Life and Times of Post-Modernity.* London: Routledge, 1993.

Vickery, Ann. "'A Mobile Fiction': Barbara Guest and Modern Pastoral." *Triquarterly* 116 (Summer 2003): 246–61.

Wallace, Anne D. *Walking, Literature, and English Culture: The Origins and Uses of the Peripatetic in the Nineteenth Century.* Oxford: Clarendon Press, 1993.

"THE ARK I": LISSA WOLSAK'S
THE GARCIA FAMILY CO-MERCY

Susan M. Schultz

I am writing this essay in the middle of the 2004 American presidential campaign, a campaign in which the word "family" sits at the centre of many issues, or what pass as issues these days.[1] The operative definition of "family" in the dominant political discourse offers us the family as a miniature version of the ideal polity: nuclear, self-contained, sacred, even "festive," as Stephanie Coontz notes (17). This family is private, composed of blood relatives, and cut off from the outside world both ideologically and architecturally (optimally, it exists in suburbs). Coontz cites a fifties advice-book which offers hope in the guise of a warning: "The family is the center of your living. If it isn't, you've gone far astray" (25). Such a view of family is inherently defensive; while promising a "haven in a heartless world," it presumes a constant threat. But it also reflects a larger society in which political discourse has deteriorated to the extent that political issues can only be discussed obliquely by way of intensely personal ones. "When the dominant political language cannot express issues of responsibility, commitment, and morality," writes Coontz, "the only vocabulary for discussing social obligations and needs comes to be the language of love" (114). Coontz does not point to a "pure" language of love, but one roped into the service of a conversation that requires another, less private, vocabulary to do its work. And, where the "family found ideological support and justification in the conception of domestic life as an emotional refuge in a cold and competitive society" (Lasch), it is *used* as ideological fodder by corporations whose intent is hardly to strengthen family ties. Christopher Lasch lashes out: "The sanctity of the home is a sham in a world dominated by giant corporations and by the apparatus of mass promotion" (xvii). Thus Hervé Varenne writes of the governing definition of family: "This is simple only in the ideological realm" (426). Varenne argues that what is central about American family life is not togetherness, but divorce. America's first divorce occurred with the Declaration of Independence, and subsequent "divorces" have manufactured many of the ideals central to the American experience. Of course, even these negative appraisals of family disregard older definitions of it; as Coontz points out, "It is worth noting that the word *family* originally meant a band of slaves" (43).[2] It may also bear noting that on my eight-page printout of the online *OED*'s definitions of "family," the term "Happy Family," or "a collection of birds and animals of different natures and propensities living together in harmony in one cage," precedes the description of a "group of persons consisting of the parents and their children."

My emphasis on the "American" family is perhaps unfair to Lissa Wolsak, who has made her home in Vancouver for decades, but she grew up in the United States, a nation she has, at least figuratively, "divorced." I would argue that these definitions of family are more typical of the western world than of the United States alone, with some variations. Ask Wolsak for her definition of family, and you get elements of both utopian and dystopian descriptions of it. After referring to her passionate attachment to what is called "her own" family, Wolsak writes:

> I've always wanted to get to the bottom of hatred, and why familiarity breeds contempt and venture my work against the egregarious [combination of "egregious" and "gregarious"?] distortions, scapegoating, atavistic charades, privilege of clan and political dissemination of intimacy. I can't help but notice that veracity more often takes place outside the family circle; this includes all manner of kin, the poets, the left, the right, nations, circles of any kind that uphold each others' lies. I see the domicile or inner circle as a prevalent source-site of love *and terror*, where we love that which reflects us and eschew that which does not. (private email, 4 September 2004)

As the neologism "egregarious" in Wolsak's email suggests, her use of language is denser and more interesting than that of almost any poet, excepting Hart Crane, in recent literary history.[3] "Close reading," so often used to unpack poems or lines of verse, is required to read Wolsak's *words*, and close reading means reading other books – dictionaries, encyclopaedias. In her 1994 volume *The Garcia Family Co-Mercy*, she uses such language to intervene in notions of "family," unpacking and at times repacking its considerable luggage. In this long poem, she puts family at the center of a utopian project – and poetics – but defines family very differently from the political mainstream. Hers is "a language of love" that attempts to reconnect small-f family with a larger, more sacred and more communal, notion of Family.[4]

So what are we to make of her book's title? **Garcia**: family name, Spanish (hence marginal in a society that overvalues northern European names like Smith and Bush); Garcia, referring to members of that family, like Jerry Garcia (whose family was a band), like Gabriel García Márquez, whose *One Hundred Years of Solitude* is a great novel about family; like Diego Garcia, a small island in the Indian Ocean, where the U.S. Navy has a base, signifying the link between "nation" and "family," to say nothing of "colonialism"; like García Lorca, homosexual Spanish poet of New York. Wolsak has said that "Garcia" is intended to represent "every family," but in the very blandness of this description we find the ordinary complexities of the Wolsakian vocabulary.[5] **Family:** as I've indicated, its origins are in slavery, with a contemporary emphasis on "love." Also: a state official in India (colonialism); a race; brotherhood or group of individuals or nations bound together by political or religious ties; members of the Mafia; family skeleton and family trees (looking nearly alike). These from the *OED*, itself a gathering of word-families. Finally, that oddly conflated word: **co-mercy.** Mercy as compassion, especially for someone who is powerless. God has mercy on us. We ask for mercy when we have sinned. We are at the mercy of forces more powerful than we are. Co-mercy would be the mercy offered by a cooperative, a family, a group, or even a corporation (co.).[6] "Co-" is a prefix that indicates community. Yet "co-mercy" sounds like "commerce," many of whose nuances lie elsewhere than in this merciful realm. The noun, **commerce**, indicates the dealing in merchandise, selling, a card game. It does involve family, but intercourse that depends on money, on objectification. Let me digress: many of Wolsak's most obscure word-choices are, in fact, the names of commodities, not by her choice certainly, but because advertisers must think that "obscurity" sells; the word "suavitas," which comes one-third of the way through the unpaginated book, is either a word for "charm, sweetness, urbanity, gentleness," or, as I found out from Google, a gourmet low-carb cheesecake. This uneasy paradox – the word suspended between the sellable and the transcendent – seems inevitable, even as poets like Wolsak work against such commodifications of language.

This is but the first of the word-fields in Wolsak's book, a field that takes us in the direction of the sacred family and the profane. As the book opens, Wolsak conflates one family member, a "girl," with the architecture of the cathedral or dome, a sacred space:

> girl   with   vase of odours
>
> cradle   one's own head . .
>
> squinches, pendentives, oculi, groin
>
> cri imaginaire   pity
>
> the river myth (7)

"Squinches," "pendentives" and "groin" all refer to parts of a cathedral or dome, and "groin" then refers further to "the river myth" of fertility, which is immediately called into question by the final two lines on this page:

> was there ever
>
> a father field

which undermines the patriarchal force of the architecture (both in stone and in words) that holds together this first glimpse of family in *The Garcia Family*. And yet what remains is the concept of "pity" that is crucial to this work, and a link between pity and family.

Father field and mother field are joined in the concept of "mumming," which appears two pages later. *Mum's the word* indicates silence; *mum* is mother in many parts of the English-speaking world. The quiet mother is *mum*, but the theatre of mummers carried storylines from father to son, giving voice to men in the family. The central question of the mummers is crucial here, namely, "are we of the same community?" "Are you an insider or outsider?" Insofar as communities are figured as family, Wolsak is introducing the question of what comprises family, and whether or not family is simply an exercise in including some and rejecting others, as her email to me indicated. One of the threads in her book is that of slang or patois or pidgin (she uses the Chinese Pidgin word "joss," which means "deity," and then refers to "patois" elsewhere), languages that generally starkly denote communities in which there are insiders and outsiders.[7]

That language functions, in part, to denote membership in a group concerns Wolsak throughout this book. A later "mother field" goes as follows:

. .   was   at first used   in pity

by running · they retracted

figura

endura

mother-tongued ·

and then, several lines down:

itinerant child-mother,

harvester and outsider (47)

The word "outsider" is significant here, as is exile ("I implant /
exile"), because for Wolsak what is generative is not so much the
reproductive realm as that of "transhumance," a note on which she
ends the book. "Transhumance" is not creation, but "migration," a
leaving the mother tongue for a foreign one, perhaps – a movement that is for Wolsak a creative and communal one. She defines
the word in *An Heuristic Prolusion*: "*Transhumance*, as understood
and utilized in late 12th C., early 13th C France, was an agricultural motion or migration, a seasonal moving of livestock, and the
people who tend them . . . but transhumance also was a possible
personal-social act of symmetry, reciprocity and redistribution" (7).
If "compassion" is generally an emotion felt by someone powerful
for someone less so, then the literal meaning of "transhumance"
applies. But Wolsak also transforms that relation into one of equity,
pointing toward "reciprocity" rather than noblesse oblige as her
governing use of the metaphor.

Wolsak makes use of what one might term "deep etymology,"
or at least "deep definition," in her work, employing words from
English, Latin, Turkish, Chinese Pidgin, Tibetan and other languages to make up her "fields." While her surfaces are exquisite,
both as arrangements of words on the page and as episodes of
sound, to comprehend her fields is to burrow, to turn to the dictionary and the encyclopaedia for word-meanings. Surface is where
resemblance is strongest; Wolsak's layered language is powerful
not because words resemble one another, via sound or sense, but
because their power lies elsewhere, where words do not resemble
each other, at least in the ways we usually think they do. If the
"mother tongue" contains a family, then Wolsak exiles the reader
(and possibly herself) from her mother tongue, either in the pal-

pable silences of the text, or in other tongues, unknown to the
reader. If sound is sense, then definition is historical, denoting an
often buried sense. Or, in terms set up by Emmanuel Levinas,
whose name appears in one of Wolsak's fields, words present themselves as Other to each other. "Words do not refer to contents
which they would designate, but first, laterally, to other words,"
he argues in "Meaning and Sense" (*Basic Philosophical Writings*,
36). These words exist in relation to one another as speaker to
listener; "that is, to the contingency of their history" (37). He
concludes this discussion of words by using a word/metaphor dear
to Wolsak, namely "rivers": "Each word meaning is at the conflu-
ence of innumerable semantic rivers" (37).

While Levinas dismisses dictionaries as places where language is
limited, his emphasis on the historical significance of language
points us back to (good) dictionaries and to their mapping of word-
meanings over time. As he writes, "There never was a moment in
which *meaning first came to birth out of meaningless being*, outside
of a historical position where language is spoken" (38). Thus
Levinas's interest is not in the *origins* (or birth) of language, but in
the way language participates in history. We are historical beings,
and therefore we do not work *for* but *in* the present, as he notes
elsewhere. In order for meaning to be understood, "[t]he whole
density of history is necessary for it" (44). Drawing from Levinas,
Wolsak's language-fields, while they exist in space, are profoundly
historical *places in time*. As historical artifacts that must be uncov-
ered before their meanings can emerge, words fascinate not for
their origins, but for their ends over time. Elements of a Wolsak
word-field do not draw close out of the magnetism of resemblance,
but because their meanings are linked historically. Often her words
come from different languages, but are related otherwise, as in the
many examples from sacred architecture, from the "squinch" of a
dome to "mihrab," the holiest place in a mosque. Here, as elsewhere, what might be considered a word-family (cathedral, altar,
nave, and so on) is extended to include difference (cathedral,
mosque). Within this difference, however, is structure, construction and a notion of sacred space.

But I would like to make an argument about material verbal
similarities and differences, and consider "sound" in poetry to participate in a (genetic) family of likenesses, while word-definition,
in its historical sense, gives us a (cultural, historical) family of differences. That similar sounds often open up a trap door to differ-

ences, and that words of different sounds and etymologies often suggest similarity, only makes my argument more complicated. Garrett Stewart has written persuasively on the power of sound (what he calls the "phonotext") to deliver messages that are not immediately apparent, by creating words across the spaces between words, for example. In "Modernism's Sonic Waiver: Literary Writing and the Filmic Difference," Stewart (while asserting that his position is suppressed by other literary critics) notes that he wants "to recast the place of vocalization (sounded or not) in the generation of literary language" (239). I want to mis-, or more appropriately (appropriatively) read his sentence through the lens of family, and note that the word "generation" suggests reproduction, fertility, a biology of sound. Further on, he notes that this generation occurs between the surfaces of words: "It is one (metaphoric) thing to have the rhetorical edge of language blunted by a cheapening wear and tear; it is another (phonemic) thing to have the surfaces of words wear away at each other, productively, under the duress of sheer attention" (240–41). While "production" moves us away from a metaphorical field of biology and reproduction toward one of reduction, wearing away, the point here is that Stewart is interested in word-surfaces, even if those surfaces blur sonically into something that resides apart from that surface, in the ear.[8] The generation of meaning from the sonic blurring of word-surfaces belongs, according to my reading, to a notion of "family" (here of sound, of meaning) based on affinity, on generation, and on sameness. If, as he points out later, the words "La j'étais" lead us to the title of a Chris Marker film, *La jetée*, then new meanings are generated through resemblances of sound. Oddly, perhaps, meanings generated out of sound-samenesses are often very different (as in the movement from "there I was" to "the fountain" in the Marker example). And those meanings generated out of spatial relationships, as in Wolsak's poem, bind different sounds into synonyms. But what I'm getting at in my argument is not so much the meanings that are arrived at, although those are crucial, but how meaning is generated, or constructed, out of words.

While Wolsak often alludes to the process of echoing, at one point using the word "echopraxia" (the imitative repetition of another's movements in schizophrenia), her word-fields differ significantly from the phenomenon Stewart is concerned with. Her wordplay is often evidently *constructed*, whether the word be "egregariously," as in her email to me, or "co-mercy," which combines "commerce" with "mercy," yoking together two apparently opposing concepts. The hyphen in "co-mercy" is integral to the coinage's effect. Hyphens join without blurring; Stewart draws us into the spaces between words where sounds bleed together, where Wolsak shows us the very suture between words. This is not Charles Bernstein's "dysraphism,"[9] however, but a conscious joining of opposites into one word, or one "family," which is then extended into the larger field of the page where words are placed separately but in relation to one another. The word "assembled" is crucial here, and it's no accident, I suspect, that this word appears in the same field as "the Garcia family / co-mercy" (24). If Stewart's ear allows for elisions of sound, Wolsak's architectural sense emphasizes the spatial, historical nature of words that are sounded.

Hence, Wolsak's spaces between words are deliberately large; she does not aim for the slurring of speech, but for distinctions between sounds that still point to relationship. In that distinction, between poetry that accrues meaning through sound (either Stewart's slurring, or through alliteration, assonance or other figures of repetition) and poetry that accrues meaning through definition, or historical depth (requiring, in my case, frequent trips to the on-line *OED*), I find an analogy in Wolsak's argument about family. If family is usually considered a field of resemblances (father to son, mother to daughter, and so on genetically), then sound is the emblem of poetry as family par excellence. To *sound* the same or similar notes is to engage in a genetic poetry, where sameness trumps difference. But where sound gives way to the poetry of *definition*, of depth, then we move from blood family to another concept of community. Wolsak began her email on family to me this way: "I take my family where I find them, wherever affinities and understanding naturally form, which means that I don't at all see family strictly along bloodlines. . . . It is not that I don't love my family passionately but that I want to, and do, keep my door open to all persons, all possibilities and further, to experience such as processual entropy and negentropy." Or, as she writes in *The Garcia Family*, "lie of origin / / avoid speaking . . . . . the / new thing is to skip / generations."

If Susan Howe's poetry is about the stutter in the text, then Wolsak's is about the skip between generations, a new concept of "generation" that does not rely on ancient fertility myths but on a gathering of words together in new families. In that sense her work builds on Eliot's *The Waste Land*, which tried to recover the fertil-

ity myth through various word-hoards ranging from European languages to Sanskrit. Wolsak throws out the fertility myth with the
bathwater, but arrives at a similar notion of family, where word
"descents" trump word "origins" and create new versions of family.
The human voice is crucial to Wolsak, as it is to Levinas, for whom
it marks an engagement with the Other; this is a voice that follows,
a "descendental human voice," but one which follows only after
a break, an exile, a loss.

What is then crucial to an understanding of Wolsak's poetry,
that its linguistic inclusivity mirrors its construction of family
(poetic, personal), enables us to see it as offering the possibility
of a new kind of family, untethered from the tribal notion of
blood, joined by "roots" of another sort indeed. Let me return to
the frame of this essay, the earlier discussion of family as a social
entity. The notion of the nuclear family presumes that family provides a private outpost in an all-too-public world, and that this
outpost is populated by individuals held together by a tight notion
of community among similar types ("family values" are astonish-
ingly uniform, not multifarious). The family community, like the
mummers, asks the question "are you one of us?" and embraces or
rejects its members accordingly. That this notion of community
echoes outward into discussions of nation, especially in troubled
times, goes almost without saying. Lissa Wolsak, keenly aware as
she is of the faults in the family landscape, writes from what she
terms "the ark I" (21), or an identity constructed (as an ark is, or as
Ronald Johnson's *ARK* was) of diverse identities. She sketches the
portrait of a family, whether Garcia or other, composed out of
migration and exile, yet held together by an architectural metaphor that suggests the family can yet be sacred – if it is defined in
a new way. This is a family composed of divorce, of loss ("the death
of a child"), of outsiders, of those who do not "resemble," but
re-assemble.

How does this re-assembly work? What we are faced with, in
reading Wolsak, is the question of who is responsible for whom,
sketched out on the level of words, but pointing toward a social
level, where human beings interact, for good or for ill. In *The Ethics
of Memory*, Avishai Margalit describes categories cultures have used
to determine an individual's responsibility toward others. Some
cultures have relatively narrow definitions of who is a "neighbour,"
while others are more open.[10] In *One World: The Ethics of Globalization*, Peter Singer argues that people must take responsibility for

others, including those who are far away or cannot be seen.[11] Singer
owes a debt here to Levinas's 1968 essay, "Substitution," described
by Robert Bernasconi as a discussion of responsibility: "Levinas
conceives of a responsibility to which one is elected and by which
one finds oneself answerable for everything and everyone, even for
one's persecutors" (Levinas, 79). The crucial word for Wolsak is
another word that begins with "co," namely "compassion."

> Compassion
>
>   is largely   exile
>
>   .. condradict
>
>   the ways in which
>
>   the world
>
>   says no (38)

She complicates the meaning of "compassion" with her use of
another, less positive, "co" word, "condradict" (or "contradict"; she
says this was an unintended typo), showing that compassion operates against the world's negativity, and is based on its existence
outside the norm, namely, in "exile" (note that the word is itself
exiled from its line). To be in exile is to be "other," even to oneself.
To locate one's compassion in exile is to acknowledge the exile of
others, the ways in which they do not "belong," at least in the
genetic sense of family or nation (which so often includes race,
religion, and so on). The compassion that acknowledges otherness
but puts its others in the same fields of words marks Lissa Wolsak's
poetry as one that emphasizes community as a union of differences
(family composed not of blood but of love's history) rather than of
samenesses.

    Wolsak thus returns us to the problem with which I began this
essay, namely that of what vocabulary to use in talking about private and public spheres. For Wolsak is clearly extending her definition of family beyond the borders of the nuclear. But is she not
employing the "language of love" that Coontz critiques in contemporary discussions of public issues? Does she not run the risk
of exploding the boundaries of family beyond what it can sustain,
and rendering it a public, rather than a private, artifact? Perhaps,
but of course hers is still the language of poetry, not direct political discourse, and her emphasis is on a spiritual community (and
love) more than one appropriated from the personal by the public

sphere. What she points toward is a notion of family that could be used, in public discourse, to expand the horizon of "ego" toward a larger place where responsibility is considered an act of love, no matter who the Other is we see, or cannot see.

While I began this essay with critiques of the mixing of political and personal language, the conflation of "family" with "nation" and with political values, I end with a defence (or, at least, a sympathetic taxonomy) of just such rhetoric by George Lakoff, whose *Moral Politics: How Liberals and Conservatives Think* argues that our politics is necessarily saturated in the metaphors of family. After describing metaphorical fields built upon Strict Father morality (conservative) and Nurturant Parent morality (liberal), Lakoff posits that we cannot talk about our public choices without using private ones as the basis for our thinking.[12] According to Lakoff, any moral and political argument in the American context needs to fall back on family; other metaphors, based on mechanics (or even car-pooling), ignore the moral sphere. Lakoff's uneasy embrace of the family-as-nation metaphor accords with Wolsak's poetic argument that what is most private (family, the insides of words) must be formed in such a way as to create a public (community of shared words) that mirrors its virtues. For Wolsak the process of reading fields of words (families of them) teaches the reader, and the poet, how to read family back into our politics in such a way that we do not demean either of them, but instead give them the strength of a sacred architecture.

Notes

1. Under the "Compassion and Values" section of President George W. Bush's campaign website, we find: "Strong families are the foundation of a healthy society." A sidebar ad for "The President's Plan for a Safer World & More Hopeful America" includes a headline reading, "Helping American Families in a changing world," though "in a changing world" is printed in a much smaller font than "Helping American Families" (http://www.georgewbush.com/ Compassion/ – this URL is no longer operative).

2. I have relied for this discussion in large part on three studies of the family, namely Christopher Lasch's *Haven in a Heartless World: The Family Besieged* (1977), Stephanie Coontz's *The Way We Never Were: American Families and the Nostalgia Trap* (1992) and Hervé Varenne's essay "Love and Liberty: The Contemporary American Family" (1996). Lasch is most concerned with ways in which family has been "socialized," or its roles taken over by public (and private)

organizations. Coontz notably pops the balloon of gender roles, and Varenne of "marriage" as the primary institution in American life.

3. In an email of 11 September 2004, Wolsak tells me that "egregarious" was a typo in her original email to me. If this typo is a "mistake," it is a telling one, as it unveils what is otherwise Wolsak's practice of creating neologisms that combine several meanings into a single word, so I hold by it. But she further relates that her book was riddled with typos by the printer, which went against her intent as the poet and likely causes confusion in a reader who does not know the difference between a typo and a neologism.

4. Wolsak's vocabulary, and her explanation of it, is very dense, indeed. In an interview with Kent Johnson, she noted: "Taking simultaneity seriously, what I have hoped is that the 'secret-seeming vocabulary' is a reclamation, a sentient interlude intriguing or familiar enough, through sound or otherwise, to etymologically span archaic-modernist-futurist memory, create space, matter, curiosity, reflection, as often many of these references possess one or more universal cultural elements which point, or are ideas, of themselves. I don't subscribe to the idea that one can speak in middlebrow, instantly accessible to all." I will have more to say later in my essay about links between Wolsak's language-use and "familiarity."

5. I had help from Google's search engine in my riff on Garcias.

6. Wolsak writes in response to this passage: "Co-mercy initiates a process of refraction, opens a field of perception, the first act of mercy primarily but not exclusively originated at face to face level, person to person, therein lies the revolution we cannot wait for any collective or organ(ization) to begin; it is about what is in our hands as individuals to do, and moreover, it is about NOT waiting for someone else to begin a kindness but to begin it ourselves" (email of 2 October 2004).

7. Lisa Linn Kanae's *Sista Tongue* investigates ways in which Pidgin is at once an insider tongue and a guarantee of outsider status in the dominant culture of Hawai'i.

8. Stewart further complicates his metaphorical field when he notes that "textual generation" comes of a "moment of sheer homophonic wordplay," indicating that his is not a hetero- theory of sound, but one that depends on words like "generation," nonetheless.

9. Charles Bernstein defines "dysraphism" as "a word used by specialists in congenital disease to mean a dysfunctional fusion of embryonic parts – a birth defect . . . Raph literally means 'seam,' so dysraphism is mis-seaming – a prosodic device!" (44).

10. In "Who Is My Neighbor?" Margalit discusses various interpretations of the concept of "neighbour," from those that universalize to more particular definitions, such as that of Maimonides, who thought only Jews qualified (*The Ethics of Memory*, 40–44).

11. Singer writes: "there are many who think it self-evident that we have special obligations to those nearer to us, including our children, our spouses, lovers and friends, and our compatriots . . . Instead, we need another test of whether we have special obligations to those closer to us, such as our compatriots"

(154). Singer's larger argument is that, in a time of globalization, everyone is responsible for everyone else, both within and without the boundaries of nation-states.

12. Lakoff's description of the Strict Father family can be found on pp. 65–67 and his description of the Nurturant Parent family on pp. 108–10.

Works Cited

Bernstein, Charles. *The Sophist.* Los Angeles: Sun and Moon, 1987.

Coontz, Stephanie. *The Way We Never Were: American Families and the Nostalgia Trap.* New York: Basic Books, 1992.

Kanae, Lisa Linn. *Sista Tongue.* Kaneohe, HI: Tinfish Press, 2001.

Lakoff, George. *Moral Politics: How Liberals and Conservatives Think.* 2nd ed. Chicago: University of Chicago Press, 2002.

Lasch, Christopher. *Haven in a Heartless World: The Family Besieged.* New York: Basic Books, 1977.

Levinas, Emmanuel. *Basic Philosophical Writings.* Ed. Adriaan T. Peperzak, Simon Critchley and Robert Bernasconi. Bloomington: Indiana University Press, 1996.

Margalit, Avishai. *The Ethics of Memory.* Cambridge, MA: Harvard University Press, 2002.

Singer, Peter. *One World: The Ethics of Globalization.* 2nd ed. New Haven, CT: Yale University Press, 2004.

Stewart, Garrett. "Modernism's Sonic Waiver: Literary Writing and the Filmic Difference." In *Sound States: Innovative Poetics and Acoustical Technologies*, ed. Adalaide Morris, 237–73. Chapel Hill, NC, and London: University of North Carolina Press, 1997.

Varenne, Hervé. "Love and Liberty: the Contemporary American Family." In *A History of the Family,* vol. 2: *The Impact of Modernity,* ed. André Burguiere et al., 416–41. Cambridge: Belknap Press, 1996.

Wolsak, Lissa. "'Ardor is its undermost shaping': An Interview with Lissa Wolsak." By Kent Johnson. *VeRT* 6 (Winter 2002). http://www.litvert.com/lwolsakinter.html.

—— (as Melissa Wolsak). *The Garcia Family Co-Mercy.* Vancouver: Tsunami Editions, 1994.

—— (as Melissa Wolsak). *An Heuristic Prolusion.* Vancouver: Friends of Runcible Mountain, 2000. Also published in *Alterran Poetry Assemblage*: http://ca.geocities.com/alterra@rogers.com/prolus.htm.

AN INTERVIEW WITH
LISSA WOLSAK

Tom Beckett

TB: I'm interested in the ways in which lyricism, spirituality, sensuality and social analysis collide, elide and just plain jam in your work. You end *An Heuristic Prolusion* with "For me, the urgent question is .. 'do we have a prayer?'" Do we?

LW: Nunc stans, yes. Of course, there is more going on here than pattern matching, circular/elliptical polarizing, my faux objectivity and blindspot. Personally and civically my hope is that we shift toward the dignity of mutual *understanding* rather than the chimera, *agreement*, to think causally about what diffusely and exactly is the concrescense of hatred and love, appearing to pace themselves within the depths of primordial matter. The world seethes on germane brinks, so too the instincts, courage, élan vital, open-heartedness and resilient free deeds of the polis. All things present at once, we are illuminable, the genius of all persons. In the deepening, taut involvement of the species with matter beheld, illumination, as opposed to limelight, is not a ruse, it is salient, actual, and has the beauty of Being, a consummate tool ~not needing sanction from hegemony and sophism. We do not wonder upon our oneness, so much as this meaninglessness amongst the usual "Fates" who foment our ends, when in pernicious degradation of trust murderous to our natures, totalitarian, hierarchic, echoic, inane; we are joined to the crawling.

Late 1970s, volunteering inside a maximum-security prison, I witnessed the inmates enact Arthur Miller's *Incident at Vichy* revealing the line "Every man has his Jew." So from within, and within our midst, chilling, horrific, and too often the case. Fascism can be just as refined as we are. It is not subject to satiric/ironic blasts. The "family" manifests everything possible, is a stage of eternal recurrance, appressed to Augustine's "I wish that you were."

Forgiveness and emancipation are not one-act wheels. There is the whirr of it which is in motion with the isness of our suffering. The message far outweighs the medium. We seem to be awakening to our duplicity, complicity, multiplicity, not to be replaced anytime soon with the brilliantly active wonder, radiant amplitude, anarchic, naked ease.

TB: "All things present at once," bassline doubling baseline. I think allegory is at the heart of your work. Am I on the right track?

LW: The works are stochastic meltdowns, entelechies in provision of a frontier for my sake, to accelerate my looking, divvied in imaginal, painty, partial pre-verbal milieux, necessarily outside agreed-upon motif-value. In contraction, syncope, they are sometime scherzi, jumpy surrealisms, bricoleurity, et al., directed toward synesthesia. I tell myself I don't impose a musculature and that one of the time-release fascinations of writing, indeed, all art, is what shows up in the after-grass. I do embed. I push against psychic containment. From here, your question causes me to realize the work contains allegory in reexamination of sanctity and fictitiousness, as in our deeply fictitious money systems, and influence of qualities supervenient on personhoods.

I think the heart of my work is the evisceration of being/its antithesis, and that which is inalienable.

TB: Pretty heady stuff. Can we slow this down though, loosen at least a little the knots of your epistemo-ontological concerns, and tease out some strands of your thinking about poetry? I'm wondering if you could speak to your process of composition – perhaps with reference to the genesis of your first book, *The Garcia Family Co-Mercy*?

LW: Experientially, it was chromatic sifting and fusing little hills of use, then sculpting in the sense of re-moving or eliminating all that was extraneous in that moment of making, nonce, letting myself tend toward inner explosive processes, metaphysical trespass and what was for me, remote sensing a full tremor of being, on its spindle of necessity. I wanted to loosehold it there, the contents .. not trapped, and simultaneously open out spatial terms, to keep it alive. The material came from accrued notebooks of reclusive experiment, "la perruque" (stealing time) over some ten years.

I had six weeks to write the manuscript. Also it came from a trenchant urge to view all the material at once, so that no part would really be refused from its entirety, I hovered and worked on the floor, hands and knees, where I could at least see the 36 pages or so, in one continuous ribbon, to begin the primitive flow, the guess-ropes.. I still like the floor as my main work surface when it is time to compose. The long-axis fix on the raw material gyrated from doing, learning and saying at the same time, while interpellating an over-lapping timelessness. I see writing as a wind-sock, which reveals to itself, ~consciousness. I truly never thought that the work would travel through but a handful of close friends. The words I now use to describe my writing, I did not know then.

TB: What instigated those early writing experiments? And what were they like?

LW: It was instigated by my experience of the complete breakdown of flow, of resonance in my everyday speech-life. Ordinary speech became such automatonic noise that I became deaf. Horribly, I could not hear what someone said to me a few feet away. I badly needed to accelerate breakthrough states and so..went looking, became deliberate. The first experiments were ideas and perceptual excursions, risky thick-pallet sound-visions, opening up for me conditions for simultaneity and individuality, placed so abstractly that each particulate could remain also, a frontier to itself.

I needed to see an emotional/perceptual free-will at work, noticeably against ideologies of perfection. The page read an infinite number of ways, much more a dynamic faltering of one's eyes over the depth-space of a canvas, from pigment to shade though even that was non-deliberate. From the first..I saw writing as a gypsy via closely related to the activity of trust, love, agape, and its counter-intelligence; deepening out one's time/perception, every which way to approach the face. It is the capacity to act. I came to make the work I did through sheer cultural necessity, as an uncertain but imaginative ascetic returning to words after having been shaped by the aero-curves of visual arts and music. My Italian mother profoundly influenced my aesthetics. Childhood contained very little money but a wealth of stimulating people, ideas, music, literature, visual arts of all ilks, gardens, arboreta, food, and too, she made palpable that culture is what happens ~here, made, in everyday life, ignited in various reciprocal moves.

Ralph Maud, the Charles Olson/Dylan Thomas scholar, in '88 became a friend and was the first to read my hitherto unseen notebooks. He urged me to do something about them. He was pivotal because I trusted him not to flatter the writing. Just after the publication of *Co-Mercy*, the Robin Blaser Conference in Vancouver '95 tore open my reading of poetry per se, which had been minute. I met David Bromige at that time whose immense and contagious freedoms I felt summoned forth by, in the making of some of *Pen Chants*. He later exposed me to Allen Fisher's work for which I am eternally grateful, as I might have gone years more, without knowing. Nate Dorward and Pete Smith most recently have influenced my reading, a difficult task as I always have my own compunctions, nevertheless, they generously provided difficult to acquire small press material and turned me toward the absolutely astonishing, compelling, contemporary poets in England and Ireland.

TB: Could you speak a bit of what you see in Fisher's work?

LW: I should only address this question in a poem, but I admire it ~because Fisher's work escapes all, even manifold definition. Idea upon idea, for me it sustains Being, wrestles Becoming, there, in the holomovement, in omnipresence of the very wildness and artistic civility of the cosmoses. I experience it as imaginatively achieved, and while magnetic, redolent with meaning, innocence, gentility and charm, in deepest personal/social critique. A threshold-free poet, knowing, pataphysical, but inclusive and further, an inutterably learned release from meaninglessness through causally fine-grained emotional IQ. There is no failure of nerve. The work demonstrates implicate and explicate orders in savvy motion, that light can and does exceed its own speed, ex animo. He is on to it.

TB: What are you working on now?

LW: A long poem entitled *A Defence of Being*, the first ana of which has been published by Spanner, U.K.; a further ana will be included in a forthcoming Selected or Collected from Station Hill Press, NY, and will also be a book from Wild Honey Press, Ireland. In addition, I am writing an essay on Madeline Gins and Arakawa's oeuvre.

TB: What, in particular, interests you about the work of Arakawa and Gins?

LW: In *Architectural Body*, The University of Alabama Press, 2002, a philosophical treatise, Gins and Arakawa's visionary social imagination factures a promontory from which even the most odious social-urban jeopardies may be negotiated. This truly is a tool "for the people." These are psycho-strategies to restore a sense of self, transforming through our experience of space and heightened sensitivity to the liquidity of surface, with ideas that engage theses of the celestial meridian to espouse a new society, still somewhat of a mirage perhaps, but an audacious shimmering bridge between wave and particle. One might say that a noun is a verb in repose. In fact, they describe the necessary path, an activity of Being, the goodness of it and what it is, to not forget. The world may not be ready for this, but these propitious blueprints are absolutely vital.

TB: "To restore a sense of self," "to not forget," "blueprints." Identity, loss, restoration, documentation of a project. One becomes, in the words of St. Augustine, "a question to myself"?

LW: I see questioning as the activation of soul, of love having eyes of its own, *esprit fort*, which wonderfully brings about apperception, uniting the contents of our intuitions. Questioning is free-will opening out an amplitude of kairological time, proceeding windward of perception; it is a new beginning, re-creative, prehensive and outstretching, an engaged antidote for static and entropy. As I understand it, St. Augustine became a question to himself when he suffered the unfathomable death of an intimate friend and was thus able to move from his previous isolation of *cupiditas*, to fathoming *caritas*, or, from the belief in appearances, to an inalterable love of all being.

November, 2002
First published in Tinfish *13 (September 2003)*

Since this piece appeared, the Gins/Arakawa essay has been published in Interfaces *21/22:* "Architecture Against Death" *(2003). Lissa Wolsak's collected poems* (Squeezed Light: Collected Works 1995–2006) *are forthcoming in late 2007/ early 2008 from Station Hill.*

"WHAT LIES BENEATH MY COPY OF ETERNITY?": A RELIGIOUS READING OF LISSA WOLSAK'S POETRY

Peter O'Leary

RELIGIOUS LANGUAGE, RELIGIOUS READING

North American poetry of the past fifteen years, especially experimental work, has been characterized by a preoccupation with clarities or obscurities of legibility. Such work seems to be a response to the question, "Can this be read?" In this respect, poetry has begun to mimic a kind of academic discourse in which *meaning* is questioned, usually suspiciously, as a way of generating theories about knowledge (or art, or political philosophy, for instance). Ben Friedlander has recently suggested a spectrum on which poetry might be understood to operate, with "intelligibility" standing on one end of a continuum, and the "registration and production of sense impressions" on the other (66).[1] I find this span useful for thinking about poetry and meaning: whether merely "intelligible" or the abstract, allusive, or surreal product of sense impressions (among which is the associative play of language itself), poetry means something, if only that it seeks to communicate something intelligible, or to record sense impressions. Readers ask, "What is this I am reading? What is this supposed to mean? How best to read this poem?" Because of our familiarity with writing built on asyntaxis, parataxis and anacoluthia, for instance, most readers, when confronted with work that is difficult to understand – work where legibility or intelligibility is called into question – feel comfortable enough registering the sense impressions of such work as its difficulties slide over them, normalizing them as a stylistic feature rather than as a challenge to sense-making. This sliding-over disengages the reader from recognizing either intelligibility or legibility in a poem. The work becomes understood, somewhat simplistically but acceptably, as "difficult." In a further simplification, such difficult work becomes "language poetry" or "avant-garde," both labels which have been used in the past as pejoratives to mark the scorn of so-called mainstream critics. Nowadays, stripped of most of their specificity, these labels typically signify a familiar mode available to a creative writer, neither better nor worse than, say, "love poetry" or "confessional poetry."

My academic training is in religious studies. This field, like that of literature, is many-plotted and subdivided, marked by various surveying techniques, as well as time-tested or novel excavation strategies (not to mention their requisite conflicts). Difficulties occupy a different space in religious studies than they do in contemporary poetry. Difficulty in contemporary poetry, as I've described, seems frequently to be used as a technique; in religious thought, it is more likely to be used as a tool, or to be seen as the product of necessary conceptions. How to understand this difference between technique and tool? In music, for instance, the use of a vibrato in singing is a technique, one that affects the way the voice sounds. A song can be sung with vibrato or without. The performance of the song will be affected, but the song itself will not. In the same example, the voice itself is the tool used to produce the notes that make the song. A song can't be sung without a voice. In this sense, then, I think when difficulty is used by a poet as a tool, rather than as a technique, the poet is getting to something more fundamental, what voice is to vibrato.

Let me give two examples of what I mean. We know from works of medieval Christian theology that it was never expected that a work – of scripture, of commentary, or of poetry – be comprehended in order for it to be useful. Indeed, difficulty was regularly built into medieval religious writings to work as keys, which, once discovered and turned, would act to open up more intimate realms of meaning. Furthermore, a work – a psalm, for instance – would never be taken "literally" in our conventional use of this term. Its meaning would be understood to exist on several simultaneous levels, of which only the lowest might be commonly perceived. Perhaps the most helpful example of this notion is Dante's sense of the fourfold polysemousness of literature, in which meanings are elucidated at the literal, allegorical, moral, and anagogical (or mystical) levels. In his *Letter to Can Grande*, Dante offers an example of these readings applied to a verse from the Book of Exodus:

> And for the better illustration of this method of exposition we may apply it to the following verses: "When Israel went out of Egypt, the house of Jacob from a people of strange language; Judah was his sanctuary, and Israel his dominion." For if we consider the letter alone, the thing signified to us is the going out of the children of Israel from Egypt in the time of Moses; if the allegory, our redemption through Christ is signified; if the moral sense, the conversion of the soul from the sorrow and misery of sin to a state of grace is signified; if the anagogical, the passing of the sanctified soul from the bondage of the corruption of this world to the liberty of everlasting glory is signified.

In Dante's cosmos, one strives through literal, symbolic and moral readings of a text to peer at the anagogical meanings underlying them. But this is knowledge arrived at only through great difficulty, and only ever partially in this life. The liberty of everlasting glory is a gift of death.

Nowadays (to give my other example), the work of scholars of early Christianity has demonstrated for us – by way of the massive discoveries of scrolls at Qumran and at Nag Hammadi – that the Christian narrative that was accepted as a monolith, arriving for us out of the Gospels and the New Testament, is in fact a kind of creative fiction – not in its contents (or not necessarily) but in its arrangement. We know now that what appears to be the continuous narrative of Christianity is more meaningfully a series of broken strands, which, over the centuries, are picked up, rewoven, twisted, snapped, lost, and then retrieved. The complexity of this new vision of early Christianity has done nothing to diminish interest in this narrative, in understanding it. Indeed, Christ – the figure about whom more has been written than anyone else in Western culture – remains as confusing and as compelling as ever when approached within this richer, more complex historical context. As the work of scholars as diverse as Elaine Pagels, Karen King, Robert Eisenman and Marvin Meyer has demonstrated, Christ's legacy in worship was twofold: there was Jesus the wisdom figure, who spoke in quasi-riddles of an interior knowledge of the Kingdom of God; and there was Jesus the resurrection figure, who defied death. The absorption of the former figure into the latter is one of the most complex stories of early Christian thought and history, as is the survival of the wisdom figure in the caches of scrolls discovered in the last sixty years.

In both examples, we encounter the value of religious language –
in terms of its complexities and its power. By "power" I mean
something similar to what Northrop Frye calls the *kerygmatic*. In
his second study of the "Bible and Literature," *Words with Power*,
Frye indicates four categories of language: factual/descriptive;
conceptual/dialectic; persuasive; and mythic/literary. Frye con-
tends – and this is behind his reasoning that the Bible, in spite of
scholarly evidence, is best understood as a totally unified book –
that in myth and literature, the dividing line between emotional
reality and mental reality, between the subjectivity of the mind
and the objective reality of the world, is obliterated. Furthermore,
within mythic/literary language, Frye posits a kind of language
unique to religious expression, which he labels "kerygmatic" language, which is to say prophetic and proclamatory. He means, in
essence, inspired language, either that spoken by God or through
a prophet. Kerygmatic language represents God's immaterial
essence, pointing to "the universe next door" (112). Religious language, in the way I'm imagining it, is powerful because it begins
in intelligibility but then begins to, or seeks to move beyond it.
Medieval Christian writers sought an excess of human meaning in
linguistic expression; the languages of the scriptures of Christ sought
to record his dangerous meanings in verifiable expressions, available for immediate adoption. My point is that the languages and
tools of religious studies, theology especially, offer a useful and
refreshing perspective on the difficulty of contemporary poetry.
Rather than shifting the blame of difficulty to the increasingly
bloviated categories of language writing or the avant-garde, why
not, when it seems appropriate, try to perceive the meaning of
such difficulty in explicitly religious terms, recognizing that from
their inception certain kinds of expression are loaded with power
such that they require special strategies for comprehension?

A MEANS BY WHICH SOMETHING IS DISCOVERED

Lissa's Wolsak's poetry occupies a mysterious, asynchronous realm
conjured from broken bits of observation, scattered neologisms,
scientific, psychological and hermeneutical jargon, and a lettristic
quasi-shamanism (best captured in the subtitle to one of her books:
12 Spirit-like Impermanences). A jeweller and metalsmith by training
and trade, Wolsak entered into a life of poetry much later than

most: her first book, *The Garcia Family Co-Mercy*, was published in 1994 when she was forty-six. Since then, she has published another book of poetry, *Pen Chants, or Nth or 12 Spirit-like Impermanences* (2000), and has issued lengthy installments (called *anas*) of a work-in-progress, *A Defence of Being*. Her work demonstrates a simultaneous care and meticulousness – something one is (perhaps misleadingly) tempted to attribute to her experience as a jeweller – and an excitement, a logophrasis of passionate engagement.

In *An Heuristic Prolusion*, her unusual poetic testimony, Wolsak identifies through the terminology of quantum physics the spiritual compulsions that generate her creative viewpoint:

~ Quantum physics engages the term "qualia," defined as those temporary states flagging our "immediate" reality . . . "no more than dispositions . . . things that can float free." The "redness of red, the painfulness of pain." The whatness . . that which gives things qualities. Qualia are the essential feature of consciousness. (16)

Her work elucidates these transient but luminous states of frequently intense feeling that underlie the normal flow of our attentions, the experience of which shapes our perception of reality. "Heuristic" is the hinge on which this observation swings. For Wolsak, poetry is her heuristic, the means through which she perceives the cosmos. When in 1916 Einstein published what the historian of religion Ioan P. Couliano calls "one of those very few books that matter in human history" (1), namely, *The Special and General Theory of Relativity*, he worried over the title before allowing it to be printed. "Theory" struck Einstein as an inapt word for what he was offering. He toyed up to the very end with calling it "An Heuristic Viewpoint of Relativity," wanting to stress the *viewpoint* he was offering in his tract. Wolsak's *Prolusion*, which like Einstein's *Theory* is meant as a preliminary set of considerations, strikes me as both a viewpoint onto and a test of reality, in her case a redolently poetic one. Take this example from *Pen Chants*, where Wolsak writes:

these arches   are but rooves

of earlier churches

cold spots where galaxies

would eventually form

I brought my sacred body

and caused it to sit . . (9)

As Einstein regarded relativity, so we should regard her heuristic as above all a theory, a provisional testing of reality. Both words, *heuristic* and *theory*, allow us to understand the hypotaxis and neologism by way of which she constructs her lyrical mosaics, as above when "rooves" (bridging a sonic image of *roofs* and *grooves*) opens to a cosmic perception of a primordial *corpus Dei* in the act of beginning its *indwelling*, a term I draw from Christian mysticism, meaning the abiding of God in the heart and the soul. (Traherne wrote in his *Christian Ethics*, "By the indwelling of God all objects are infused, and contained within."[2])

As a "heuristic," Wolsak's work is very much an experiential probing, rife with play and invention in words (among those to be found in the first ten pages of *Pen Chants*, for instance, are: *diaphane, luo, ingled, tungusic, gnos, devastatrix, sauvis, rhus, oospecie*), punctuation (most notably her characteristic "double-point" [..] which frequently begins or ends lyric installments in her poetry, acting as a visual stutter, a lyric hiccough), and page layout/prosody. *The Garcia Family Co-Mercy* is her most daring-looking poem, with words and syllables scattered across the page, generating a mosaic appearance. *Pen Chants* is a little more conventional in appearance, with most of the poems flush left and double-spaced, instead making use of abrupt linebreaks and enjambments; *A Defence of Being* duplicates this format, adding an even greater emphasis on enjambments, such that words are frequently broken at syllables or even letters – in one lyric, we find both "be- / cause" and "h- / and."

Among "theory"'s meanings, buried in its earliest usages – ca. 1600, according to the *OED* – is the act of looking at something, or contemplating it. In Christian history, *theoria* has frequently been understood in this light as a synonym for contemplation, which in Catholicism and Orthodox Christianity means the same thing as the Buddhist understanding of *meditation*. (The range of spiritual reference in Wolsak's work stretches from Christian notions of negative theology to Jewish mysticism and ethics, especially those of Maimonides, to the Buddhist mystical philosophy of Nagarjuna and Madhyamika Buddhist doctrines.) Contemplative, *theoretical* prayer is prayer which loosens itself from reason to focus on the Divine in a reflective, ruminative way. Which is to say that if I call Wolsak's poetry "theoretical," I mean that it is mystical/anagogical (in Dante's sense), or perhaps more accurately, *pneumatic*, which is to say "breathed out" from the *pneumatikos* or *spiritus*, the breath-source, which is the insitting soul.

AN ICONIC BEYONDSENSE

The "somatics of openness" that drives Wolsak's work, to use a phrase from *Pen Chants*, is the source of the disorientation that makes her poetry – in its searching and its grasping – both possible and ecstatic:

> eustasy, erosis, predicta, illusionism . . . ,
>
> lustral, tribulated, august . . .
>
> misnomers all (17)

These misnomers lead into the negative but sensuous light in which to perceive her poems, a kind of "divine darkness," perceived through apophatic devotions, understood through a simultaneous derangement and arrangement, or conscientious organizing of the disordered states out of which her poetry arises. "Apophaticism," warns Orthodox theologian Vladimir Lossky, ". . . is, above all, an attitude of mind which refuses to form concepts about God" (38–39). To this Lossky adds a sense of the contemplative imperative such refusal inspires: "[Negative theology] forbids us to follow natural ways of thought and to form concepts which would usurp the place of spiritual realities" (42). Poetry, for Wolsak, is the sense by which unusurped spiritual realities are perceived, in a "beyond-sense" she cultivates through active, Olsonian apprehensions and language:

~ I delimit my world through interoceptive (a receptor of the viscera responding to stimuli originating within the body), proprioceptive techniques, assembling, phrasing multiplicities where the containment of all possible meanings moves beyond its own oscillation, toward a relation to some or all of those juxtaposed but shifting magnitudes. Atomic reflection, in beyondsense. (*HP*, 32)

I want to think, then, of Lissa Wolsak as a theological poet, not in order to bolster an orthodoxy or to suggest her work represents any explicit faith. Rather, theology permits us to consider her work's mode of giving pleasure through experiment; furthermore, it allows us to regard her work as an intuitive functioning of the creative imagination, one shaped by a desire to articulate the deep space of beyondsense into which her poetry sends exploratory probes.

So how do we understand Wolsak as a theological poet? What are the terms of her theology? In an important essay, "The Icon and the Idol," from his book *God Without Being*, the Catholic theologian Jean-Luc Marion proposes of theology, first of all, that besides being the writing that gives its writer the most pleasure, it is also that for which its writer must obtain forgiveness in every instant, in that such speech can never satisfy its Author, in this case Christ, the ultimate *theo-logos*, or Word of God. Marion speaks of the idol as a dazzling spectacle that captures the gaze, such that "the gaze ceases to overshoot and transpierce itself, hence it ceases to transpierce visible things, in order to pause in the splendor of one of them" (11). "The idol," he asserts, "thus acts as a mirror, not as a portrait" (12). Beyond the dazzle of the idol, which blinds us, is the *icon*, emerging in the invisible. The icon is never seen, but *appears*; or, better, *seems*. It is energy and not essence (which belongs only to God), such that its semblance "never reduces the invisible to the slackened wave of the visible" (17). In the invisible, we stand "face to face" with ourselves, "our face as the visible mirror of the invisible." This is a semantic reorientation of *reflection*: not looking or gazing but being seen, *seeming*. Marion asserts:

Thus, as opposed to the idol which delimited the low-water mark of our aim, the icon displaces the limits of our visibility to the measure of its own – its glory. It transforms us in its glory by allowing this glory to shine on our face as its mirror – but a mirror consumed by that very glory, transfigured with invisibility, and, by dint of being saturated beyond itself from that glory, becoming strictly though imperfectly, the icon of it: visibility of the invisible as such. (22)

Wolsak's poetry, according to these terms, is iconic in its restless, relentless transfiguration of self-knowledge – a kind of mirroring of the self – into an *iconic* knowledge: a revelation of things invisible in the visible through an intuitive cohesion of language. This cohesion, which might also be called "epinoia," which in Christian Gnosticism means creative or inventive consciousness, prompts the qualia, or temporary states flagging immediate reality, that form the essential features of consciousness.[3] Marion's sense of the divine icon is synonymous in my mind with Wolsak's understanding of beyondsense, which is, for her, poetic knowledge – *gnosis* – never grasped, only received, epiphanically.

How does one – how does Wolsak – articulate this consciousness? In contemplative terms, only by backing into an expression of it. Sometimes this is accomplished through negation, as in these disorienting lines, where accent marks represent the blindfolded embodiment of silence: "I am mostly silence . . . distaff // but it is not so // as I have heard from ```` // that blindfolding eliminates stress" (*PC*, 60). At other times Wolsak presents a fragmentary, mosaic set of perceptions, so that broken bits of language contribute to a holographic vision of the consciousness expressed in the poem:

.. go with me,

disquisit ·   hour of terse ·

touch and sight,

transhumance,

fever them · selves

In these lines (the conclusion of *The Garcia Family Co-Mercy*), the reader fills in the remainder of the words implied by the symbol of the dot, leaving us with "disquisition" and "terseness," but the same dot severs/fevers "themselves" with an aporia neither touch nor sight can completely fill. Wolsak alights on consciousness through an excited quasi-silence, ordained through a linguistic geophagy:

arouse then
my tungusic.. my gnos...
I am full of rammed earth (*PC*, 13)

The call to "arouse" here serves as a kind of invocation of the spirit (proxy for the muses, perhaps?). It is preceded by a statement about the "speech-blows" of the "many-bodied // suspensi spiritus" who "is not our own" and who "is waking, just as I sleep" (12) – a hypnotic juggernaut who delivers potent messages. The poet's arousal – her coming into wakefulness or contemplative attention – is stymied by two interferences. First is "tungusic," which blends the English *tongue* with the Swedish *tung* (for "heavy") in a neologism drawn from *Tungus*, the eastern Siberian people thought by ethnographers and scholars of religion to be the group from which shamanism originated.[4] This she follows with "gnos," the root of knowledge, clipped by a characteristic ellipsis. Rather than ascend into some trance-realm of higher gnosis, the poet-shaman at this moment devours earth, or recognizes the humus packed deep inside her. This moment reveals to her an abiding, necessary "via immanencia," a way into the present.

TRANSHUMANCE AND CO-MERCY

I don't want to take Wolsak's work as entirely oblique in its references, nor made up exclusively of a reality revealed to her fragmentarily. The iconic beyondsense her poetry emerges from is perhaps best thought of as made up of quantum particles, surrounded by the qualia of perception that make a nimbus around the actual. Her theology, such as it is, feels experiential, its expressions necessitated by epiphanies and insights culled from her everyday life. Take this lyric from *Pen Chants*, for instance:

> ....in bussing silence.
>
> then it is *we*
>
> allow the cello to wander
>
> open among
>
> aestheocratic
>
> gift economies, grok
>
> therapeutic America, expire my
>
> omni-range, my mordant jealousy of space, my
>
> permanently blowing curtain, my
>
> breastlessness (26)

Let's try to reconstruct the scene in which this lyric took shape: she's on a bus, experiencing a kind of communion with the other – her own otherness? – inviting a kind of perception or potency of language and understanding, signalled by the wandering away of the cellos. Is she listening to music on headphones? Or is this an aural hallucination, an imagined accompaniment to her vagarious thoughts? She's trying to connect – to her fellow passengers, or to the world visible outside the windows of the bus? "Bussing" also carries the archaic sense of "kissing," which adds to this scene a level of intimacy. In any case, this feeling is opening her to the "aestheocratic / gift economies" of "therapeutic America," which she wants to "grok," a coinage of Robert A. Heinlein in *Stranger in a Strange Land*, meaning "to understand intuitively." Her desire to grok what she is seeing/imagining leads her into a purgative, plaintive mode in which she asks to be "breathed out" (*ex-* + *spirare*), or that these lingering qualia of hers be breathed out of her body: "omni-range," "jealousy" for "space" (which can be taken as a desire for possession, for a house, for land, for acquisitions), a "blowing curtain" (representing transience, perhaps – I'm reminded of Wallace Stevens's poem, "The Curtains in the House of the Metaphysician"), and, at last, her "breastlessness," the most startling word in this lyric. Does this indicate an actual condition – a mastectomy – or is this in reference to a kind of spiritual state? Most likely, it's a reference to the lack of such a spiritual state, or the difficulty of attaining a kind of communion in the current American world, supersaturated as it is with commerce and greed, driven by aesthetic and religious misconceptions that justify economies and hegemonies that render even a healthy woman feeling "breastless," in a state of surgical incompletion. It also hints at or echoes with "breathlessness," which reconnects this line, through a kind of erotic intimacy, with the closeness of the bussing silence with which Wolsak began this lyric. "Breastlessness" is a condition I don't imagine being imagined by or spoken from the voice of a man. I move through this set of readerly questions not to demonstrate explicit meanings in Wolsak's poetry but, rather, to suggest that her work feels based in the realities and materials of life, her life or an imagined other's life, one whose otherness is distinctly feminine.

Wolsak's poetry can best be construed as consciousness mirrors – reflections of an eternal state gleaned in the motion of words and thoughts through the imagination. We might perceive, then, some of her stylistic quirks – the frequent neologisms and punctuation oddities – not as poetic fancies but as survival techniques: a means of recording the transpiercing transience otherwise lost in the fleetingness of thought. In an interview from 2000 with Pete Smith, responding partially to his question about her late appearance on the poetry scene, she addresses the silence out of which her art arises:

For me, to speak at all, is suspect, just as it is almost always suspect to speak under the constraints in linearity, where the main question is: which surface must I appear on? In my work I presume to move through that silence which linear language admits, its lack of fullness, its utter necessity, placing a slight emphasis on the grace/civilizade/intuition of one who interprets its urgency. From silence of early and late dogmas, of duplicity, of closed human circuits, of refuge and resistance to cultural engulfment, of fixed and encrypted ideas, and obliteration that also naturally inheres in the language, then of all that had gone before, and that which holds love in fear. Very much from the silence of reflection, strong wishes, autonomy,..a vulnerable defense of being. (33)

By her own admission, "co-mercy" and "transhumance" are the terms through which she composes her poetry. Transhumance she amplifies as: "acts of symmetry, reciprocity and redistribution of generosity, forgiveness, love per se, and in doing so, ceasing or suspending the revenge cycle" (34). "Co-mercy" we can understand as a kind of compassion via alienation – the merciful feeling that ensues from recognizing one's otherness as something shared by each person you encounter. In *The Garcia Family Co-Mercy*, Wolsak puts it this way:

> Compassion
>
>   is largely   exile
>
>   .. condradict
>
>   the ways in which
>
>   the world
>
>   says no

But perhaps the strongest statement Wolsak makes about these terms is in the opening of *An Heuristic Prolusion*, where she connects co-mercy and transhumance explicitly to silence, which we can understand – through a synaesthesia of Marion's terms for understanding the icon – as a mode of listening to the invisible, to the reflection of the divine infinite. She writes,

~ I speak as one silenced. *Transhumance*, as understood and utilized in late 12th c., early 13th c. France, was an agricultural motion or migration, a seasonal moving of livestock and the people who tend them . . . but transhumance also was a possible personal-social act of symmetry, reciprocity and redistribution. Co-mercy, the art of harmlessness, equivocating sexual/theological, fiat, fiat lux . . . to lay the supremely ambiguous, phantomatic faces .. to let, to kneel, along the place of the abyss, to linger as long as possible .. where the same relation may be observed throughout the whole universe, where significance "bleeds into an unconstrainable chain."

What lies beneath my copy of eternity?

What coils-up .. in spoken space?

Even though the words come from different sources, I can't help but hear in Wolsak's "transhumance" Dante's assertion in the first canto of *Paradiso*, "Transumanar significar per verba / non si poria; però l'essemplo basti / a cui esperïenza grazia serba."[5] *Transumanar* = passing beyond humanity. There's something of this in Wolsak's migratory "transhumance," a motion beyond the human, pulled into the spiritual by an unearthly signal, an inward migration. Note how during the course of the main paragraph in the quotation from *An Heuristic Prolusion* her sequence of observations breaks down, as signalled by ellipses and then double-stops, a kind of hesitation as she imagines the lip of the abyss (which she feminizes in *Pen Chants* as the "upflung abysse" [13]). This leads her to two questions that serve as Virgilian guides to her work: the Dickinsonian "What lies beneath my copy of eternity?" and the more distinctly idiomatic "What coils-up .. in spoken space?" Beneath her copy of eternity is *beyondsense*, an iconic thrumming of silence, source of spoken space. "Coils-up," hyphenated as it is, feels adjectival, descriptive, rather than verbal. The double-stop seems to indicate a missing participle, for which "coils-up" is an adjective; or perhaps a missing noun: an announcing source of spoken space. In either case, it is absent. Wolsak's disruptive grammar leads us here into that space, peeling back the copy of reality she reads from to see what reveals itself underneath.

MORTISCIENCE

Underneath her thoughts, in the blackness of creative origins, there is also, strangely, a morbidity: death, in fact. Much like the Tibetan Buddhist understanding of the *bardo*s the departed soul passes through – thronged with fantastic figures of death – Wolsak's conception of "Being" is one rife with dead bodies. Her newest work, *A Defence of Being*, proceeds more apocalyptically than her earlier books. It is presented as a series of lyrics, divided into sets of *ana*s, by which she means collections or books of memorable or odd sayings (personal email to the author, August 14, 2004) – though one can hear as well the Greek prefix "ana-," which denotes *up, upon, back, again, new, throughout*. Wolsak appears in *A Defence of Being* to be compiling the elements of a revelation, but also to be looking into the moment of a vast catastrophe, one in which death and destruction are, as ever, sources of knowledge. Wolsak's poem occurs under the sign of another orienting term of hers, *fencelessness*, which we should add to *transhumance* and *co-mercy*. Fencelessness is a state of being "defenced," which she describes as meaning "that there must be a turning point from revenge, a completely new mode of *commerce*, so that rather than the capitalistic taking advantage of a person, place or thing, one . . . is inspired by compassion, and acts accordingly, and this is an initiatory opening process which must be begun by each of us . . ." (email, August 26, 2004). The imperative of defencing one's self, which is a challenge toward personal/social insight, is nonetheless fraught with ardour. She characterizes this imperative in the poem by imagining the underworld – both as Hades and as Hell-on-earth. The following two passages, for instance, are less Dantescan tours through Hell than Vajrayana imaginings from a new *Book of the Dead*:

> Perhaps..I say,
>
> love's whipscorpian cadaver
>
> omnivorously wavers *be*
>
> 'tween feeding and lidless
>
> vigilance, yet . . . free to reply to
>
> human prayers
>
>   . . .
>
> Awing us
>
> in the open place
>
> which inflects
>
> being . . . as in union or rapture,
>
> aside not yet all that would be
>
> fatherhooded
>
> will of nations, how much
>
> iconic depravity in play,
>
> on paths unknown to any vulture,
>
> the algebraically intractable corpse-vine
>
> bore on us

matchless

monuments to ascending vanity

in superposition just

enough death-rouge

holographically at hand how

then . . . ought each of

the said things intrude upon us now?

being scient is of

minute moment

loom-shuttles still (*DB2*, 6–7)

In the first lyric above, Wolsak connects Eros and Thanatos in the image of a poisonous scorpion who acts as predatory muse for Being itself: consumptive and watchful. Implicitly horrible. None-theless, to this god-thing humans pray – even as it preys on us. The second lyric gives an awful but appealing form to death, which "Aw[es] us / in the open place / which inflects / being" but is also figured as a patriarchal monster, "fatherhooded" and clothed in "depravity" and constricting "vine[s]." The question nestled in this poem – "how then ought each of / the said things intrude upon us now?" – is asked of the thanatoptic oracle that is the poem. The oracle answers: knowledge is only ever glimmering, a momentary still point in the shuttling of the loom. ("Scient" is an obscure adjective for "learned." Thus, to paraphrase Wolsak above: being learned – having knowledge – is of the fleetingest instant; death is always at hand.) "[M]inute moment" also refers to "enterprises of great pith and moment," in Hamlet's soliloquy (III.i.86), by which Wolsak intends to suggest moving power, importance, and conse-quence (email, September 13, 2004). Like Hamlet, Wolsak is medi-tating here on death in the face of being, the "dread of something after death" that makes life momentous. I'm compelled to coin words to describe the knowledge of death Wolsak is working toward/ out in these poems: *thanatognosis* – an intuitive knowledge of the meaning death shadows underneath our copies of eternity; or *mortiscience* – a prescience of death, a learnedness of the "unthought known" in which our true body abides.[6] It's important to recog-nize that Wolsak's prescient sense of death is not liberating, at least not here. What is represented in these lines is very much a hellish oppression. Part of the awareness of death – the knowledge that you will die and the knowledge that the world is made of death – is the repulsion of that knowledge.

One further passage from this second ana of *A Defence of Being* elaborates the Dantescan scene by way of Gustave Doré's renowned illustrations of the *Inferno*:

> Perhaps..
>
> Dore's throngs *fff* tremolando with
>
> covered heads in
>
> their origins from mercy, tell
>
> what birth-throes and pan-
>
> ic-stricken volleys, which
>
> of its sacral self, in
>
> suppurating shirts of blood shout-
>
> ing intimacies that
>
> they should ever feel wonder,
>
> *Ex Ante*
>
> according to what lies ahead
>
> it is enough that
>
> sapience before
>
> all else piing and a-
>
> loof under mocking fire, we,
>
> disclosively welling up, shall
>
> cling to nothing, tidal-
>
> tugging on our ex-
>
> cruciating wet rock, wrap-
>
> ped in willow-splints (*DB2*, 44)

The possibilities of this scene – introduced to us through that "Perhaps" followed by the double-point – come into focus in the following lines. "*Ex Ante*" is a curious inclusion in the poem, since it is a term derived from economics, meaning based on forecasted, predicted results. (Its literal meaning is "what lies ahead, before-hand, as before," which would trigger Wolsak's attraction to the term, in that it ciphers *beyondsense*; but it also injects a sense of economics into her critique: fencelessness requires new, more gen-erous, less murderous bartering among poets and the rest of the world.) The economies of the dead in this lyric work on punish-ment – a torturous clinging to a "wet rock," wrapped in "willow-splints." Our knowledge of this impending state determines our punishment in it. Knowledge is the coin of this realm. Being is something "piing and a- / loof under mocking fire," so that pi, the calculation of which is infinite, is a numerical equivalency for our self-knowledge or awareness. I think Wolsak is also saying here that foreknowledge is infinite (that is, "sapience before / all else piing"), and even as we may be punished for casting our thoughts endlessly ahead into the unknown, in this life or the next, we shall remain "aloof" under the mocking fires of eternal punishment, because knowledge informs the "sacral self" toward which we feel abiding wonder and awe. The flesh is refigured as a garment of our suffering: "suppurating shirts of blood" in which we "shout" (or are the shirts somehow vocalizing?) our "intimacies" – a bleakly ironic portrait of our condition in this life. Despite the horrors of this scene, Wolsak presents it as co-merciful, a picture of the sacral self originating in mercy. The lyric is a redemptive song.

HORIZONTAL READING

In passing beyond humanity, in rising into the imagined infinite in her poetry, where death and transfiguring knowledge await, Wolsak requires a different strategy of reading, one that deliberately engages her obscurities and seeming difficulties of legibility and meaning. I propose we read Wolsak, as I have been attempting, horizontally rather than vertically. I take this notion from the arguments of John Dominic Crossan, a scholar of early Christianity who has suggested that the four canonical gospels yield a vastly different – implicitly more interesting – story when read hori-zontally. Crossan suggests that because the four gospels were chosen for deliberate theological reasons to represent the "true" story of Christ, they each offer consistently different versions of his life and teachings, which, through the centuries and through negligent reading habits, we have synthesized into a whole, "true" story of the life. So, for instance, we might speak of Christ's sufferings in the Garden at Gethsemane, without realizing that Mark's Gospel speaks only of a garden where Christ went to suffer on the night before his crucifixion, begging mercy from the Father, while John's Gospel speaks of Gethsemane, where Christ triumphantly confronted the Roman centurions, willingly giving himself over to his captors.[7] Over the centuries, Crossan claims, we have moved from understanding these gospels as *interpretations* to perceiving them as immovable, literal fact. He implies, then, that horizontal reading of gospel texts – a method re-opening them to interpretation and heuristics – reveals meaning, whereas reliance on vertical, consecutive readings tends to obscure meanings and the theologies that drive the sequencing in the first place. By invoking Crossan's understanding here, I don't mean to suggest we take Wolsak's poetry as gospel. Rather, I want to appropriate Crossan's notion of reading toward understanding Wolsak's writing. Reading *Pen Chants*, for instance, as a consecutive sequence might distort its meaning, misleading one to a progressive reading of its lyrics. Reading it mosaically – or horizontally – allows for its images and ideas to settle into a holographic image.

Lest there be confusion here, let me state that Crossan's understanding of horizontal reading is spatial rather than sequential. A horizontal reading would consist of reading the first verses of the Gospel of Mark, followed by the first of Matthew, then of Luke, and finally of John, instead of reading the whole of Mark's Gospel first, followed by Matthew's, and so on. The purpose of such a reading is first of all to highlight differences (Mark begins with Jesus being baptized; Matthew begins with the genealogy of Christ; Luke begins with the Nativity; John begins with a Christological rewriting of the opening verses of Genesis); to indicate contradictions (Mark concludes with the tomb in which the body of Christ has been laid found empty by his mother and Mary Magdalene; the Gospel of John concludes with Christ's reappearance on a beach of the Sea of Galilee, frying fish); and to demonstrate motivations, hidden and revealed. I am not entirely certain what a horizontal reading of Wolsak's poetry would look like. I take my own reading of her work as a provisional beginning. The real difficulties of her work – a kind of (en)tranced grasping after gnosis – are too easily sold short by a fixation on the veneer of lexical, syntactical diffi-

culty, which can flatten the effect of the work. In bringing some of
the tools or ideas of religious studies to looking at poetry, I want to
suggest a different – let's call it *horizontal* – approach to difficulty.
Rather than excusing difficulty as a byproduct of a manipulation
of language, let's use it as a door into another room, or universe of
thought.

Wolsak's composition practices bear out this notion of a hori-
zontality at work in her writing. The production of a poem for
Wolsak is a layered, cumulative process, one in which she immerses
her senses into the act of writing. She begins by noting words,
fragments, sound-bites, and neologisms in a notebook she carries
with her everywhere. She then highlights what seems important
from these notebook fragments, writing them out longhand onto
"great big drawing sheets. I pour over these spread out on the floor
so I can see everything at once." At this point, she begins to "listen"
to her writings, letting them begin to "speak to each other, forming
affinities." This part of the process she likens to a kind of chemis-
try, one in which word-molecules join together intuitively or
thematically. From here, she begins another set of longhand drafts,
one in which she brings the poem together in a manner that allows
for maximum saturation of her creative senses, most especially the
ear, "with particular attention to meaning." She describes this process
as a "froth of confusion, so much going on at that point I can't see
anymore, but in some way I think it is all about not seeing at first
and 'going' blind until meaning springs forth." At this point, then,
she begins to compose drafts on a word processor, whose function
is to allow her to see the work again, to work on it further (email,
August 1, 2004). In this sense, Wolsak brings a normative, vertical
conception of poetry into her work only in the last act of composition. Prior to this, in listening to the pleromatic invisible of her
beyondsense, she is compelled into apophatic, horizontal acts of
reading and writing.

Not all difficult poetry is religious poetry; nor are the languages
of religion and theology necessarily helpful toward understanding
even such transparently spiritualized writing as Wolsak's. We need
to tread carefully when insisting on religiously inflected readings
of contemporary poetry, for fear of losing sight that it is poetry and
not religion we are talking about. I don't want to suggest that
Wolsak's poetry should be treated exclusively in light of religious
discourse and language. Hers is vigorous work as responsive to
contemporary strategies of literary appraisal as to religious thinking

and consideration. But I do want to suggest that an academically
inflected culture of reading contemporary poetry imposes constraints on literary thinking that are ultimately as transient as their
dogmas are inviolable.[8] Work such as Wolsak's suffers from the
constraints of an academic perception, in that it seems to welcome
reading strategies that are looser, more intuitive. I don't think of
religious studies as a great liberator for thinking about poetry; but
I do find its premises and its tools helpful, because more open, in
considering work like Wolsak's. Rather than glossing over her
difficulties, a horizontal reading of her poetry cultivates an environment in which to perceive its strangeness, and to accept its
prospective ventures toward meaning. What lies beneath Wolsak's
copy of eternity? Poetry. Let it be so, then, for each of us who
read her.

Notes

Many thanks to Lissa Wolsak, who provided biographical and bibliographical
information for this essay, as well as offering insights into her compositional
methods.

1. Lest it appear that I am trying to co-opt Friedlander's terms here – he is
interested in defusing notions of any native difficulty in his subject's poetry
while preserving the experience of reading work that is manifestly confusing –
I want to say that Friedlander's essay has been helpful to me in constructing
ways of thinking about Wolsak's poetry in relation to other so-called experimental work of the past ten years. It's helpful as well that Wolsak's poetry
resembles Jenks's rather a lot.

2. I found this citation in the online second edition of the *OED* under the
definition for "indwelling."

3. Elaine Pagels writes that *epinoia* conveys genuine insight, and might be
translated as "imagination." The term appears in the *Secret Book of John*, a work
of early Christian Gnosticism, which speaks of this "luminous *epinoia*" as a
creative force virtually endowed with consciousness. Pagels says that "*epinoia*
conveys hints and glimpses, images and stories, that imperfectly point beyond
themselves toward what we cannot now fully understand" (165).

4. See, for instance, Mircea Eliade, *Shamanism: Archaic Techniques toward
Ecstasy* and I. M. Lewis, *Ecstatic Religion: A Study of Shamanism and Spirit
Possession.*

5. "The passing beyond humanity may not be set forth in words: therefore
let the example suffice any for whom grace reserves that experience" (*Paradiso*
I:70–72). Dante, having ascended from the Garden of Eden at the end of
Purgatorio, is ascending from earth into the heavenly spheres. Commenting on

this word, Singleton writes: "As a verb, the coined term is striking enough; but it is the more so in being, in this context, a verb of motion" (*Journey to Beatrice*, 26). He goes on to equate this verb with the *lumen gratiae* of Beatrice, which he compares to the light of Virgil's guidance, which he calls "*umanar*," or "within the proportion of our human nature" (33). Making my own comparison: Wolsak's transhumance is Dante's *transumanar*; her co-mercy is Virgil's *umanar*.

6. "The unthought known" is psychoanalyst Christopher Bollas's concept for the instinctive knowledge – which he separates from acquired knowledge – that characterizes the thought and feeling of the True Self, a notion Bollas borrows and amplifies from the writings of D. W. Winnicott. See, for instance, Christopher Bollas, *Forces of Destiny* and D. W. Winnicott, *Human Nature*.

7. Crossan writes: "differences and discrepancies between accounts and versions are not due primarily to vagaries of memory or divergences in emphasis but to quite deliberate theological interpretations of Jesus" (*The Historical Jesus*, xxx). Elsewhere, he writes, "It is precisely that *fourfold* record that constitutes the core problem. If you read the four gospels vertically and consecutively, from start to finish and one after another, you get a generally persuasive impression of unity, harmony, and agreement. But if you read them horizontally and comparatively, focusing on this or that unit and comparing it across two, three, or four versions, it is disagreement rather than agreement that strikes you most forcibly" (*Jesus: A Revolutionary Biography*, x).

8. I'm indebted to Robert von Hallberg for this idea, who passed it along to me in a personal communication, August 11, 2004.

Works Cited

Bollas, Christopher. *Forces of Destiny: Psychoanalysis and Human Idiom*. London: Free Association Books, 1989.

Couliano, Ioan P. *The Tree of Gnosis: Gnostic Mythology from Early Christianity to Modern Nihilism*. Trans. H. S. Wiesner and the author. San Francisco: HarperSanFrancisco, 1992.

Crossan, John Dominic. *The Historical Jesus: The Life of a Mediterranean Jewish Peasant*. San Francisco: HarperSanFrancisco, 1991.

——. *Jesus: A Revolutionary Biography*. San Francisco: HarperSanFrancisco, 1994.

Dante. "Epistle XIII" [Letter to Can Grande]. In *The Letters of Dante*, trans. Padgett Toynbee (Oxford: Clarendon Press, 1920). *Princeton Dante Project 2.0*. http://etcweb.princeton.edu/dante/pdp/.

——. *Paradiso*. Trans. Charles S. Singleton. 2 vols. Bollingen Series LXXX. Princeton, NJ: Princeton University Press, 1975.

Eliade, Mircea. *Shamanism: Archaic Techniques of Ecstasy*. Trans. Willard R. Trask. Bollingen Series LXXVII. Princeton, NJ: Princeton University Press, 1964.

Friedlander, Ben. "Philip Jenks and the Poetry of Experience." *Chicago Review* 48, no. 4 (Winter 2002–3): 65–81.

Frye, Northrop. *Words with Power: Being a Second Study of "The Bible and*

Literature." New York: Harcourt Brace Jovanovitch, 1990.

Lewis, I. M. *Ecstatic Religion: A Study of Shamanism and Spirit Possession.* 2nd ed. London and New York: Routledge, 1989.

Lossky, Vladimir. *The Mystical Theology of the Eastern Church.* Trans. the Fellowship of St. Alban and St. Sergius. 1957. Crestwood, NY: St. Vladimir's Seminary Press, 1976.

Marion, Jean-Luc. *God Without Being.* Trans. Thomas Carlson. Chicago: University of Chicago Press, 1991.

Pagels, Elaine. *Beyond Belief: The Secret Gospel of Thomas.* New York: Random House, 2003.

Singleton, Charles S. *Journey to Beatrice.* 1958. Baltimore and London: Johns Hopkins University Press, 1981.

Winnicott, D. W. *Human Nature.* New York: Schocken, 1988.

Wolsak, Lissa. *A Defence of Being [second ana].* Bray, Co. Wicklow, Ireland: Wild Honey Press, 2005. (Cited as *DB2.*)

—— (as Melissa Wolsak). *The Garcia Family Co-Mercy.* Vancouver: Tsunami Editions, 1994.

—— (as Melissa Wolsak). *An Heuristic Prolusion.* Vancouver: Friends of Runcible Mountain, 2000.

——. "Lissa Wolsak Interviewed by Pete Smith." *Six Poets: Views and Interviews.* Willowdale, ON: The Gig, 2000.

——. *Pen Chants or Nth or 12 Spirit-like Impermanences.* New York: Roof Books, 2000.

63 OUT-TAKES
FROM THE D.F. SHOW

Pete Smith

This work arises from trawling through D.F.'s poems, from brief encounters with her & some location spots in Cranbrook & Canada's poorest postal district in Vancouver, & from fascicles of gossip.

"*Unlimited Growth Increases the Divide*"

1.

There is failure of community in the poem-world of Deanna Ferguson. The reader reflects.

One doesn't know which side of whose mirror one is on, do you?

2.

They don't look like sisters. Make the one on the right look less

visible

wouldya

3.

Odd about the Jesus. He was God's way of getting Even with us: straining the self out of righteousness; pouring vinegar back into the sponge. Papal infallibility for Gawd's fake? Two thousand Hail Marys and two weeks flipping burgers in Hope – ahh, the good burghers of Hope.

But, cheap puns notwithstanding, from the cloister of choice enlightenment's always been an outing.

4.

The poem teetered on the edge of the 32nd floor. Its own yells of Jump outshouted the crowd of eager enablers.

5.*

Emergency. Drain the Ocean – we're missing a body. Anybody(?). Will do.

6.

Let me introduce you to my anthology. Your absence will guarantee you pride of place.

7.

Wait a minute, wait a minute, I'm confused.
No you're not. You're refused.
Refuse?   .

8.

Water or Knife. The real cold shoulder doesn't discriminate edge from edge.
Precipice shower: prospect point.

9.

Link fantasy to what?

10.

Cranbrook – home of theories, as in *mental conceptions*, e.g., hockey dad & gourmet logging-camp chef. Wait a wee minute: just cuz he's a drool case, there's no need to get peevy.

11.

Cranbrook: the *Daily Townsman*
                          tells her story?

12.

If you hit Louis Zukofsky with a 2 × 4 twice you'll get a demi-semi-quaver discount of Coltrane or a Sophie's Cosmic refund at 4th & Arbutus. Not both. Not likely.

13.

A word in your (ear). The poem as high chthonic lavage or syringe me an aura, Poe, peel me a bell. Both. And. Trinkle tinkle.

---

*Written months before December 26, 2004, as a riff on DF's poem "My Body Lies Over the Ocean": her pun and the fact that her erstwhile press is called Tsunami are facts beyond anyone's control – in another century other claims would have been filed & salted.

14.

Whisper it not in Goth
>   home of No Theory.

15.

Shut the window. The stench of bad poetry is affecting my equilibrium.
A pocketful of posies is no help.

16.

Fear is Gaelic for *man*. Fear goes on. US policy: them murderous unbelievers.
The domestic, the foreign, subjected & objected to.

17.

The thought of an audience, that's scary.

18.

You can read my *Writing*, Tom.
Yeah, then I can stand beside my text, be a para/graph.

19.

Blazoned on the Ferguson clan heraldic crest, a heart with nails through it.
So bleed, language.

20.

The thought of a reader, that's scary.

21.

It is true that Oprah refused to appear on The Deanna Ferguson Show
>   & then she declined.

22.

She was happy as a Vancouver riot when she construed her name as *teargas*.
Happier than Larry.

23.

At the AmLit/CanLit border the guards have dropped theirs. Keys. Lids.
Hastings deserted: Hamilton abandoned. Acid Speed Toxi City. Not every
blue-eyed blonde (Beckett-blue; platinum blonde) sports PKU's stigmata, but
an absent enzyme makes for present danger.

24.

D. Ferguson & T. Raworth read *together* at the KSW. Not together, she first.
Her words so angry she whispered them & we groped round in that lacerated
silence; his so fast, we lashed ourselves onto the raft of her silence & went over
the falls together. Oh, it was a good day to be alivened, to see the sepia picture
colour. (Who *we* were is removed. . . .)

25.

Ground swell   water OK   air fair
                                    -to-middling.

26.

Lines in the sand for those who cannot read the signs in the land.
The waste. Not whatnot. If oysters turn sand into peep-holes
then Tom's a-cold, but a dry cold.

27.

Someone was watching, always is, while hair & common standards fell. Tom,
Hugh Hefner's little page-boy, who saw him peep? Godiva didn't. Her collective
eye was on the way her smooth hair swayed with the horse's wind-roughed
mane: the illusory politics of freedom. Leofric breathed a corporate sigh.

28.

Hello you little Bombshell. I was just thinking plastic explosives need a lot of
room to grow in: neglect of poverty to acidify the soil. The rich have problems
too: first, vertical running water at False Creek, then a high-priced flotilla
weeping all the way to the bank-on-it.

29.

She daughtered well, but there was a huge draft when she quit her post
          at the lacuna between door and stoop.
                    Muck thirst ensued & matching of teeth.

30.

Carrying on down the line. Lots of fuss over Onan's lack of determination. He
wasn't such a bad wanker: interruptus was the issue. Refusing to co-sire through
his dead brother's widow. Not following the line of morbidity. Patriarchy required
such hankies.

31.

She lives way up there. Doesn't connect with the Collectif any more.
Disowns her (previous) poetry.
Does it still speak to/for her? Six/eight then?
Even as time's signature shifts the relative minor may still bring gladly home.

32.

I say/cannot say: indignant is as disgust does.
Gust of foul wind
                    hard gist
                                    expelled guest
aghast
        sex-ghost
                    gloss this.

33.

A tidal-wave of p.r. orgies accompanies the launch of Reader's Disgust Compact
Books.
        Vol. 1 groups *If I'd Been Able I'd Have Cut More Cane* with *If You Can See
My Epiglottis, You're in the Wrong Opera* and *Jack & Jill Fell Down the Hill
Because It Was There.*

34.

His eyes grazed her chest caved in ertia ertia all fall down. *It Must Be Artificial*
to be real.
        Dr Susan Miller says disgust is the gatekeeper human emotion: it would be
hard to represent that, so we'll just reinvent it.

35.

The putative stars of *The Little Coup That Could* accepted a time-shared condo
in the North of Contention in exchange for revolutionary fervour. Proof: every
reaction produces an unequal and opposite inaction. Don Carlos Williams
produced Don Paterson out of inert matter – a three-step program where twelve
were needed. Being one of the boys is the apotheosis, but notice how quality
control always rises to the top of the boot.

36.

I is a maze, an amazed and amazing am. I am a part of the most intricate
cornutopia of wishful filaments in the whole blazing trail – bright shiny &
something illegible.

37.

Seep if veined like Creeley: signed, the Kis of Dea.

38.

In group therapy the key is to subordinate the *maladaptive*
in opera if you lose the key six degrees of grin & tonic will see you home
in both, sign by sign, the show must go

39.

To Elvis. What the USArmy needs in Iraq is to Elvis
have benign capitalist pill-poppers show how easy
the Good Life is for all
in a non-prophet society.

                   (Jesus Christ? Trademarked by WalMart.)

40.

Love-lies-bleeding. Inca Wheat. Pigweed. Tumbleweed. Amaranths. Amen.

41.

Deplaning in Cranbrook the first time just naturally levels everyone to the
same caste – decelerated acculturation. The support group meets nightly at
the Bar None.

42.

A river runs out of it
        keeps girls & co-eds tamed
                clouds the fact
that Hero was a woman
       fell
             for that drowning boy betide

43.

Disarmingly, the tree was perchless for the bird.
Chopped & lopped & follies ahoy.

44.

Or not to Elvis. Splick, splack I was taken aback.
                Hard rock, hard island,
                   hard line
     Eye to eye looking   like want wants want.

45.

> Swayed & stormed
He wishes us, from the City of Men,
> a health of ripe waters.
Hero still woman
> also the Beloved.
>> (Where it says *Yield* read *Meet.*)

46.

Everyday dust say You rather be a poet or write poetry?
Just dessert is more than I can afford.
Nevermore than an extension of Raven.
An ought is a naught is an ort.
> Alice, be tactless.

47.

Silence then. An honourable estate. After all there are already so many more poets than poems in the world.
> Unsay. Unsing. Steel home.

48.

Half of me thinks stand-up comics should stand in buckets of their own piss and half of me thinks a sentence is a pustule of fascist pus while half of me idles in neutral and dreams of fifth and a ten K passing lane in the always up-ahead . . .

49.

Political heartsickness for *asphyxia.*
Don't you wanna choke on that?
> Hot bush   Singefingers
> Preresuscitated angel spirochete
> President of an abject state
Katydid or might have if Remorse hadn't winged by.
"We will find Original Sin whatever rock he's hidden under: we got him on the run . . ."

50.

It was tomorrow when the magic meanings pulled apart
> a petal of pulchritude
>> & encunted themselves in self-effacement.

51.

How do you turn your back on yourself?
　　　　When the learning-curve turns into a cul-de-sac
　　　　　　　there's no stopping progress – is there?

52.

The story goes round and round:
an intimacy shared is a braille invitation – unopened.
　　　　The ubiquity of bullshit makes detection difficult:
　　　　the chosen forget the choosers by nightfall – apparently.
　　　　　　Until representations　　no fear

53.

A yawn of clomipramine.
The atomic part tickles –
　　　　fields where late the sweet burns

54.

A pall borne is a corse untethered.
An umbrellafall of sky to patch the ript blue.
　　　　We shift shapes & remove stains & put the dog out,
　　　　　　　yes, Snuff.
Succour the born every day.

55.

Hush, what erotic breezes drift over the marsh.
The subsequent renga to be published by Sudden Change Press.
No matter how softly, vengeance is a mine of hideous non sequiturs.

56.

He thought you could only use a Swipe Card if it was stolen.
Like a urinal with no brain-pan.
Back at the store, when the spleen was removed the poem was
nothing but cut fist.

57.

The stand-in person eschewed blotting paper
spat out wasp-sting.
　　　　　　　Hey, you, mean like you act it
　　　　　nerve-pulped
　　　　　　　　& easy on the butter.

A rougher prejudice writes without dallying
                                          the bluest fade

58.

Tinge me an orifice, won't ya.
Hang & clang
                  until the rats say it wasn't so
                                          total eclipse

59.

They told us a little economic SSRI would fix our Recession, so we borrowed it
from the future. Not ours. Some other losers'.

60.

It's the Law of the Biggest Dipper, the one whose ante is so far up everyone
& her philosopher folds. A silent bid on eBay will at least raise an old hope for
new heaven & a private government will clean up here, in our time on our
dollar. There is no way. Out.

61.

She's uptown now
                  home of no
                              poetry

62.

As punk as you wanna be. It's not just attitude, you know, it takes some bleedin'
talent to get to the trough while there's still some (& more to leave some behind).
On yr Marx. As punk as you, wannabe.

63.

Those are words that were her poems
                  (chiastic chasm)
When you amputate your poem-self
          do its nerves still twitch
          in the night   at lunch   at sex
                  in mid-conversation
                                    that phantom limb
                                    & its gathering brood?
                  Och, pull the other one –
                          tintinnambulate yr crippled poems outa here.

ON COLLABORATION

Nancy Shaw & Catriona Strang

1. *Arcades Intarsia*

For a Love of Knitting

A love of knitting and Walter Benjamin's *Arcades Project* inform our latest collaboration, *Arcades Intarsia*. Like the Arcades, our work intersects with the public space of the street and the spectacular interiors built for dwelling, consumption and entertainment. Like Benjamin, we want to unravel the conditions of our engagement. We liken our writing to knitting; we provisionally stitch and restitch, ravel and unravel. We shape our writing in light of the mosaic knitting technique Intarsia's distinct, yet integral, sections as compositional fabric. We apply this patterning to our research into the shifting boundaries of affiliation and disaffiliation, inclusion and exclusion. As such we crave history and alliance in all their variances: in their numerical, gestural, musical and discursive configurations; in their textures, designs and colours. We blend, traverse, contest, hash and rehash, translate, adapt, and intersect. Rather than prescribe rules and regulations dictating conduct, we braid and cast, blend, hem and trim disparate and related skeins, spinning time and weaving spaces for people to eke out their possibilities and limits. Our arrangements are aimed at the curious and restless, at amblers, perusers, and fellow travellers, as well as at the dispossessed, excluded, and silenced. In our collaboration, we seek out multiple processes that are neither unified nor univocal. We are committed to activating, reorganizing and redirecting these processes toward ends that are flexible and inclusive.

from ARCADES INTARSIA

"Vows to Carry On"

1 – Fragments of a General Layout

Question One: "What is the historical object?"

These can be messed with; the shawls were not documented. Here a defiant venture, a combat paid without approval, and an empire of a-certain shame-world poised to sprint from recapitulation to sell-off. And there our tasks are slightly easier? It was nothing more than rational convenience; that there is a rational connection may safely be doubted. As for my own personal terror – in order to decipher the contours of the collective dream, we must find space for provisions of all sorts, and coax a proliferating collectible context, i.e. envy-portfolio.

41 – Syndicates

moreover, he is no buyer

*Three habits not to be shared:
 Life-style terrorism
 randomized home-off
 peer purchase, or: anti-largesse

Down-ante
 that is, thick with, and fringe
 driven

17 – A kindred problem arose

A catalogue, in which we witness the convergence of forces mercantile, hygienic, and military, and the concurrent rise of the parasitic elements.

45 – shawl passage

I.   ? (in the eaves)
II.   Phantasmagoria
III.   Progress

[these MUST follow the same trajectory
                i.e. le spécialité]

43 – disorderly, or libertinism

Chiefly transposable visor sucks

51 – Shawl again, but presented as living images, as intransigent as "a careerist in the service of a usurper" (I have long been a generous donor). Here we expose the slurry wall, for a series of highly articulated slopes do not reflect at ease, or vainly exceed the hired sit-down/stand-up presumably left behind. Structure, circulation, interior organization: are they not worth the increased expanse? What below-grade uses would a completely illegal structure incur?

[Note: amend obsolete patches]

2. *Cold Trip*
(*Schubert's* Winterreise *Meets the Ramones*)

Written with composer Jacqueline Leggatt.

Version 1: for voice and hurdy-gurdy mechanisms
Version 2: for voice (both sung and spoken), clarinet,
violin, viola, cello and piano.

In *Cold Trip*, we probe the relationship between music and poetry, as well as romantic and contemporary conceptions of the lyric (Schubert meets the Ramones). We dwell in multiple time scales conjuring the past through sensations of the present, while eliciting the present through residues of the past. More pertinently, we mess with time scales as they both accelerate and slow down. In

Cold Trip, we interlace notions of speed, efficiency and instantaneousness with melancholy, sluggishness and breakdown. Like Schubert's, our songs are queries of the sublime – its envelopment of the beauty and/or horror of the self, nature, war, kindness, passion and disaster. Through song, we perform in musical and verbal scale, comparing Schubert's intense commitment to nature and inner life to our encounters.

Our conjunction of the Romantics' time with our own leads us to delve into the machinations of the free market and artistic expression. As such, our lyrics excavate the historical and spatial connections and disjunctures between market liberalism and free expression. We are concerned with these processes as they work within and against our locations in their political, economic and discursive guises. We consider song to be a vehicle of cultural traffic – multilingual and polyphonic – which not only disturbs traditional and contemporary practices but gleans from them, while facilitating charged interchanges. We conduct conflicting and collaborative trade between a plethora of perspectives. Further to this prospect, we address the self-estranged and self-conscious (à la Schubert), as well as dissenters, the exiled, disaffected and disenfranchised, in their dealings with the powerful.

Song operates not only as entertainment, but as a genre through which cultures and languages express, preserve, emerge, clash, revive and transform. Our adaptation and translation of Schubert's song cycle *Winterreise* will venture through sonic scenographies infused with love and generosity, fear, greed and loathing. Therefore, we work in and against the production of emergency, segregation and fear.

COLD TRIP

Must be razed
rent, or rapped
far, far again
my stray moves strange, for

Here I cannot
vote, cannot
travel, cannot
flag, shall no longer
long

All this crazy stay I

Can't remember
what I'm
lookin' for

TAKE A SHINE

Here I go
I shine
I shine
I should be high
Cover me
Better than I

Rant:
I don't know who
I don't know why

Therefore, this is the New Year
And I have not the decrees
For the state induces perjury

Without permission
Thinly disguised
As I forsook
As in those days
Not in those days

Then I could have travelled
Or been avenged

3. *IDR: Manifesto*

Who among us, in his idle hours, has not taken a delicious pleasure in constructing for himself a model apartment, a dream house, a house of dreams?
> – Charles Baudelaire, in the introduction to his translation
> of Poe's "Philosophy of Furniture," which originally
> appeared in October 1852 in *Le Magasin des Familles*:
> cited in Walter Benjamin, *The Arcades Project*

To live an ordinary life in a nonordinary way.
> – Institute for Domestic Research, 2004

Under the umbrella of the IDR, we engage in collaborative projects
with poets, visual artists, musicians, dancers and composers, all
friends. Most of our time is spent hanging around, watching movies,
eating, going for walks, telling jokes, and gossiping. Sometimes
out of these informal encounters workable ideas emerge which we
transpose into notes, manifestos, internet exchanges, poetic and
photographic treatises, musical and multimedia performance and
recordings as well as forays into the domestic arts (knitting, bead-
ing, sewing, crocheting, renovation, interior decorating, cooking,
entertaining, playing with and caring for children). We explore
materials such as heirlooms, textiles, photographs, letters, portrai-
ture, scrapbooks and diaries.

We engage with the domestic because it is the locus of our creative
production and casual interaction – to say nothing of the domestic
sphere as a site for everyday life as well as work. Many of us are self-
employed and work from home. As a result, we regard as unten-
able separations made between what is considered to be public
and that which is private. We cannot conceive of the home as a
reprieve and refuge from the world although it is often treated as
mere shelter.

Nevertheless, we realize that this construct of the domestic is
historical and rooted in the rise of modernity, the middle class,
and the association of women and their femininity with purity,
privacy, virtue and frailty. As such we conduct research into these
conditions, scouring novels, pattern books, cookbooks, how-to
manuals, self-help literature, historical conduct manuals, as well
as tomes on home décor and the fabric arts. Thereby, we seek out
genealogies of the home, the domestic sphere and its environs.

Within these genealogies, we query the home as a sphere of the heteronormative, patriarchal nuclear family, which sanctions intimacy, and is utilized as an index of the health and wealth of the city and nation. The home, moreover, is a major source of economic growth, as is reflected in the rise in property values, homeownership, and the profitability of do-it-yourself and big box stores. Within this conjunction, domestic arrangements can take on a different hue when they are engaged by single parent families, gays, lesbians, queers, feminists, the homeless, migrants, immigrants, refugees, and the indigenous – all those who do not fit easily within normative formations of home, family, marriage and the constitution of the domestic sphere. Indeed the tenets and regulatory regimes of home simply fail those who are without one.

The domestic is a rubric through which fear, belonging, security, and emergency are defined. As of late, home operates as a metaphor eliciting nationalism – it shapes domestic and foreign policy, and allows for the suspension of civil liberties and perpetration of war under the rubric of "homeland" as in the "war on terror" and conflicts in the Middle East.

For the IDR, the domestic operates as a space for self-fashioning and contestation for living an ordinary life in a nonordinary way.

IDR Members: Jacquie Leggatt, Catriona Strang, Nancy Shaw, François Houle, Jim Smith and Bernard Sauvé.

4. *On Collaboration*

Writing in collaboration creates for me a sphere, a little shifting spot my comrades and I inhabit together. As the other kid-filled spheres I more often frequent are delightful but very demanding, I could not access our humming, cooking and regenerating space on my own. I literally could not get there, nor could I write without the ideas and impetus my cohorts provide. Collaboration offers me love and possibilities unattainable in any other land.

(2005)

THIS THEN WOULD BE THE CONVERSATION

Christine Stewart

> Mid-ocean on a raft palms extended but a horizon but the open as hunger every which-way; and this is perhaps one of them, this gap, across which you face me, absorbed, spectacularizing. I, you, we use the text as our occasion. – Clark

I will not analyze these traits.
I will not ignore the invitation.
I will read slowly.
Oh anachronistic readers take time –
the future is generous.
My service is total.
The rules are the eyes of the future.
The ashes are central to the argument.
"We use the text as our occasion."

> The nightreading girls are thinking by their lamps; we make use of their work. We cannot contain our pleasure. – Robertson

I am reading Susan Clark, Lisa Robertson, Nancy Shaw, Catriona Strang and Lissa Wolsak. In reading, we are writing; in writing we are reading, conversing, waiting, listening and no longer waiting. This is a discussion. We are around a table. We pass warmth to our left, cool glass to the right. There is a clatter of plates and implements. Our human becomes un-human as the possibilities for being extend into the furthering edges of words. There are many metaphors (table, fluid, edge, field, conversation, tiger, horse) and they extend space into new surface and relation.

There is an encounter. There is a discourse. There is a grammar.

> These are the subject of conversation. – Robertson

There is a sentence I have. It happens to be a motive for things that I am not, but which I do . . . attend to. I am not free than otherwise to perceive.

This then would be the conversation. – Jack Spicer

I'm reading Clark's *as lit x: the syntax of adoration* (2001),
Robertson's *The Weather* (2001) and *Debbie: an epic* (1997), Shaw
and Strang's *Busted* (2001), Strang's *Low Fancy* (1993), Wolsak's
An Heuristic Prolusion (2000) and *The Garcia Family Co-Mercy*
(1994). These texts bear their readers to conversations of light and
dark, to rage and quietude. They are a *sensus communis*. They make
a sense, as Hans-Georg Gadamer says, that founds community.
This community is reasonable in the way that Baruch Spinoza
understands reason. That is, the community is the result of relations made and these relations constitute positive and necessary
compositions. From these compositions there are other relations
and from these relations we experience new and active feelings. For
Spinoza, for the city, for the sharp forest at dusk, for the stone
green sea at noon, this abundance of reason creates a real.

songliness

inutter

office

book of offices   Horary   hour angle

whore as forgiver   reef

the flock twists

– Wolsak

ONE: MEMORY THEATRE (SPACE)

A great and beautiful invention is memory, always useful
– Fragment from the *Dialexeis*

Memory: the tremulous agitation of the seen, the perforation of
description, a heard belief.

Memory as we have clung to it can be newly conceived. – Wolsak

Perhaps, newly conceived, memory is no longer an activity of pres-
ervation. It is constitutive. It activates relation and every subject is
subject to its own memory theatre, its own crazy sudden theatre.
Its conventions are scenes that interest us, hold us and distract us.
Memory stages belief.

So free to the showing. What we praise we believe, we fully believe. Very fine. Belief thin and pure and clear to the title. Very beautiful. Belief lovely and elegant and fair for the footing. Very brisk. Belief lively and quick and strong by the bursting. Very bright. Belief clear and witty and famous in impulse. Very stormy. Belief violent and open and raging from privation. Very fine. Belief intransient after pursuit. Very hot. Belief lustful and eager and curious before beauty. Very bright. Belief intending afresh. So calmly and clearly. Just stiff with leaf sure and dear and appearing and last. With lust clear and scarce and appearing and last and afresh. – Robertson

Memory pictures belief with small stiff stitches and ties us to ourselves. Memory leaves holes in the image. The rain gets in and thus belief extends.

> Memorize being sequined
> to something, water. – Robertson

Description is belief. It ties the object to the observer. Fettered, we ride its/our wave.

> – And again, physics has equivalence in its description that the very existence of an observer causes the collapse of the wave function. The wave function is a mathematical description of all the possibilities for an object. – Wolsak

The fluctuations constitute all the possibilities for an object.

> huge things of girders greased. Say
> the water parting about the particular
> animal. – Robertson

An eye can be the witness of these shifting events. Memory, belief, described. Walter Benjamin's secular ecstasy – the way the water parts around a particular animal. Our seeing is subject to its own shifting.

How does this work in words?

Giambattista Vico's metonymic/metaphoric science clears a previous symbolic space or it shifts the press of no space. It is a clearing that both configures and reconfigures the subject and it is the slipping space through which the subject perceives itself as other and so names another real. In the *New Science*, Vico writes that the first forest clearings were round. They were called *lucus*, in the sense of an eye. The clearings were made by the giants who had just become human – after they heard voices (their own voices)

in a thunder-split sky. Hearing themselves in the sky, they remembered themselves for the first time.

We have been in that round space for a long time.

> The long time in the round space – that's not bad. Anyway, "Nice To Be
> Able To Say Thanks To A Giant," our virginity drama's subtitle/last
> line – slick, kind and still damp with a heaven's dew, I write as one jealous
> of myself – "You were made for this." – Clark

Vico also writes that Vulcan set fire to the forests in order to
observe in the open sky the direction from which Jove sent his
bolts. Finding space, we find narrow openings. We find seeing and
seeing we are describing.

> All plain. All clouds except a narrow opening at the top of the sky. All
> cloudy except a narrow opening at the bottom of the sky with others
> smaller. All cloudy except a narrow opening at the bottom of the sky.
> All cloudy except a narrow opening at the top of the sky. All cloudy. All
> cloudy. – Robertson

To make fields for seeing so that being clouds and reveals being.
This is time and space.

> As if time got through – intransitive, felt, and *about* space – or showed
> itself to itself there. Where adoration might imagine extreme distances –
> the past, e.g. – and long to submit to what resembles it in no way – like
> any good field, lying under its sky. – Clark

For perspicuity, the clearing (the *lucus*) is necessary. We require a
clearing.

> > this place overwhelms
> > me I require a clearing just for a
> > moment please cancel this earth. . . . – Robertson

The round clearings, made in the thick forests to see the sky, to
hear Jove, were necessary spaces. Out of the spaces occurred new
relations: humans, "local temporary coherences" (Clark), "hot-spots"
(Wolsak).

> Or, in order to perceive, I create distance, and re-situate my own epistemo-
> logical ideas of causation, separation, and otherness. To find axis, or, an
> orbital angular moment, in rejection of its own centrality, always already
> disturbing its own refinement. – Wolsak

There, in the settling distance, (shifting) bodies can be observed,
held in abeyance, perceived in their relations – angular movements,
intersecting relations disturbing our own refinements.

Our pearls broke. We are watching ourselves being torn. It's gorgeous; we accept the dispersal. It's just beginning; we establish an obsolescence. It's petal-caked; flow implicates us. It's so still; ease of movement is possible.

– Robertson

New proximities – illuminating, moving with ease and mutilating.

The nightreading girls are thinking by their lamps; we make use of their work. We cannot contain our pleasure. The rain has loosened; we engage our imagination. The sentence opens inexpensively; we imagine its silence. The shrubs and fences begin to darken; we are deformed by everything.

– Robertson

Giulio Camillo Delminio (1480–1544) made a memory theatre. It was the literal, imaginative space where he could observe from beyond the trees. It was his clearing.

If we were to find ourselves in a vast forest and desired to see its whole extent we should not be able to do this from our position within it.

– Camillo

Camillo's memory theatre represented the universe expanding from First Causes. It was meant to "keep the mind awake and move the memory" (Camillo).

To be absorbed, and to wake – Wolsak

In *The Art of Memory*, Frances Yates says that Camillo was abundant in body and an able Petrarchan poet. In order to understand the universe, he released rhetoric from its narrow classical role into the most "ample places of the whole world." Shifted awake, the intellect is drawn from the substance of divinity. The world and the mind are divine. Camillo remembered the beginning of the universe.

But Giordano Bruno (1548–1600) was the radical. He traced the history of the human. He revived the magical religion of the Egyptians and used the magic image of the stars in *Shadows* (1582). For Bruno, memory was a hermetic secret. It was magic: extreme rational thinking, technologies, procedures for inventions. Our history could be remembered by assembling the symbols and stories of humanity. There the mind could be harnessed to the universe for purposes of reflection and control. Bruno sought One, not the Trinity. He did not look above but in the world. The powers of the cosmos are in the human. The universe is infinite. Christ is a magician. There are infinite possibilities for other worlds.

Bruno was tried by the Roman Inquisition and burned at the stake (February 17, 1600, Campo dei Fiori, Rome):

gimme gimme

halfy
scorched-pokey
   unsecuritized or overpaid attic
     glitter
     beam
     drool scrawny

     rotating crystal
     counter-load us crowd rats
     bully-pulpit
– Shaw/Strang

Ut pictura poesis – to think is to speculate in images. Images exist in time and space.

> Down etymological spillways, a sensual oral audio-optic fibre, reaches across time and space, to begin a weave, or a cross, the meta-religious image, par excellence .. Standing inside the ancient echoes . . . – Wolsak

A confusion of verbal theories. To be burned alive. We are not always at liberty. Are we ever?

    I DON'T FEEL AT LIBERTY . . .
    11. Sometimes in a flash.
    12. I talked to you.
    13. At the edge of myself.
    14. All but a twin.
    15. In the house of self evidence.
– Shaw/Strang

Do we write to see, to re-remember, to re-see? To face or duck the "bully-pulpit"? In the house of self-evidence, memory makes the real portable, recognizable, pellucid, flammable.

> We are almost transparent. We rest on the rhetorical face. Body of cloud through the night. Now we will be persons. Body of cloud by the fibres collapsing. We rest on erotic heart-love or resist. Now we persons are breaking open. – Robertson

Persons breaking open, the theatre of memory is the conversation we have always had. A conversation seen and heard. Heart-love, we love what we have been made from. Sometimes even when it/we work/s to annihilate us. Breaking open, are we audience and players? Camillo reverses his theatre. A single subject stands where the stage should be and looks toward the doors at the back. Watches the symbols there. Looking back for the way out or in. Benjamin's angel, again?

> I call a theatre (a place in which) all actions of words, of sentences, of particulars of a speech or of subjects are shown.
> – Robert Fludd (1574–1637)

Is memory a kind of taxonomy?

> Implicate order is the ground of perception, but also the process of thought. – Wolsak

You would say that Vico would say so and that Bruno made Vico careful. Vico stayed away from the divine and memory was the taxonomy of the human. Words in thinking by thought extend into thing and so implicate order.

What Vico found astonishing was not so much what is, but that anything is. How do we compose being? What are our compositions of being? Are they taxonomies? Spaces of being hewn in thought, strewn in an entire present. Who decides? Who cares? We are born in and of narratives that precede us. Who has cared and why? Who has thought us into being? It's not so much Descartes' *cogito ergo sum* as "I was thought and therefore I am."

We were refigured. Born in someone else's memory. Araceous and complected.

> It's intransitive and about space; or is space or shows itself to itself in it
> – Clark

Then we are born, shown a self. We mean as beings within terms that are not our own. How to investigate this Absorption? This Inner, Impressionable space of being?

Aside: I am certain that these hot bodies communicate their heat to cold ones & Words – Opaque Bodies. Their surfaces are pored and susceptible to agitation – illuminating and susceptible to illumination and mutability.

> As if lit, we or I or you are in a field and don't know where the field is.

> We are waiting-forgetting; it's *of* thought like vision; plain and thorough sight you can walk in.

> It's sweet here with the early bees. And it, and nothing, and here. – Clark

This waiting-forgetting being is constituted in a radical passivity. But what if language and so being occurs on a Spinozist plane of immanence? On this place, bodies are in motion, moving toward pleasure or away from pain. Their movement is angular and the angle of its refracted light determines our (words) species and colour.

> When conditions of freedom come. When cormorants play. When corn comes. When dogs lick. When newness and shame, come we now throwing. When glittering, we're slapping. – Robertson

In this way, writing perfuses the body thinking – illuminating and susceptible to illumination. Carbonic. Antagonistic particulars. Striving for being. Spinoza's *conatus*. A persistent desire to be is the innate resistance to the totalization of power.

Spinozist being interrupts being and so insures being. The multitude carries its own agency, bears its own revolution, its own revolutionary pace. Bodies moving on a horizontal continually disruptive plane.

> Come we now walking. Now also be here. Now bending, come we crawling. Now crisp, come we falling. Now sparkle, eating. Now swagger, drinking. Now transmit, smelling. Now yellow, sucking.
> – Robertson

Transmit diotropic: that is, refractive and tremulous. Words surface. Smelling. Beaming. Dissipation. And oscular. Kissing contingent and sucking. Touching on all sides. The skin timberous, struck thin: tympanic. Struck thick: the soft lap of flesh.

> Our mind is a skin – Robertson

Arc and lintel.
Affects of Urge and Pergola.

> "Pray undo this button" – Wolsak

Words are the affects by which we make the tender opaque body visible. Words are ways in which we make the body and remake order and orders and chaos. Interrupting the totalization of power.

But often we write into totalizing places of power. Why did Leonhard Euler tell everything he knew about colour to the German Princess? And Descartes had to get up too early for the Queen of Sweden. It was his habit to rise at eleven in the morning. She made him start at dawn, and he died of it. It must have been too cold and too dark. This can be the problem with universities, God, the Princess, the Queen, and Manfred. The places we choose to write to (or must write to) are the places where thinking goes. Ideological, and sometimes black holes. Reifications, jamming human liberation, tireless and oppressive. What Adorno calls "bad contingencies" or what Clark (and Hegel) call "bad infinities." These places are the instigators of antagonistic mental blockage.

But, maybe, we need to be writing something, somewhere. To be somewhere. To be something.

> however momentary .. – Wolsak

> ~ A thing is a phenomenological presentation, with a depth, a complexity, and a purpose in a world of relations, with memory, history, and also possesses subjectivity, appreciated in how it presents itself, speaking to the imagination. – Wolsak

To be chained outside is also, sometimes, the way out.

> a delirium of syntactic destabilization. – Clark

A practice of "being held" (Clark).

> *You see that it's the beholding you're doing that's holding me in this exaggerated pose.* If you weren't there, I'd wait-forget.

> You see, where the beholder threatens to theatricalize what's beheld by an adoration, and where the refusal of that theatricalization by the beheld is a task or talent of her absorption which is a capacity of the love of nothing, *in* it – the beheld's own diffuse attention to which she abandons herself, given to herself and nothing, distended, sovereign – as syntax took the mind which allowed it. – Clark

The practice of being held as syntax takes the mind that allows it. Adoration. For example, talking to God took St. Augustine into a delirium of syntactic self-destabilization: "I have become a question to myself" (St. Augustine).

For Vico, to be held is metaphoric. Freeing, determining. To watch and so make the world, the self, the other, from across space – that allows being.

> Metaphor, *glorying* in its own clumsiness. Its own clumsy toss across the chasm . . . – Clark

To be held is to be human, to extend oneself ecstatically into the world as a body, into the world as the unreachable other. The spaces between us are never bridged.

The irreconcilable, restless, mindless, essential erotic distance – dynamic, empty, blissed, inhuman – which puts an other somehow "beyond recognition" as the self. . . . – Clark

Elaine Scarry writes, "to have a body is to finally permit oneself to be described." That is, the practice of being held is constitutive, materializing, linguistic. For Vico, the body is linguistic permission of place, a *topos*. The body is extension and vulnerability. This is what Judith Butler calls impressionability, the possibility of harm and the necessity of influence. The body is a metaphor of place, an extension of space. A place of profound vulnerability. It follows a relation. In extending it describes and is described. Its edges expose the linguistic body to the limits of representation, to the beauty and harm of being and to the endlessly flawed performance of reiteration. The Viconian metaphor means by virtue of its relations. It is not based on similarity – there is no like or as. Vico departs from the Aristotelian concept of metaphor. The Viconian metaphor is an ecstatic throw into space, a meeting with whatever edges one might find there. It entails recognition and loss. Its loss is its constitutive capacity.

> 1. METAPHOR. Woe to you who first dissed metaphor in my hearing! that *move across what* is a delirium of destabilization that feels like an abandonment inherent in language. I want to let the beauty of its doomed effort show. What are you afraid of? Its thrownness is yours. If "we" live *like* and *as* whatever whatever, *that's* toxic; leave metaphor out of it.
>
> – Clark

The skin of the Viconian human is porous, a delirious linguistic proposition. It rests next-to. Simply it stretches into the world. Next to the world, it is the world. Does this make the life of meaning infinite? If meaning relies on the possibility of relations, where might meaning end?

> *spotless heathen*
> *gregarious avatar*
> *pure goofer, hey*
> we were never actually
> getting there
>
> – Shaw/Strang

Never arriving, inhabiting the flaw, having a body opens speech to gesture, the ear to eye, the public to the intimate, the intimate to the public. It is a capacity for change, the manifestation of change. Which, as Robertson once remarked, is "interesting."

On Mount Tabor, Peter and James hear "this is." Vico's giants hear "this is" in the thunder that cracks open the sky. It is the "this is" of the thunder that makes them human.

> It, and the thing that lies between it, it-and. No eternity in sight but this is. – Clark

There is no eternity in sight. No Godhead. The "this is" heard by Vico's giants is the sound of human existence. For Vico, human truth is actively made by humans: *verum factum.*

> the mind it's made itself. – Clark

And the mind-made human is metaphoric, metaphysic. That is, a delusional, utopian, dangerous, boring, beautiful, hideous, heal- ing, wounding space: an image. More motile than solid, more pored than impermeable, tremulous with its own agitation: lit and lighting.

Linguistically the human is the transfer of relation into some- thing. If the human is a metaphoric vehicle to the tenor of the world (which is the space of being [which is the human]) and vice versa, it's complicated and structural and contingent. If the human is a metaphor, the embodiment of relation, we are place of being – the *topos* of relation. The impressionable subject is self-substanti- ated in relation, in metaphoric contingencies:

> Come contingent . . . – Strang

Is the human subject a figure of speech, a poem, a formal lin- guistic shape, a trope – turning both literal and figural? Figmental? In poetry, the loop of meaning is exposed, elastic and reconfigured. To mean "human" is never simple and literal but standing impres- sionable, dependent. Capable of being wounded, of wounding, isolated, displaced, requiring it.

> That it could be that they showed them this
> But not this that they showed them they showed them that
>   or only one or not with not only as only not one
> Could they come where they were
> Not only so much but also this much. – Gertrude Stein

TWO: SEEING – *UT PICTURA POESIS*

Is the human a metaphor that makes itself seen? Language stretches us before the eyes.

> What a pretty thing it is. – Robertson

Charles Bernstein – Language is our lens of sight. "The eye of sense is slow, because it is the eye of sense," say Clark and St. Augustine.

> Description decorates. – Robertson

Is the word the human witness of its own event?

> What shall our new ornaments be? How should we adorn mortality now? – Robertson

If the human is description and forms community through repetition and improvisational response to indeterminate stimuli, then we are convention's trammel plus what Robertson calls an "expressive contingency." Or what Wolsak calls originary, revolutionary space.

> ~ Latent in speaking, in language, are freedom and hope, erecting a figure for the moment in which they are propounded, as advocacy for originary experience and revolutionary space – Wolsak

THREE: LISTENING

> the difference
> is phonic – Shaw/Strang
>
> 14. Infinite decibel – Shaw/Strang

The sentence is sonic.

> I am not myself indivisible. Lucent fugue of inner snow so abruptly vegetal. Gulf of diminutive affliction, reams like a shred. – Shaw/Strang

A thin membrane closes in on eternity.
Sump a ball cock as if manifold.

> lovely, all
> in a fluent and double grooving – Shaw/Strang

Think of our ears as eyes (Gertrude Stein).
Triangular metrical pediment and ordinary telephone.

I scarify hot-spots, with up-and-down octave listening. – Wolsak

Derrida says that listening is our political responsibility.

Writing is my way of listening and ventriloquising until I reach the place of speaking. – Wolsak

The erotic auricular.

> I'm vernant, knocked over, the, uh
> fruit you pulsed for times renewed
> and interminable rigid dolts.
> Spate. Swank like lilacs
> though a lewd calm might cap
> this fulgid verging. – Strang

Cathexis sung frictional.
Language sounds a world.

I want not to be metaphysically tone-deaf: the reedy vibration of sound . . . urgent affinities tell me so .. of authenticity of time and timelessness ..
– Wolsak

Can we listen to what we can't hear? Somebody else's necessity is not necessarily apparent. This aids the human project of oppression. In this city, on this street, next door. In neglect, people die drastic and in terror. Some of us hear too many voices; some of us hear too few.
A swallowed figura sung
Voices emptying into space. In impossibly broken impossible speech.

In world-wide ideological deadlock each part of the planet, persisting terrorism, and urging war. Enervated surfaces, against an arras of overwhelming bathos, in everyday speech.

Capitalism's everything and nothing .. depthlessness, euphoric waves of consumption, mimetic desire .. disillusions of autonomy, hunger, and grasp .. – Wolsak

Floating in a syntax of terror and lies, we are tone-deaf. According to Nietzsche, big ears bend toward the pavilion.

State? What is that? Well, then, open your ears to me. For now I shall speak to you about the death of the peoples.
State is the name of the coldest of all cold monsters. Coldly it tells lies too; and this lie crawls out of its mouth: "I, the State, am the people."

That is the lie! . . .

Confusion of tongues of good and evil: this sign I give you as the sign of the state. Verily, this sign signifies the will to death! Verily, it beckons to the preachers of death. . . .

"On earth there is nothing greater than I: ordering finger of God am I" – thus roars the monster. And it is only the long eared and shortsighted who sink to their knees! . . . – Nietzsche

According to Nietzsche, small ears are attentive.
Fremescent in self pounce
The membrane tremulant lucid; its production
Listening to the generation
Of historical forms of
Consciousness in order to
Note how they represent and misrepresent actual social relationships. Listen and rail against historical forms of domination. Note the tonal differences between the ideal and the actual. Reconciling ourselves to our historical possibilities and historic relations.

What coils-up .. in spoken space? – Wolsak

And in listening language will sound an animal somewhere – a bird surface and verge. Emergent frog in the ripple of auditory surface.

a sensual oral audio-optic fibre, reaches across time and space . . .
– Wolsak

Writing as listening.

And if writing is listening – a distension – no less – and listening is waiting . . . – Clark

Attentive to and poetic by the gatherings of communities: dead, living, animal, vegetable and textual. These are the narratives that precede us. For Levinas listening is waiting. Awaiting the other. We are only beings in relation. Thus, the sound of this world requires our complete attention.

Sort through my pale heaving verse. Such is a scruple or slander orgy. Thus, pronounce potentate as stunt blow. Prompt. Objectile scoff. Manner is not strictly classical. Your memory's margin of frugal syntax. Hock the sentence. The lout boot or darling league of pro-moral verbal barge. Stoop peep Venus. Rave imperial hollow. We are diffident guilt.
– Shaw/Strang

There is "the necessity of a chorus" (Derrida). Antiphonic: wiring the horns of balance, *duende* (Spicer). The pellucid sings in fulgent illuminants.

> in
> ruse
> seek
> rank
>
> *slink*
> *or slanky*
> — Shaw/Strang

vexing the word
pushing to aural
hard & pricking out the said
busting and ape to its own succulent lyric
word smatter forms the aggressivity of clamour
write into the eye of collision
intersect, indent & posit-matter
unstable landscape, tectonic
This is

> the uncomfortable music of the poem – Spicer

> The autos of the receiving self is displaced by the otos, the ear of the perceiving subject. – Derrida

> Thus, pronounce potentate as stunt blow – Shaw/Strang

Does the ear hear sound-waves against the edged trees and carry the tension of their clearing? Is the ear a portable lens? Listening, the mind looks toward the word and its edge where language invents the mind. Maybe there the mind is roused to itself – sung and seen.

> It's sweet here with the early bees. And it, and nothing, and here. – Clark

> Edging a rise or
> extol all means of his
> absence in it; tell us carmine, delect
> and do – I sang rind. – Strang

Its own site of productivity: that would be us. Words are their own bellows, eared, edged and seen, creased to broad light air.

> In seeing we are saying – Heidegger

In listening, perhaps we are singing what we are saying.

> Torch Songs 1–7
> Publicly sung . . . these songs are intimate.
> May also be sung in pairs, or with supportive background. But always
> remember, you are singing for Liberty, never forget, you are singing for
> Liberty. – Shaw/Strang (written with Monika Kin Gagnon)

This is the conversation. There is a common sense. There are songs. They make a real and we are listening. And we are wondering. We are writing ambitious surfaces becoming ornament; we are naming mortality; we are patient with rhetoric; we are in an un-calm space; we are floating in a bursting space; we are astonished.

CODA

What is the potential of poetry? In part, poetry's capacity for witness is determined by its capacity to inquire into the linguistic conditions of the real. Like a mirror, language reflects us. By observing its machinations, can we observe our systems of thought? Closely mapped our grammars reveal our methods of perception, abstraction and cognition. Yet language as a site of inquiry and as an investigative tool reveals us strangely to ourselves. Maurice Blanchot asks, "is man *capable* of radical interrogation, that is to say, finally, is man *capable* of literature?" (quoted in Derrida, *Writing and Difference*). Perhaps man is not capable of literature. Perhaps literature requires "surreptitious rhetoric's" dream of "the groin's slack gender" (Robertson). Maybe, in order for the human to be capable of investigating itself, it must discontinue the murder required in bogus modes of representation (like the word *man* for *human*, like the word *human* for that that exists with [or without] significance). Perhaps if we look into language and note the deep vagrancies of human identity, we can understand that in fact *man* is not capable of literature. But a new public "slack gender[ed]" un-human subject might be. A radical interrogation requires a full textual avowal of our absence in structures of established subject identity.

Language that works to investigate itself cannot simultaneously work to conceal the emptiness that lies behind its claims of truth and knowledge. Language that is used for purely referential purposes must conceal the space on which meaning rides. Within systems of referentiality, the relativity of meaning, in language, is seen as an abyss of nihilism, moral decay and deep existential anxiety and despair. But Derrida writes that absence is the letter's "ether and respiration" – that is, the life of its meaning. The breathing letter is the place where "meaning is liberated from its aphoristic solitude."

In reading these poems, I ask if I can read *absence* as *space*. Can I read language as that which constitutes and is born out of the spaces where we are – in that common place: the word/world: the full emptiness of everything? There I perceive possible circumstances in their infinite relational variations. These poems write within a poetics of inquiry, where the loosening of language from its aphoristic solitude is essential. They are the gorgeous disruption that occurs when language looks at language.

A practice of poetic inquiry prods language into its semiotic and symbolic potentials. It is where language produces its own space and is utilized in its own dimensions: its volume, its pale undersides. Representation occurs as linguistic visibility, audibility, sensibility and vulnerability – as soothe and scrape. Linguistic surfaces of inquiry contain their own dynamic of division and disposal and thus previously unwritten subjectivities are written toward their dispersal and return:

> This is not to say that we abolish poetry, nor that the self is invented by the alphabet, but rather, so fucking early, that vexed double sense: "to be sung, and words spoken." – Shaw/Strang

The poetic dismantling of syntax space and word relation makes language transparent. Poetic dickerings make spaces and lay bare "the flesh of the word, [lay] bare the word's sonority, intonation, intensity – the shout[!]" (Derrida). To dismantle requires a stage for language that does not pacify the clamour of words:

> Said it hums to a durity
> (fuck!) or able, it, ridge of a glacier
> is brumal, as fur, ready *as it is*
> to pour, or – improbable – Ignite! is
> colour, ire at pallor. – Strang

Here language can offer itself as an absenting manifesting astonishing present. It sublimates and subverts its symbolic orders. It is not of simple origin; it is permeated by its own absence and immanence, its own impossibility, its own beauty and hideousness – to reveal the lush surfaces of language is the production of this poetry.

When the surface of things, soft restraint, motility, girls grouped on the lawn. When the trees, licking nothing, greeting fantasy, subsist by these glances. – Robertson

In these poems, words are held in abeyance, on the lawn, in a greeting fantasy. These poems peruse the linguistic unit, graze the other, swing the metaphor and rouse the subject. They bear us to the pellucid surface of things. They are round fields edged with bright trees, the trees of periphery (licking nothing). These poems subsist by our glances as we read them. They give us wide rooms of sharp air and quickening light.

exact idiosonic decor – Shaw/Strang

Words are fleshy ducts. Description decorates. As for us, we like a touch of kitsch in each room to juice up or pinken the clean lines of the possible. – Robertson

"You were made for this." – Clark

Note

This piece is a shortened presentation of a longer, still ongoing project. It originally began as a talk about *as lit x*, *Busted*, *The Weather*, and *An Heuristic Prolusion* for Aaron Vidaver's "Anomalous Parlance" series at the Kootenay School in 2002. However, I have also spent the last few years reading Robertson's *Debbie*, Strang's *Low Fancy* and Wolsak's *The Garcia Family Co-Mercy*. As a result, these poems have also entered the conversation.

RADDLE MOON:
A TALK

Edward Byrne

This talk was given on July 25, 2003 at the Kootenay School of Writing, to honour Susan Clark on the occasion of the launch of the final two issues of her journal Raddle Moon.

> Out of desire for this "hidden," "displaced" and "imperious" centre [Blanchot], and out of ignorance of that centre, *Raddle moon* has, I think, become a kind of psychogeography [Debord] – which rightly resists description but which nonetheless brings towards it the work which belongs to it. A haunted, porous "no-place," implicated but motile, built of little but the trace of the work that's appeared there – agglomerative, bulgy, made and unmade – what I've called a "utopia of shoddy upkeep," despairing of time, money and energy.
> – Susan Clark, "dear Ccc&Cie" (*Sulfur* 44, Spring 1999)

Struggling to begin this, I open my notebook and happen upon the word *cyclothemia*. In the dictionary I find only *cyclothymia* – "a temperament marked by alternate lively and depressed moods." The suffix *-thymia* is defined as "condition of mind or will." Therefore, perhaps, a better definition of cyclothymia would be: a circular condition of mind or will. This definition is really closer to my neologism, my misspelling, which I at first took to mean something like a circular thematic, or maybe a cyclical thematism. So maybe I will say that *Raddle Moon* is cyclothemic. I hesitate over the word "theme," it having been in bad odour for about forty years. But I want to convey the notion that this long project, *Raddle Moon*, has displayed a constant changing, a reaching forward, a becoming, that is also a restless returning, a gathering back, a consistency. That it has an overall shape or trajectory and that, in a sense, it has an author. I think the evidence is there.

The Red Ochre Moon. *Raddle Moon* does not editorialize . . . much, at least after the first issue. But self-description persists in one manner or another for a long time. That first editorial displays a sense of certainty, of definition, that never reappears. And yet it will be a long time before *The Raddle Moon* completely drops the definite article from its title. It persists on the spine from the fifth issue to the ninth and then disappears altogether.

Raddle Moon's self-descriptions are always changing, never adequate, always reaching after a program. This sense that it's trying to find definition disappears eventually and another kind of certainty surfaces, one that's quite distant from, even opposite to that *original certainty*, which was false to begin with, a false beginning.

The first issue (1983) describes itself as follows on the masthead: "a magazine of contemporary fiction, non-fiction, essays, reviews, poetry and short plays." It also describes itself as "international" – an accurate definition that will hold. Its feminism, on the other hand, is muted and, in fact, contradicted by some of the content. It's really only evidenced by the gender of its editors and the inclusion of Phyllis Webb's Janus-headed address to the Women and Words conference in 1983.

This first issue, in fact, displays various kinds of closure that one would have to say *Raddle Moon*, by its overall practice, anathematizes. Such closures are definitively addressed by the publication of Lyn Hejinian's "The rejection of closure" in issue 4. By closure I refer here to such matters as the predominance of male writers, the dedication to the master (Robin Skelton) and the creative writing department, the misogyny of George Faludy, the unexamined metaphysics of Pierre Reverdy, women writing about fruit and earth (Borson, Bowering), the specificity of genres and the modernism of writers like Crispin Elsted, Calvin Wharton, Antonio Porta and James Reaney.

Issues 2 and 3 continue in much the same manner. The format and the cover, while attractive, are fairly standard-issue for a literary magazine. What continues to mark it off is its internationalism. Issue 3 expands and rewords the self-description in the masthead, promoting poetry from fourth to first place in the list of genres: "contemporary lyric, epic and prose poetry, fiction etc." Also, beginning with issue 2 there are more women writers than men.

In issue 3 there is a short editorial – an editorial which states explicitly that it is not a manifesto, "only questions, and a few comments." This brief editorial is significant for the way it characterizes the project: "The current issue surprises us. We do not plan these things." "Editing, like [life], we find, is impatient with hesitation." We are also given the etymological definition of edit: "edi: to give, to give out."

Issue 4 is the "international women's writing issue." The writing itself begins to open up with the inclusion of writers like Louky Bersianik and Giulia Niccolai. Lyn Hejinian's essay serves as a clear indication of the direction ahead, its discussion of "the open text" itself offering an opening to *Raddle Moon*. This opening, this concept of textuality, ties it to a practice that is first theorized within late modernism: Duncan's "opening of the field," Eco's *Opera Aperta* (1962), the poststructuralist "text" and "*écriture*" of *Tel Quel*, the "writerly" and "readerly" text of Barthes, and what Johanna Drucker later (in *Raddle Moon* 11) englishes as "feminine ecriture." Hejinian, moving from this ground, says:

> The "open text," by definition, is open to the world and particularly to the reader. It invites participation, rejects the authority of the writer over the reader and thus, by analogy, the authority implicit in other (social, economic, cultural) hierarchies.

She also introduces form as determinative, relying on the Russian Formalists. She says that "the conjunction of form with radical openness may be a version of the 'paradise' for which the poem yearns – a flowering focus on confined infinity." In this vein, she also speaks of "women's language" and references Irigaray and Cixous: "A feminine textual body is recognized by the fact that it is always endless, without ending. There's no closure, it doesn't stop" (Cixous).

Raddle Moon 5 was guest edited by Jeff Derksen. The cover changed dramatically, becoming distinctive in layout and texture in a way that continued until the end. At the same time, however, the cover of issue 5 strongly echoes the cover of issue 1, making it appear to be not just a change but a new beginning. The self-description disappears from the masthead, but now the cover contains the rubric "open texts, the new lyric, translations." "Translation," a marvellous word altogether, comes to replace the modernist term "international."

Issue 5 was the first issue I ever bought, at Octopus East, where Brownie and Ingrid always gave it a prominent place. A new issue of *Raddle Moon* was an event there. Issue 5 is, understandably, like an expanded issue of *Writing* magazine: American language poets and the KSW apparatchiks. It also included important work by Michel Gay and Maggie O'Sullivan. Although it marks a new beginning, issue 5 is also somewhat different from what *Raddle Moon* would become.

On the back page, editor Susan Clark outlines an extremely ambitious program for future issues, much of which was realized, in one way or another, over the years. She also defines "the open text" as the future of *Raddle Moon*. Issue 5 also introduced the first photo-based textual work, a selection from Joseph Simas and Tim Trompeter's collaborative work *Orientation*. This type of image/text work appears over and over in the years to come.

Issue 6 was the first issue with photographic work on the cover. From here on *Raddle Moon* has a completely distinctive appearance. This issue is also the first to feature a long work, Simas and Trompeter's "The glass house" (the first section of *Orientation*). In the future *Raddle Moon* would always make a place for longer works.

Raddle Moon 6 includes Bruce Andrews' first appearance in the magazine, with the memorable line "She blames all the language males for having bigger dicks than her." It also includes the first of several forums, this one on "the open text." With the inclusion of Crispin Elsted, a contributor to the earliest issues of *Raddle Moon*, this forum has the appearance of a belated, unnecessary debate over the very direction *Raddle Moon* has announced for itself.

Raddle Moon 7 (we're now up to 1989) is a kind of American invasion: except for Tom Gore's cover and Steve Forth's work, the writers are all Americans and mostly men, including P. Inman, Stephen Rodefer, Robert Mittenthal, Norman Fischer, Tom Mandel and Ray DiPalma.

One tends to think of *Raddle Moon* as a feminist journal. In fact, the overall proportion of male writers in the journal was about 40%. This is not to say that feminism is necessarily undermined by the presence of male writers. However, I think that the closed forum on "Women / Writing / Theory" in issues 11 and 13 is an indication that the notion of women's writing is still a question for *Raddle Moon*.

Raddle Moon 8 is the one with the great Renaissance magic universe on the cover. It has faint touches of colour which Brownie told me were added by hand. I bet that issue was delayed! *Raddle Moon* 8, "The Known – part 1: knowing," includes the journal's first appearance of Lisa Robertson and Norma Cole. It is also the first issue with a "theme." In future, *Raddle Moon* will alternate between anthology-style issues, and issues with a designated theme. Issue 8 also includes a photo-based text work called "The Bloody

Sunday riots of 1938" by Jeff Derksen and Roy Arden, and a review of P. Inman's *Red Drift* by Ben Friedlander.

Raddle Moon 9 continues "The Known" – part two is "the self." It's 1990. The mix of issue 9 is somewhat typical of *Raddle Moon* from here on in: canonical language poets (Bernstein, Silliman, Hejinian); women writers often associated with language poetry (Abigail Child, Hannah Weiner, Tina Darragh, Joan Retallack); photo-based text work (by Leslie Scalapino in this instance); the French connection (Norma Cole, Emmanuel Hocquard, Claude Royet-Journaud); the Zen Buddhist axis (Norman Fischer, Leslie Scalapino); the Canadian avant-garde (Christopher Dewdney). The KSW is conspicuously absent from this issue, but the absence is brief.

From issue 13 onwards, it is announced on the masthead that *Raddle Moon* is "published by the KSW." This has sometimes been represented as an administrative necessity related to the need for a tax number. However, Susan was part of the KSW collective for many years and quite a bit of the writing that appeared in *Raddle Moon* in the nineties was solicited from writers who visited the KSW. So I see the connection as being considerably more intimate than it may appear to be on the surface.

Raddle Moon 10 again introduces a completely new look, a new texture and colour – that marvellous chiffon yellow, green and purple that persists until the final issue, first as ground and then as coloured type. Issue 10 is the "Translation" issue, guest edited by Steve Forth, featuring translations and writings on the practice of translation, including Benjamin Hollander's remarkable essay "In the extreme of translation," Catriona Strang's stunning *Carmina Burana* translations, as well as Nicole Brossard and Yoshida Issui, among others. Also included in this issue is part three of "The Known," "the unknown," with Norma Cole, Rosemary Waldrop and Norman Fischer.

Raddle Moon 11 is a large issue, including extracts from the discussion "Women / Writing / Theory," part two of the Translation dossier, and several long works. It includes an important article by Susan Gevirtz on Dorothy Richardson, as well as Norma Cole's talk on translation which was presented at the KSW in 1991. A long essay by Cid Corman. And work by Clark Coolidge, Erin Mouré, Lise Downe, Diane Ward. The "Women / Writing / Theory" forum was initiated by Johanna Drucker and included statements and responses by Abigail Child, Jean Day, Norma Cole,

Kathryn MacLeod, Chris Tysh and Laura Moriarty. This was an urgent discussion of the relations between gender, theory and writing practice.

Raddle Moon 12, "The Known, part IV: description," included work by Caroline Bergvall, Margy Sloan, Fiona Templeton, Lee Ann Brown, P. Inman and Peter Gannick, among others.

Raddle Moon 13 came with a major change in editorial personnel and the design of the journal. At this stage the editors are Susan Clark, Catriona Strang and Lisa Robertson. The size and shape of the journal change significantly. The ground becomes grey/black, but the lettering retains the colours of issues 11 and 12. So, again, there's a certain continuity indicated even in a sudden shifting of ground. The cover of issue 13 is a photograph of the destroyed National Library of Sarajevo. The covers from here on in are photo-based and mostly somber or ghost-like.

Dan Farrell headlines issue 13. It also contains "round two" of the discussion of women's writing and theory that began in issue 11. This was supposed to have been taken up in the "new, small, casual irregular . . . notebook project" called *Q'ir'i*. I never saw an issue of *Q'ir'i*, which is not to say it never existed. *Q'ir'i*, like other projects that ran "beside" *Raddle Moon*, such as Sprang Texts, was clearly intended to provide something more immediate. Sprang Texts were chapbooks meant to supplement readings. There may have been four. I don't think that relevancy has ever been a problem for *Raddle Moon*, but immediacy has. *Raddle Moon* has always operated on analog time rather than digital time. Issue 13 also featured: an excerpt from Christine Stewart's *Taxonomy*, a Scalapino/Hejinian collaboration, Sianne Ngai, Stacy Doris and Juliana Spahr.

Raddle Moon 14 featured mostly long works, including Bob Perelman's "The Manchurian Candidate: a remake" and "A False Account of Talking with Frank O'Hara and Roland Barthes in Philadelphia." It also featured Kevin Davies and a large amount of work from artist Anne Tardos.

The cover of *Raddle Moon* 15 is by Rhoda Rosenfeld. There is also an insert booklet of her work. The issue also includes performance work by Fiona Templeton. Plus Denise Riley, Fanny Howe and Alan Davies.

Raddle Moon 16 was guest edited by Stacy Doris and Norma Cole, and consisted of an anthology of new (to North America) French writing translated by Canadian and American writers. The heart of the project was the careful coupling of its writers and translators. These were, in effect, collaborative translations. The high points for me were Dodie Bellamy and Sabine Macher, Sianne Ngai and The March Hare, and Fiona Templeton and Christophe Marchand-Kiss.

Raddle Moon 17 was called "Some Vancouver Writers." This issue is primarily a large anthology of KSW writing to set beside Andrew Klobucar and Michael Barnholden's "official" anthology *Writing Class.* Not an alternative, but an expansion, an update, another version, less historically oriented. More than half of the writers in this collection are also represented in *Writing Class.* This is also the first and, I think, only time that Susan has published her own poetry, a selection from *Tied to a Post. Raddle Moon* 17 also nicely situates Vancouver at the centre – the next section of the issue is called "Elsewhere," a neat psycho-geographical reversal. "Elsewhere" includes Jean Day, Rae Armantrout and Jackson Mac Low. There is also a section called "New Writing from Quebec," curated by Nicole Brossard.

Raddle Moon 18, the penultimate issue – since 19 and 20 came out simultaneously – is called "bewilderment, transhumance, ghost." The "ghost" relates to the work by Alice Notley in the issue, including a talk given at the KSW, and to Christine Stewart's remarkable "Jack," being letters to Jack Spicer. "Transhumance" refers to Lissa Wolsak's "An heuristic prolusion," also presented at the KSW. "Bewilderment" is the title of a piece by Fanny Howe. The issue also includes Robin Blaser's "Thinking about irreparables," a talk given at the KSW on the occasion of its tenth anniversary. Also included is work by Barbara Guest and an over-the-top review of Colin Smith's *Multiple Poses* by Kevin Killian.

Raddle Moon 18 has the feeling of joyful death. This may be the real last issue of *Raddle Moon,* 19 and 20 being a coda, or even a new beginning. As a set they display two faces of the journal – the anthology and the overarching theme. In fact, they package all the faces, or facets of *Raddle Moon.* They fulfill the multi-generic man-date of issue 1, and bring the project full circle. In doing this they also demonstrate, perform or rehearse the nature of the whole project: the uncentred and circular, changing and consistent project of the editor and her friends.

I've used the term "*Raddle Moon*" throughout, when often I've meant to say Susan Clark. *Raddle Moon* is both a vast collaboration and the singular project of Susan Clark. With regard to the "vast collaboration," a glance at the editorial board provides evidence of this – editors, associate editors, assitant editors, advising editors, international editors, even a "scout." These editors included: Kathryn MacLeod (1–7), Pasquale Verdicchio (1–12), Jeff Derksen (5–7), Steve Forth (8–12), Hilary Clark (10–12), Lisa Robertson (13–20), Catriona Strang (13–20), Norma Cole (16–20), Nicole Brossard (17–20), Erin Mouré (17–20). Several issues, or sections, were "guest edited," but other than for issues 13 to 16, Susan was the sole editor-in-chief.

Raddle Moon 19 finds a way to have the visual work inhabit the inside and the outside at once, which was attempted less successfully in earlier issues. In this way it has a "new look," odd for the final issue of a journal. It also presents some great new work by "established" writers: Aaron Shurin, Lisa Robertson, Erin Mouré, Ammiel Alcalay, Tom Beckett and Jessica Grim, Geraldine Monk.

Raddle Moon 20, numerically the last issue, is also "new" in the sense that it is the most visually oriented issue ever. All of the work includes images, and two of the works are print versions of performance works. This just doesn't look like the end of a project. And yet it also does provide a kind of summa, a perfection of all the earlier ways and means, a kind of certainty (in uncertainty) that the first issue of *The Raddle Moon* only pretended to have.

STRAIGHT FORWARD APPROACH: ANNHARTE'S *EXERCISES IN LIP POINTING*

Reg Johanson

> shoulda been the poet
> at Oka, sneak up in monk habit   fire words
> take the straight forward approach   fire at
> choppers   write poetry on walls waste less
> paper, words
>
>   – Annharte, "I Shoulda Said Something Political"

Having thus foreclosed upon all options for concrete engagement as mere "reproductions of the relations of oppression," the left has largely neutralized itself, a matter reflected most conspicuously in the applause it bestowed on Homi K. Bhabha's preposterous 1994 contention that writing, which he likens to "warfare," should be considered the only valid revolutionary act. One might easily conclude that had the "opposition" not conjured up such "postmodernist discourse" on its own initiative, it would have been necessary for the status quo to have invented it.

      – Ward Churchill, "The Ghosts of 9-1-1"

Annharte (a.k.a. Marie Annharte Baker) is the author of *Being on the Moon* (Polestar, 1990), *Coyote Columbus Cafe* (Moonprint, 1994), and *Exercises in Lip Pointing* (New Star, 2003). I wanted to write about Annharte for this volume because she has not previously been associated with writing that is "experimental/avant-garde/innovative." Though she has begun to receive some critical attention as an "experimental/avant-garde/innovative" writer,[1] Annharte's work causes trouble in, and for, many of the places where she would seem to fit "naturally" – as "feminist," as "queer," as "native," as "native writer" (maybe especially as native writer), as "experimental." Her radicality may lie in these refusals of seemingly "natural" locations, refusals which are also a subversive critique

133

of writing, language, and nation. My comments here are limited to her most recent book, *Exercises in Lip Pointing*.

MEMORY AND RESISTANCE THROUGH THE MOTHER

Annharte's language for and methods of talking about "mother" are dissimilar from those adopted by many of the writers in this anthology, so they provide a good place to start thinking about the way in which Annharte is "experimental/avant-garde/innovative." If I want to talk about Annharte as an "experimental" writer, I have to take up that strain of the experimental that is motivated by political commitment. But the critique offered by the "experimental/ avant-garde/innovative" in that strain is often restricted to language- or genre-centred registers. Moreover, as Roger Farr points out, "in recent discussions of the Canadian avant-garde, the notion of 'oppositional writing' is often paired with 'radical,' which refers to writing with an 'innovative' or 'experimental' form and which works towards entrance into 'the social imaginary' and for a 'share of discursive territory.' . . . Because such criticism leaves a capitalist model of society intact at all points, it reduces the sphere of 'opposition' to reformist legislation" ("Against Stratification"). While Annharte's writing does critique representations and discourses, the territory she's after is more than merely discursive. She's less interested in the representation of territory than in the territory itself. Also, David Marriott's critique of language- or genre-centred experimentalism is relevant to the way I want to imagine Annharte as experimental/innovative/avant-garde:

[Practitioners of] Language writing, by breaking down the semantic and syntactical codes of discourse and representation at the level of poetic form, [claim to] make manifest the ideological workings of realist discourses and representations. In order to make these claims these critics and poets have had recourse to linguistics in its Saussurean version, ie language as a system of differential relations which precedes and makes possible the speech of an individual speaking subject, consigning speech to a secondary consideration. Or as Robert Grenier has said, rather loudly, I HATE SPEECH. [However,] marginalized voices . . . have traditionally had their claims to representation, their positions of performativity, silenced, ignored, and oppressed. Grenier's dismissal of speech has a different ring entirely if one's speech has not been a privileged source of positionality and individuation but has been the source of an agonized attempt to make oneself HEARD.

While Annharte's language is in fact full of syntactical play and does ignore many of the regulations of the colonizer's grammar, she has no privileged position to renounce; the exchange-value of her commodity-speech is already devalued, and she feels responsible to a larger community than the one usually addressed by the avant-garde. Annharte's work challenges Ward Churchill's dismissal of the radical possibilities of writing in the epigraph above, yet at the same time confirms and instantiates his indictment of the passivity and cop-out of what he calls "postmodernist discourse," exemplified for Churchill "in the fact that, since they were published in the mid-1990s, Jean Baudrillard's allegedly 'radical' screed, *The Gulf War Did Not Take Place*, has outsold Ramsey Clark's *The Impact of Sanctions on Iraq*, prominently subtitled *The Children Are Dying*, by a margin of almost three to one" (8).

Annharte's work with the trope of the mother is most usefully understood in the context of her critique of the pervasiveness in "Indian"[2] communities of the language of the "social services":

Even the most personal thoughts or intimate experiences may be articulated in the strange lingo of cultural outsiders. Some conversations are laced with words borrowed from A.A. meetings, government-sponsored conferences, educational workshops, and from a mere glancing through handouts or manuals. . . . Sometimes I find A.A. talk particularly horrible. We are forced to hear about everyone being "healed" or in a state of "recovery." So much emotion or action is glossed over when someone refuses to give any detail of experience by saying simply that they are "healing." It's become so cliché that it is a type of code that silences the actual telling about a survivor's experience. ("Borrowing," 63)

In Annharte's work mother is just such a survivor, an icon of resistance through which Annharte works back to make ab-original claims for rights as first people, claims that state-sponsored workshop language is intended to defer and deflect.

On the one hand, mother is absent: "a hole in . . . memory when . . . mother left / a suitcase of shells beads and a moosehide vest" (7); "she was supposed to visit me / that time she got out of jail" (17); "my mother kept me waiting / for affection time after time . . . / she left memories in me deep hurts / stab my heart velvet soft and worn" (17–18). In terms of syntax and of lexicon, where "experimentalism" is often marked, Annharte writes very plainly: "waiting," "affection," "hurt." But these complaints and injuries are historicized and understood in the context of poverty and its violence:

her terrified girl story kept hidden
from the mother with a loaded gun
pointed at what now is a smiley face
she remembered that mother with tears
so we young ones would tell her forget
this misery mother needs to be told

get lost
      not wanted back mother
      unless you behave better
      more like a mother
she stayed a scared woman years after (16)

Yet this mother is not a victim: "She posed for the camera proud to tell / everyone in this part of town her rights / she won because she fought back fierce / a slum landlord, street punks, drunks" (16). She needs, however, to be re-membered, put together again:

I set up archaeology expeditions
but digging up mom takes work
news of where did she go abandon me
I turn instead to a faded old newspaper
clipping to brag about this fighter mom

this mom is not in a skeleton closet (17–18)

"Archaeology" and "skeleton" remind us of the grave-robbing of colonial scientists. But Annharte turns her archaeology of the mother into militancy in the poem "Half Light Weir I Lie Down." Fishing spots (using weir technology) are sometimes handed down through the mother. So for Annharte

what is known   where I lie
     is recorded in clay

    dream canal

        help me take back land
           attack
red out
red riot
    red right
red writing
red people read
rights read out (5–6)

To go back to the mother is to go back to the foundations, the lineage, of an ongoing fight. While there is not much here that would be recognized as "experimental," the call for a "red riot" is certainly radical. Most writing about mothers, "experimental," "feminist" or otherwise, does not conclude in a call to "help . . . take back land / attack." The critique of the discourse of social services is intended to reveal the extent to which the "language of cultural outsiders" has obfuscated "the actual telling of a survivor's experience." But the "digging up" of the mother, the telling of the story of one such survivor, does not have as its goal a mere discursive correction of an oppressive narrative; we know where we can stick our "imaginary." The point is to show that the land belongs to the Indians.

BAD WRITING, WHITEBOY STINK, FAKES

For Annharte the stakes of writing are high. She takes on the appropriators, in this case Gary Snyder:

> white boys
> claim to be artists first
> like Indians are supposed to be
> artists first
> to write whiteboy stink
>
> if we are artists first
> then we don't need to be Original People
> first is a first for first nations (34)

But those are easy targets. She has a harder critique of "the easy Indian life," which for her develops out of the use of generic "Indian" signifiers:

Questionable phrases or buzzwords such as "trickster," "shaman," "traditional," "two-spirit," "windigo" and "contrary"/"heyoka" are tossed around in conversations. . . . We still seem to know so little about actual differences among our own people. We are always lumped together. . . . We also have logos like peace pipes, feathers, or other icons to represent us, whether or not our own ancestors or relatives engaged in these particular cultural practices. So much pretentiousness is exhibited by people's ability to manipulate these symbols to be "politically correct." Whenever I hear the word "shaman" I get apprehensive because I think that whoever is using that word might be referring to a variety of performance art, or a new age cult conversion, or even the equivalent of the English word "doctor." For me, I begin to distrust such speakers and their loose language. And I cannot always rely on other native writers or readers to understand the disadvantage of using other people's names for us. ("Borrowing," 65)

This "loose language" is one of the things she has in mind when she talks about "bad writing": "Given enough poison / Indians will die out but who will give us / the secret remedy or cure for bad writing?" (55); a friend who has passed away "will escape bad poetry nights" (19). "Bad writing" is what's produced by fake "Indian" culture, represented in her writing by the recurring figures of the "shake'n'bake medicine man," the "instant elder cult vulture" (19). It is, simply, deadly. In the poem "Got Something in the Eye" the literary industry in general is implicated in the problem of "bad writing." Annharte imagines a male "Indian" writer as a victim of "celebrity status": "His claim to fame was writer working on the next novel. Drunk and disgusting came later with offer of special discount price Only five frog skins. Boozer breath too much." (39). The writer is found dead, "Mirrored disco ball lodged in eye socket": "He never looked up to his own kind. Publisher cranked out Indian books. Portrait on cover made so easy to hitch a ride" (39).

"I DON'T WANT TO BE AUTHENTIC ALL THE TIME"

Annharte is quick to call out the fakes, but she also problematizes "authenticity," most powerfully in "In the Picture I Don't See." Reporting out of Oka, in the midst of the crisis,[3] Annharte finds herself

> in the home of a pink lady
> with a pink & grey decor
> I sit on a mexican blanket
> draped over a grey loveseat
> a thin rosy pink stripe
> offsets blue and black geometric
> runs parallel then intersects a line
> that points to my crotch
> pink ruffled curtains
> match with a pink carpet complement
> grey endtables are coordinated by
> grey & pink flowered mirrors hang
> on the wall above my head

I am a slight off pink accent
a shade of blush soon overtakes
welfare blues hidden by too sharp
contrast for an undertone of shame
feel temporarily out of place
in an ostentatious perhaps typical
mohawk warrior residence
maybe I have wigwam wonder
"who lives here &
am I at all related to them?" (12)

The incongruity of the scene – these people are "mohawk warriors," yet "pink," and with dubious taste in decorating – produces an ambiguous discomfort. She makes fun of their "ostentatious perhaps typical" taste, yet she's aware of a class difference; at the same time these are the people taking the fight to the cops, standing on the blockades, confronting the Canadian army:

I notice how warriors are organized
in kitchens both women & men
sip coffee & talk to mothers
sisters brothers & other first nations
the terrorism of my hosts is casual
but touches on an innerspring of silence (14)

"Terrorism" is the description of the Mohawk resistance proffered by the Canadian state, which describes it as such not least of all because of the middle-class accoutrements of the warriors. This experience of the Mohawk warriors raises the question of authenticity: the decorating is not "authentic," the colours don't match, the activity of fighting for decolonization doesn't line up with the racial markers, with skin-eyes-hair, which exposes the "racial" as bogus and arbitrary:

I get told the identity problem
is 100,000 Indians do not know
tribes of origin but make up lies. . . .
I have tattooed the verification
of Indian status on my big toe
band number without the photo
I will show it if I'm ever asked
when I sneak behind the lines
next siege demo protest to help out
I have provable identity in case
clan membership expires annually

> or my traditional but urban story
> requires I reinvent my ancestors (14–15)

So the truth of identity is in the struggle – Annharte relishes her "pink" hosts because their identity is in the fact that they fight, not fake:

> I don't want everyone to be Indian
> or to be too suspicious either
> they should have interesting bric brac
> with pristine impeccable backyards
> keep on decorating interiors
> I don't want to fight for exteriors
> fight for home fight for sanctuary
> defend status regained
> a right to being Indian
> is not a pretty picture
> an identity made questionable
> by invasion or evasion (15)

The "exteriors" of race – who is an Indian, who is entitled to "status," who isn't – distract from the fight for "status regained."

LIP POINTING

Despite this poetry's directness, it is also frequently ambivalent about speaking. A description of a rape – "scary hips held down / I don't want to hold out hold back hold in / cherry scream defiant silence" (10) – suggests that there is a desire to speak back to this brutality, but silence is also defiance. This problem appears again in "Who Am I to Judge," in which Annharte struggles with speaking and keeping silent as she overhears the conversation of "a family court judge" who presides over the removal of children from native women, the placing of native children in foster homes, and over adoptions of "'papooses' from up north who return / for adult sentencing" (53). She's aware that "it's rude to enter / private conversations" (51), but the judge's own conversation is "rude enough to ruin my dinner / the white noise at the next table / I want to shush them quiet, complain / typical racist ambience ruins a dinner out" (53). The poem is full of "I want to," full of revenge fantasies: "I wish the Native woman lately / who lost kids would drop in here / say something to ruin his reputation / shoot straight arrows into his back" (53). But the poem does not offer this satisfaction. Instead: "I'd make a poor defence / not one to shield her [the "Native woman"] / from the judicial x-ray stare / or conceal the whole truth / white noise is used for torture / the sloshing in my stomach / gives away my presence / the gurgle is in resistance / to white noise in the background" (51). Literally, the stomach turns. Yet Annharte finally refuses the terms of the legal discourse which would require her to make a "defence."

As a response to the brutality of the discourse of law, however, it's not very satisfying, even if it does ring true. But the problem comes back again in the poem "Exercises in Lip Pointing," this time suggesting a more liberating use of subversive codes. "Lip pointing" is "signals // watch ahead to the side / either side / take a peek / but don't say anything out loud / to Mr Mrs Ms Authority Person In Charge / don't say   aw fuck off either / you bug me   aw come off it / enough enough / that bullshit" (40). Here it seems that the secret "signals" of lip pointing don't overcome or seriously undermine the "bullshit" – it seems clear that at this point for Annharte saying "fuck off" would be better but she is constrained by not only by the rules of politeness, but more importantly by the fact that speaking back to "mr mrs ms authority person in charge" can result in punishment. Yet later in the poem Annharte recruits the lips to make war: "command / lips move / quick march / single up / form a circle around the wagons // hey lips over there doing nothing / lips don't pout / grab those arrows / start firing // lips on the other side of the face / light a few guided missiles // to Hell with Tomahawks / let's Scud doo" (41–42). Here the secret code of lip pointing is militantly subversive. And yet: "remember the cowboy Indian movie / especially starring in it // don't get lines / just come out trilling / give us lots of tongue / pow wow lips / contest time / ceremonial lips action" (42). The non-speaking "Indian" has a degrading past; maybe it is better to tell the oppressor off in a language he can understand. But:

Jimmie Durham, a Cherokee artist, has stated his position that Indigenous people shouldn't "educate the oppressor" because anything said or written in English will be used against us. Check any court record for quotes by anthropologists or other Indian experts. Sometimes, the words of our own elders are twisted out of context to support our so-called "non occupation" of the environment. Obviously, our words will be used by "the enemy." Governments will want to take our land because too many of us speak English and are not "as Indian" or culturally pure as we are expected to be. ("Borrowing," 62)

Annharte's "lip pointing" is an example of language use by marginalized people that complicates David Marriott's formulation above. Because speaking for Indians is a double-bind (to be capable in the discourse of the colonizer is to reveal the extent to which the speaker is no longer "really" an Indian and therefore has no legitimate claim, yet to keep silent is to remain under the oppression of that discourse), making oneself "HEARD" may not always be the wisest course. Under these circumstances Annharte reveals the operation of a covert language that finds a third way, speaking around or underneath or behind the back of the authorities and that can organize solidarity and resistance against power in the same moment as it seems subjugated by it.

COPS, PRISONS, SOCIAL WORKERS, WELFARE

If the cultural fakery and homogeneity of symbols of the "Indian" "poison," sell out and appropriate, the courts, prisons, cops, and social workers carry out the real dirty work. "JJ Bang Bang" directly attacks police brutality, exposing the absurdity and hypocrisy of the "cultural sensitivity" initiatives that inevitably follow, and precede, yet another police brutality scandal:

> After a lengthy inquiry police need
> time to fabricate events records heal
> go to sweat lodges pow wows
> next police class is at least half Native
> but native what?
> half Native part pig siouiii
> Aboriginal cop out (48)

And in prison: "I start bawling humiliated by the hygienic measure of an Indian matron who searched me because she had been especially hired to touch me. . . . She didn't feel my crotch – her job. I'm sure a whitelady would've jumped at the opportunity" (49).

In "JJ Bang Bang" the paternalism of the Canadian state is represented as a mania, an insanity. The cop/repressive state apparatus says:

> I told you go back up north
> quit hanging around here
> get off the streets
> get a job go to school

you need a counselling referral
I want to see you in detention. . . .
I told you stop accusing me
my job is to look after you
but I'm not responsible to you
just for you your damn nation
give me good reason, one, why
I feel guilty what happens
to you when you go out wandering
alone at night (45)

The discourse of cultural sensitivity, generated by both white guilt and as a strategy of amelioration and containment of demands for decolonization, merely disguises the older genocidal imperative. "Indians" interfere with the total (fascist) alignment of the non-native body with the land – the failure elicits rage among "Canadians," who can never get body, land, and nation to line up.

The critique of aboriginal cops and prison guards as "cop out" is the "racism" referred to in the poem "Woman Bath," in which Annharte and white feminist social workers discuss the murder of a native sex worker. The paternalistic (maternalistic in social work) attitude of the nice liberal is offended by Annharte's critique, implying that it's Annharte's *attitude* that's the problem: "Curious I have been discussed as to how my racism prevents treatments deserved by other Indian women tending to trust not disappoint or please others who work for them" (32). Her "whitewomen buddies," social workers, accuse her of this. But these are the same women who "witness gay pride": "An Indian woman leaned against a pillar jiggling tiny tits then slunk back to white lovers who witness gay pride but she doesn't like me" (31). And: "Nazi women torture on command all the slim girls dancing for them" (31).

But Annharte recognizes her own complicity in this: "One Eye ["One Eye Annie," Annharte's imagined guardian angel of sex workers] quit working with my sisters now each one is mine & worth many zeros to fill a blank cheque that won't bounce in my face & make cash now out of my sweat" (32). And she's implicated not only by her job, but also by her mixed race: "One of me doesn't fit in a women crowd   often left in complete rage because the white twin belonged better" (31).

I've heard it said that Annharte "goes too far" – as she reports that accusation, "I need to take it easy I am too hard on myself they rush to tell me when I think I am just about to figure it out" (31). For Annharte the going-too-far is necessary to the figuring-it-out. She can't rest in the "easy Indian life," she can't be comfortable with her "white twin," she can't glibly get paid for working as a social worker, which is to say, for managing poverty on behalf of the Canadian state. If my comments at the beginning of this essay seem anxious about Annharte's reception by and place among experimental/avant-garde/innovative writers, it is an anxiety about the possibility that her inclusion, though deserved, is also a containment and recuperation of work that in many ways is hostile towards an avant-garde whose members too often prefer to "ignore their role in the reproduction of social hierarchies" and who "imagine themselves to be occupying the role of specialized leaders . . . directing their energies into reforming a society that can't be reformed. . . . [T]hey may be removing themselves too far from the struggles they claim to represent" (Farr and Johanson). To what extent does the adoption of Annharte by the experimental/innovative/avant-garde allow us to ignore the literally un-settling implications of her work?

Notes

1. See Pauline Butling and Susan Rudy's *Poets Talk: Conversations with Robert Kroetsch, Daphne Marlatt, Erin Mouré, Dionne Brand, Marie Annharte Baker, Jeff Derksen, and Fred Wah*. For a critique of the representation of the "radical" in this and its companion volume, *Writing in Our Time: Canada's Radical Poetries in English (1957–2003)*, see the review by Farr and Johanson.

2. Annharte uses the term "Indian" throughout her work. I follow her practice but put the word in quotation marks when I use it, to indicate its problematic history.

3. In the early spring of 1990 the town of Oka in the province of Quebec was granted permission to expropriate burial grounds from the neighbouring Kanesatake reserve to build a nine-hole golf course. "Indians" from all over that part of Quebec and elsewhere in Canada and the U.S. helped to put up barricades that blocked the development. The "Indians" were attacked by the Quebec provincial police forces. One policeman was killed. The Canadian army was brought in. The stand-off lasted through to the end of September 1990. The golf course was not built.

Works Cited

Annharte. *Exercises in Lip Pointing*. Vancouver: New Star, 2003.

—— (as Marie Annharte Baker). "Borrowing Enemy Language: A First Nations Woman's Use of English." *West Coast Line* 27, no. 1 (Spring 1993): 59–66.

Butling, Pauline and Susan Rudy. *Poets Talk: Conversations with Robert Kroetsch, Daphne Marlatt, Erin Mouré, Dionne Brand, Marie Annharte Baker, Jeff Derksen, and Fred Wah*. Edmonton: University of Alberta Press, 2005.

——. *Writing in Our Time: Canada's Radical Poetries in English (1957–2003)*. Waterloo, ON: Wilfred Laurier University Press, 2005.

Churchill, Ward. "The Ghosts of 9-1-1." In *On the Justice of Roosting Chickens: Reflections on the Consequences of U.S. Imperial Arrogance and Criminality*. Oakland, CA: AK Press, 2003.

Farr, Roger. "Against Stratification: Dorothy Trujillo Lusk's *Ogress Oblige* and the Poetics of Class Recomposition." Forthcoming.

—— and Reg Johanson. Review of *Poets Talk* and *Writing in Our Time*, by Pauline Butling and Susan Rudy. *Vancouver Rain Review of Books* 3, no. 4 (November 2005/January 2006): 6. http://www.rainreview.net/rain-030406.html.

Marriott, David. "Signs Taken for Signifiers: Language Writing, Fetishism, and Disavowal." In *Assembling Alternatives: Reading Postmodern Poetries Transnationally*, ed. Romana Huk. Middletown, CT: Wesleyan University Press, 2003.

TOWARD A POETICS OF THE COMMONS: *O CIDADÁN* AND *OCCASIONAL WORK*

Miriam Nichols

PREAMBLE

As I write this, the processes of globalization have left no aspect of life untouched. Among the effects are a decline in the autonomy of nation states and a corresponding democratic deficit, the concentration of wealth in the hands of a small, owning class, the privatization of essential resources such as water and seed, the patenting of life forms, the destruction of cultural and ecological habitats, and the impoverishment of whole populations. This is now our condition, rather than news, and there are countless organizations around the globe already devoted to protest and amelioration. It is not news either that world events are of concern to the humanities: any serious art faces up to its times in one fashion or another. It is the arts which give shape to human life,[1] and to which we look for a social imaginary. But the humanities for many decades now have been out of step with globalizing tendencies in trade and technology. By this I do not mean to diminish the considerable accomplishments of postmoderns and contemporaries, but to suggest that the whole push of humanities discourses and art forms since the mid-twentieth century has been to establish difference rather than commonality. If deconstructionists sounded the last death knell of the old humanist subject (rational, free, centred in itself), feminists, postcolonialists and sexual difference theorists worked for the validation of new identities that respected differences of gender, sex, race, class and ethnicity. For some time now, it has been enough to pronounce the words "humanist" or "universal" to dismiss a work of art or a critical commentary – and understandably so, in view of the exigencies facing the early postmoderns: the horrors of authoritarian states, rigid ethnic and national identities (still a major source of conflict), and the effects of imperialist conquests. But the result of this focus on difference has been to render unfashionable the discussion of humanity at the species level. While other disciplines like ecology or law have been able to respond to globalizing trends, arguing the inter-connectedness of ecosystems and weather patterns, or devising models for global human rights, the humanities have not produced a strong, alternative vision to the prevailing neo-conservative world-view because difference – social difference as well as *différance* – seems to lead to cultural and ethical relativism. From such a stance, it is difficult to construct convincing versions of agency or compelling world-views. I want to qualify these remarks as generalizations meant only to describe major theoretical moves rather than individual voices, and as coming from an academic perspective: in my view, it is the theorizing and the interpretive skills that need adjustment more than the arts themselves. More nuanced readings of the postmodern legacy and of contemporary art practices would yield a different story than the one we have, I think. My immediate purpose, however, is to look at two poets who have taken on the challenge at hand of imagining a new human universe.

Erin Mouré and Lisa Robertson both write big, ambitious poetries that address this most consequential of contemporary tasks. The necessity of such creative work is urgent: as Dany-Robert Dufour remarks in a recent issue of *Le Monde*, the reluctance of the intelligentsia to address the question of human values in a global context leaves the field open to the discourses of neo-conservative expediency and religious fundamentalism.[2] In *O Cidadán*, Mouré asks what citizenship might mean in a global era and what its virtues might be; in *Occasional Work and Seven Walks*, Lisa Robertson invents a "soft architecture" through which to reconfigure civic spaces and challenge the prevailing narrative of lack which underpins capitalist political economies. I have juxtaposed these writers because I think they offer complementary poetries that lay out some of the groundwork for a new commons.

O CIDADÁN: THE EXISTENTIAL BOND

O Cidadán is a complicated book with a high level of indeterminacy, even higher than that of most poetry texts. Although predominantly in English, the text also includes words, phrases and passages in French, Portuguese, Latin, Spanish and Galician. The title is

Galician masculine, "[a]s if," Mouré says, "'citizen' in our time can only be dislodged when spoken from a 'minor' tongue, one historically persistent despite external and internal pressures, and by a woman who bears – as lesbian in a civic frame – a *policed sexuality*" (v). Right away, the reader, whatever her mother tongue, must confront an array of "foreigners," and in a text which immediately problematizes the foreign (who is "us"? who is "them"? who do we wish to police and why?). The collection consists of three series of poems with occasional pieces interspersed: a set of love poems called "Georgettes," a set of "Catalogues of Harms," and a set of "documents" that archive the poet's readings and prosey meditations. These series are interspersed throughout the book, so that "Georgettes," "Catalogues," and "documents" push up against each other. This complex, contrapuntal structure offers virtually unlimited possibilities for combination that extend the potential for meaning well beyond single poems and the skills of most readers. The structure, in other words, pushes readers to accommodate the foreign and relax into probable misunderstandings. The movement back and forth between the love poems and those that seem to bear more directly on public matters suggests at a formal level the impossibility of separating private and public spheres. The human subject in its inner complexity (its memories, its singular experiences, its emotions, its material body) and the citizen (the person who circulates in public, a "mobile complex of . . . rights, obligations, dignities, and virtues" [7]) twist into each other, and the twisting point is the "Harms." Affectability, and hence susceptibility to "harm" as well as to love, is the hinge between subject and citizen, and Mouré's insistence that the citizen be embodied, rather than abstracted as a legal entity, is crucial to her sense of the virtues that global citizenship requires. This kind of citizenship has "nothing to do with country or origin," but is rather "a seal or bond with this world" (9).

The philosophical groundwork for the bond mostly comes in the "documents," which include many quotations from those postmodern philosophies which have made sociality constitutive of subjectivity. As Judith Butler says in a passage quoted in "document20 (sedition's *abrigar*)": "Subjection marks a primary vulnerability to the Other in order to be" (53). This is the precondition of the ontological, as explicated in the otherwise variously inflected philosophies of Levinas, Derrida, Jean-Luc Nancy, Kristeva and Lyotard. Yet primary sociality cannot issue *binding* ethical imperatives because the givens of existence – the gift that each inherits at birth – can be rejected, as it is daily in gestures that range from discourtesy to genocide and environmental pillage. There is nothing at all that can *compel* ethical behaviour other than the bond with which each may tie him- or herself to the world – or not. What *is* imperative about the human condition, however, is its "being-toward," as Nancy puts it: we cannot not respond to that *existentiale*, even if we do so negatively by insisting on our self-sufficiency or by trying to dominate others. If we can make that response more conscious and artful, we may begin to see the possibilities of mutual dependency as an alternative description of planetary life to that of self-sufficiency. The global citizen, the one who practices civility, accepts the existential given as *gift*, rather than instrument or obstacle, and this acceptance opens up a different logic than that of exchange. We affirm the various modes of life around us because they *are* givens, not belongings, and we accept their claims on us in order to pass the gift on to future generations.[3] Such a fiduciary bond with the world can be denied, but we have to see that rejection for the enormity it is, a form of nihilism that points to planetary destruction.[4] Acceptance of the bond, on the other hand, can provide the grounds for ethical judgment. In *The Imperative*, a phenomenological revision of Kant's categorical imperative, Alphonso Lingis gives several examples of the kind of affirmation and acceptance which I think is characteristic of Mouré's global "cidadán." When we stub out the smouldering cigarette that may destroy a sequoia forest, or when we dive into a lake to save a drowning person, Lingis says, we do not reason out the merits of the forest or the drowning person, nor do we stop to consider whether we are in fact acting freely by giving a moral principle to ourselves. We respond to the exigencies of the modes of life that confront us because we can recognize them as modes of life. Our recognition is already implication, entanglement. We already know, because we are embedded in the life-systems of the planet, *what is to be done* (219–20).[5]

In *O Cidadán*, primary sociality is the point of departure for a poetics of receptivity. How might we respond to strangers and enemies as well as intimates and fellow travellers? How respond to the "babel" of foreign voices and manners? To misunderstandings? And most importantly, how might we respond to modes of life incompossible with our own?[6] I have selected three tropes that recur in *O Cidadán* to indicate some of Mouré's answers to these questions: sense without sense; the fraction; and giving face.

To begin with the first: Nancy's *The Sense of the World*, a book which turns up repeatedly in the "documents," treats sense as a primary orientation outward that for Nancy *is* the world: preceding signification, sense precedes cognition, as if thought were suspended over its object of attention (10–11). Sense without sense, as I have adapted the concept to *O Cidadán*, means a way of approaching others that suggests acknowledgment without cognitive grasping. As Mouré writes in "document3 (hieratic and paternal)," the point is "To resist the 'hieratic and paternal' pose of touch – of access to a surface as appropriation (à la Heidegger); think touch, rather, as quiver or thresholding, mark and threshold//" (12). For Heidegger, the world was what stood forth in the light of Being (truth is *aletheia*). If we are sighted, the eyes are the first to *take* the world in. We receive others as objects of knowledge by sight: we scan for recognition of the friend or stranger, for social position, for danger or advantage. At closer range, we listen, too, because by tone, accent and idiolect we place the other; we register age, education, person-ality, ethnic identity and class. These are the senses that put the other in her place. But touch is full of risk and indeterminacy. Even in permissive, secular societies given to violent or erotic media spectacles, real touch is tightly regulated in public places – the handshake, the buss on the cheek – and more often reserved for friends and intimates than strangers. When touch becomes pub-licly erotic or violent, we watch appalled, excited or frightened, unable to turn away at this breach before us of the comportments that make up our fragile civilities – that make the city "safe." But the ever-present need for safety underscores the vulnerability of the body to touch. This little "Georgette" of Mouré's catches a mode of sensing that respects our *exposure*:

> tardily entrance me now
> her sill
>
> her hand bearing shock of what my
> mandible
>
> a jaw or seer
> copious
>
> hand's mandible to the
> why

+ (25)

In the first two lines, the syntax sets up a "between" without clearly identifying the positions of the speaker (me) and the third person (her): more than the two persons, it is the "between" itself that is constructed. Who is it, for instance, that is to be "entranced"? Is the first line an imperative, addressed to a beloved, as in "entrance me now, tardily, since you did not before"? And if the line is to be read in this way, are we to take it that the speaker wants entrance, as in "let me in, I have been waiting outside your door," or entrancement, magic, fascination? Or should we read this line as reflexive, as in "I have been tardy, but now I am ready to enter or to be entranced"? In either case, the entrance or the entrancement seems about to happen, but is at this moment suspended in the "not-yet." The poem, along with speaker and reader, lingers on "her sill," at a spatial point between inside and outside, and a temporal point between not-yet and already. This temporal point is nothing but the "now," the ever-moving "between" of past and future, conveniently there at the end of line one.

In the next two lines, the spatio-temporal "between" of lines one and two finds a correspondence in an emotional "between" generated by the speaker and the third person. *Her* hand bears the "shock of what *my* / mandible." The oddness of the word "mandible" stands out here, as does the slipperiness of "bearing." "Mandible" denotes an insect's feeding apparatus, but that apparatus is also used for sensing and picking up food: it functions as both mouth and hand. Moreover, the word "mandible" rhymes internally with "hand" in English, and with "main" in French. But what exactly is between the hand and mandible? Does the hand of the beloved "bear," as in endure a shock coming from "my / mandible"? Or does it "bear" as in carry toward? Where is the shock coming from and where is it going? In the poem, it is between the "hand" and the "mandible," which through their rhyming begin to sound like two sets of feelers. Mouré's diction and syntax underline the diciness of drawing close to someone – that mutual exposure of flesh that makes us as vulnerable to shock as it does to love. Hands and mandibles can be dangerous to whatever they identify as desirable or edible. In the next lines the jaw and seer suggest the double function of an apparatus made for eating the world as well as seeing and greeting it. But hands and mandibles can also evoke a way of proceeding by touch, of feeling one's way toward the other, of being careful. Notice that the "seer" evokes visionary seeing as well as looking, while the word "copious" hints of that pleasure

a skillful hand or mouth can draw from the body of the beloved.
The last two lines, however, give the poem a twist so that what
seemed intimate and lyrical – between a "me" and "her" – suddenly
sounds more public. The hand now has a "mandible to the / why."
"Why" asks after the purpose or end of an act or thing. It is a
question that asks for reasons. To touch such a question with the
"hand's mandible," however, suggests just that suspension of
thought over its object which does not close itself off with a concept.
As the "+" at the end of the poem seems to say, there is something
yet to be articulated. If we read this sign as a "plus" then it suggests
(endless?) addition; if we read it as a cross or cross-road, then it
indicates alterity in the form of a trajectory that momentarily crosses
ours, in the magic and peril of touch. In "document9," Moure
says it this way: "How to think along the edges of something that
is not yet a thing, using one's own 'not yet' which is anterior to
our 'our'ness, to any 'my' or any *sum* . . . and which creates the
'our'ness too as a further (always further) 'not-yet' superimposed
or perhaps coalescent with an 'our' that is tentative (but oh this is
beauty) and urged up and forward by the 'not-yet'" (28).

But why linger over this suspension of the *coup*, the cut of meaning or form that the mind requires to understand and *act*? Why
this *staying of the hand*? As the "Harms" poems show, affectability
means a dangerous vulnerability. The social is bounded on one
side by intimacy, beyond which lie the solitudes of love-madness
or mysticism; and on the other by the "harms" which point to
violence and death. The "Georgettes" and the "Harms" thus represent the two poles of affectability, between which is the living
space of human sociality. Citizenship rooted in strong, national or
ethnic identities has played out in the twentieth century and continues to play out as blood and soil. This is theological politics,
and it has meant repression of whatever is perceived as foreign.
The suspension of judgment, the holding back, suggested by sense
without sense is one tool to be used against the kind of raw terror
in which social and political life simply ends: there is no social
living room when the hands close up the space between you and I
or us and them in violence. As the "Georgettes" gather up intimacies, the "Harms" poems catalogue with devastating thoroughness
the modes by which "harms" may befall any one of us. In the first
of these, there is "armistice day," so we think of the harms of war (6).
Then there is "Debt's harm," conjuring the multitude of harms
that befall those in poverty, including the devastation of whole

countries burdened with debt. "Debt" morphs into "Depth" (we are in the hole) followed immediately by "Debit," which Mouré glosses as "a ditch where they buried the shot children": economic harms easily segue into violent conflict and bodily harms. It is the "extensibility of the body into a world" which makes us vulnerable to harms large and small: "Her torn muscle in the arm / 's shoulder that makes 'shaking hands' difficult." The "shaking hands" hold in a simple trope the potential and the risk of bodily "extension": hands shake in fear, in illness or in greeting. But in this poem even those invisible mental spaces that are not so extended are exposed in other ways. The line "At that moment, she remembered 'Sharon Thesen'" reminds us that memories can intrude suddenly, just as this line suddenly intrudes in a poem that is about something else. And even if the memories are pleasant, they rend open the unicity the conscious mind thinks it has – they expose consciousness as a suturing up of heterogeneous moments and point to the instability of memory banks that we cannot fully account for or control. There are no corners of human life, in other words, not even the secret spaces of thought and feeling, that are not exposed for good or ill.

   From the perspective of the "Harms," self-sufficiency is a fantasy born of the desire not to be vulnerable. The poems give formal representation to human affectability through a series of fractions. Thus the "Second Catalogue of the Substitution of Harms":

harm	harm	harm	harm	harm
-------	-------	$\sqrt{}$	-------	-------
forms	term	devices	units	count (11)

The obvious point is that the fraction dramatizes our lack of wholeness. The dotted line between the words that form the two halves of the "fraction" relates the words that it separates, and once relationship is established so is affectability. The square root sign – or is it a check mark? – between "harm" and "devices" serves the same purpose but directs the relationship differently: are devices (prosthetics, technologies, strategies) the root of harm, or is harm the root of such "devices"? We devise *technés* to protect ourselves from harm, but these devices (weapons of mass destruction?) can increase exponentially the possibilities for harming. Or, to take another example, what do we get by dividing "forms" into harm? Endless substitution, of course, as the title of the poem says. The word "form" can suggest almost any articulation at any level of reality –

linguistic, social, physical and so on. All *may* "divide into" harms or harms may be divided into uncountable forms. And similarly with the other fractions. As this poem unfolds, the bottom "divisors" are not limited to abstractions but include words like "bath," "abs," "kid" and "comedies." The simple contiguity of "harms" with each word, however, multiplies the occasions and means of harming. Consider "bath" into "harms": scalding in a bath, slipping in a bath, drowning in a bath, bloodbath, electrocution in a bath. And so it is for each fraction.

The "Third Catalogue of the Temperament of Harms" (14) is also written in fractions, but these are composed of two, seemingly unrelated words. Yet again it is the contiguity of the words, in the context of a poem that invites us to consider the "temperament of harms," that multiplies the potential for harming. Consider, for instance, "cliff" and "wit." The two words denote different levels of reality, one geographical and the other behavioural or perhaps cognitive. But "cliff" gives us some edge or precipice that presents the danger of falling, and "wit" evokes the need for vigilance in dangerous situations – keeping one's wits about one. In its older sense, wit denotes awareness or knowledge of something, and of course it evokes its opposite "unwitting" and all the attendant dangers of inattention. Wit in the sense of "wittiness" or being a wit evokes the kind of social repartee that can be very edgy, somewhere between cleverness, humour and discourtesy, if the wit falls flat. A wit may be a social cliffhanger, vulnerable to disapprobation. Of course a similar commentary can be given to *any* two words, given that the indeterminacy of the relation between them is such that almost any reading is possible and no reading is definitive. But in the context of Mouré's cataloguing of harms, the effect is to demonstrate the potential for an unlimited range of affects and thus raise the stakes in this inquiry into civic virtue.

The "Harms" poems suggest that we fancy ourselves beyond the lessons of the postmodern at our peril. The whole push of those philosophies of the subject which Mouré references has been to challenge identities deeply implicated in blood and soil and imperial aggression. The intense performances of affectability in the "Georgettes" and the "Harms" demonstrate anew the dangers of theological politics, realist epistemology and narrow definitions of personhood, ethnic boundaries and national borders. All these potentials for harm continue to exist, especially now, when religion and politics have taken the central place on the world stage

once more. But the contemporary task is no longer just to decon-
struct. If deconstructive strategies suspend judgment – and how
often is just such a suspension needed to stay the hands, and make
time for judgment – they suspend any new constructive envision-
ing of the world as well. How, then – to return to Nancy's question in *The Sense of the World* – can we imagine a politics that is
based not on self-sufficiency but on interdependency? In "docu-
ment11 (ni circonscrire)," Mouré writes:

What opens itself over and above any being is hospitality, says Lévinas. D insists
that Lévinas says literally: intentionality is hospitality – a threshold without
derivation or closed borders, thus without opposite -> "les phénomènes d'allergie,
de rejet, de xénophobie, la guerre même manifestent encore tout ce que Lévinas
accorde ou allie explicitement à l'hospitalité." *Intentionality* nudges at the word
"enactment." Looking here for a way to call up or name that relation with the
other that is not amorosa but cariñosa, cara being "the face." Is the face, too, an
enactment? "To face up to." But even *la que es cariñosa* can't help but risk
"harm." (32)

The receptivity that Mouré unfolds in trope after trope comes
to this facing of the other, such that "facing" means not only to
greet (by or with "shaking hands") and face up to (as in take responsibility for) but to give face – to respect, but also to give, through
mutual recognition, each a tolerable identity to the other.[7] Hence
in "document15 (differential plane)," the example of Captain Paul
Grüninger, who "altered 3600 passports to permit Austrian
Jews entry to his country" – a "prosthetic application of 'Swiss
border'" (42). In this same poem, Mouré remembers Christoph
Meili, a bank guard, who saved Nazi-era documents from the
shredder: as C. S. Lewis wondered, "How can God meet us face to
face, *till we have faces?*" (42).[8] In another poem on the face-to-face
relation, Mouré writes:

. . . Lévinas's take on "hospitality" is one that interrupts interiorization/
incorporation of an other, is instead a space of interruptibility or leakage where
there is no claim to totality. The one welcoming the visitor is already in the
visitor's debt, for visi-tor is also visi-ble, brings the visible into being. *Tor and blé.*

Tor y trigo.   *Isthmus.*

Which honours "the space between" and does not produce a subject/object
relation; both faces remain present unto each other. (103)

As Mouré writes in the preceding poem, "visitor" brings about
"a certain symmetry of i's around a curved channel" (102) – the

mirroring of "i" around the letter "s" becoming a metaphor for the
face-to-face encounter between human "I's"/"eyes." The word "tor"
is the root of the French "tordre," to twist, and Spanish "torcer," to
twist, wind or distort. "Tower" is here as well in the Spanish "torre."
By sound, the Spanish words "toro," "torero," "tornado" and "tornar"
may also come in, the latter meaning "to turn" or "return." The
French "blé," taken from the spelling of the English word "visi*ble*,"
doubles with its Spanish counterpart "trigo," meaning "wheat."
Facing the other is an act fraught with possibility and danger: it
may result in twisting, distortion, misunderstanding, a deadly playing of the other as the torero plays the bull, or a fortification against
the other as suggested in "tower." But it may also come with "wheat"
or bread, and hence companionability (literally, "with bread").
What Mouré suggests is that the facing makes both "I's" visible as
"I's." In the meeting they become (first) persons.

   Or not, if the gaze is turned away. In one of the last poems of
the collection, Mouré evokes the extreme right-wing politics now
afoot in the world – "Rio's street children excised by police, por
exemplo" – by way of counterexample to the citizen's act of giving
face. "Genocide's seedlings" grow out of a refusal or inability to
face the other:

Not Lévinas's face to face but José Antonio's *face to the sun*.

Where *l'accueil* is impossible, for the eyes go blind to the other, thinking they
see god. (137)

The image poignantly catches the premise of the book. Human
eyes are made to look across rather than up, or as Mouré says
elsewhere, the citizen is one who acts across, rather than one who
holds a line (94). This is a form of humanism, based on the de-
instrumentalizing of the *existentiale* – an obvious move, perhaps,
but one which implies the profound transformation of societies as
they now exist. The turn toward the other in the act of giving face
is a gesture that activates civility through a primary orientation
toward *persons*, before these are sorted into friends and enemies. In
his writings on the Trinity, Augustine argues that a word in a foreign
language strikes us as meaningful even if we do not understand the
language, and he conceives of our desire to understand as amorous.
When we recognize meaningfulness without grasping the meaning,
or when we see in the gestures of others analogies to our own
thoughts and feelings, we are inspired to learn more for love of the

meaningful as such.[9] In that orientation is already a recognition of personhood in the voice of the foreigner. We are at a point, as Mouré says, where "'the rights of man' confronts 'the Nation'" (116), and the first "right," on which citizenship is predicated, is the right to have a face.

OCCASIONAL WORK AND THE POLITICS OF FREE TIME

I think *O Cidadán* is most deeply concerned with the extension of personhood to the whole of humanity and therefore situates itself most often at the level of the existential. Lisa Robertson's *Occasional Work and Seven Walks from the Office for Soft Architecture*, however, strikes me as social and political in its pitch. The point of intersection between the two books is that each articulates a commons. Robertson's *Occasional Work* (rather than the *Seven Walks*) is my focus. It consists of a series of "essays" commissioned for various art shows and journals. I put "essays" in quotation marks to note that Robertson's prose is never academic, although it is carefully researched: rather, it is closer to prose poetry than to conventional art criticism. The thematic link between the pieces of "occasional work" is Robertson's focus on the various surfaces of public and private spaces. *Soft* architecture means just that: the draperies, temporary scaffoldings and decorative surfaces that go up and come down.

In the introductory "Soft Architecture: A Manifesto," Robertson begins with bedding and baby clothes, the "curious histories of shrouds" and "[m]emory's architecture" which she says is "neither palatial nor theatrical but soft" (13). In this category are the draped gods of European oil painting and classical friezes who have disappeared into the "latent conventions of canvas, or in the draperies and *objets* of the rooms themselves" (14). The association of memory with soft architecture here at the beginning of the book is a significant move because it begins to lay the framework for a certain temporality – "our temporary commons" (67) – that develops in the essays which follow. Through a temporality which fuses memory and desire into a utopian "now" Robertson is able to turn her cosmetology into a kind of sabotage and counternarrative which strikes at the enabling premise of capitalist economies. Capital exists through deferral. The investment or hoarding of wealth and the lending of credit all construct the present as a time of unfulfilled desire, or desire deferred to the future. But this deferral actually

makes the future atemporal, both because it is owned by the credi-
tor or investor and is to that degree determined, and because it is
a time of imagined enjoyment and expenditure that will always be
deferred. The worker, on her part, not only mortgages her future
literally if she is a borrower, but also lives the present as lack, despite
whatever enjoyments her debt may have afforded. Work defers free
time and pleasure to a future which will never arrive because it has
been taken out of circulation, so to speak, by the owning class, not
only in the form of interest and surplus value but also through the
endless production of items that stimulate desire and hence create
lack. Lack is the first, enabling product of capital, and because it is
based on desire, not need, it can be extended endlessly.[10] Under
such a system, the given, including the cultural past and the earth
itself, appears as material for new production. Memory, however,
is harder to bring under the rubric of lack, and this is where
Robertson's revisiting of "memory's architecture" gets interesting.
Memory *wants* nothing because it already has, and yet as it repeatedly returns in the present it is a never-ending source of the new,
the fascinating and the counternarrative: memory is a renewable
resource and there is plenty of it.

   The correlate of the abandoned baby-clothes of memory or the
discarded draperies of the gods is the clothes rack in Robertson's
"The Value Village Lyric." At Value Village, superfluity, rather
than lack, is the order of the overstuffed rack, and the "new" is
always already recycled – a "simultaneous proliferation and cancellation of origins" (217). In this atmosphere of plenty,

Anything is possible. We'll conduct our life unrecognizably. Recombinant figures of memory present themselves. We'll untwirl that life. Sociology becomes
ornament, like a decorative scar-work. The seam has been caringly mended.
From random documents of uncertain provenance, unstable value, and
unraveling morphology, we produce new time. (217–18)

"New time," I would suggest, is a "recombinant" such that desire
invests itself in the *trouvés* of memory and history[11] rather than in
a future that is really atemporal. "New time" works on the logic of
transmission rather than exchange: as in *O Cidadán*, this is gift
logic. At Value Village, clothes are donated and passed on for
minimal contributions. They thus represent a "gift" bestowed on
the present from the past (217), and one that is widely distributed. In the virtual Value Village of the world, the gift is the
heritage ("all that is defunct, such as Europe and America"), here

available for recombination and transmission, such that "we luxuriate in the unoriginality of our desires and identities" (218). Just about everyone can participate in the "economy" of Value Village, where the means of creative production come in bales and "[t]here is always more" (217).

"New time" is about process without teleology: there is, after all, no imaginable end to time that is not nihilistic or theological. In an essay called "Spatial Synthetics," Robertson writes:

Everything glimmers, delights, fades, goes. We drift through the cognition with exceptional grace. Attached as we are to the senses, we manifest the sheer porousness of boutiques. The boutiques are categories. We have plenty of time. The problem is not how to stop the flow of items and surfaces in order to stabilize space, but how to articulate the politics of their passage. (78)

If we stay in a time that has unhooked itself from metaphysics, there is always "plenty of time" – in fact there is nothing but time and nowhere to go but here. Were such a temporality to be installed in the marketplace, "items and surfaces" would circulate without the reserve capital requires. In postmodern philosophy, there is precedent for a "politics of passage" in Deleuze and Guattari's transvolumed analysis of capital, in Lyotard's *Libidinal Economy* and in the more recent *Empire* from Hardt and Negri, all of which propose that the problem with capital is not the circulation of goods and services but the capture of those flows for "consumptive hoarding" (Lyotard's phrase). The postmodern response to the excesses of capital in a global era is thus to suggest strategies that promote flow without capture – in other words, a radical democratization of the market and a socialization of investment in public goods and institutions in order to pass on the wealth of the human heritage. But such theoretical liberation, enacted at the textual level and through philosophies of the subject, has barely registered in the world of real events. As Robertson remarks in *The Weather*, "the socius / of 'le texte' / is bullshit" (75). The current disaffection with things postmodern perhaps comes of the recognition that a change of consciousness may be a necessary condition but is certainly not a sufficient one to produce change in the world, especially when by its very nature the language of process and expenditure does not translate well into institutions.

Soft architecture finesses this story. Robertson's choice of architecture as a key metaphor opens up a whole series of spatial tropes such as the installation, the ornament, and hard versus soft structure.

A "soft" architecture supposes a contrary "hard" structure, and this key opposition seems contrary to a poetics of the fluid. Mouré's language can help with the seeming contradiction, I think.[12] The point is "not to deny borders," she says, but to render them porous, such that the relation between the two sides so articulated is "tensive and productive": "What's key is not to ignore this relation or sublimate it in a *dialectic*. But to make apparent or work / function with the tensilities. To allow porosities or what might be 'penetrations' across a liminal surface" (*O Cidadán*, 112).

Two examples from *Occasional Works* illustrate Robertson's version of this strategy. In an essay titled "*Rubus Armeniacus*: A Common Architectural Motif in the Temperate Mesophytic Region," Robertson explores the history of the blackberry vine in North America, an "illegitimate" plant that "seems capable of swallowing barns" (125). The Himalayan blackberry escaped its first cultivators to morph "from aestheticized exotic, to naturalized species, to invasive alien" (127). The "*Rubus*'s habits are also democratic," Robertson says.

In Fordist fashion it maximized distribution through the temperate mesophytic forest region. . . . But what we have come to appreciate most about this *Rubus*, apart from the steady supply of jam, is the bracingly peri-modern tendency to garnish and swag and garland any built surface it encounters. In fact, the Himalayan blackberry insistently makes new hybrid architectures, weighing the ridgepoles of previously sturdy home garages and sheds into sway-backed grottoes. . . . (127)

Notice that the blackberry is "peri-modern": it does not try to get past the modern with its lingering affection for hard forms, but rather to work upon its surfaces. As political metaphor, the vine is subversive of the structure (the institutions) it covers: by growing *around* and *through* the structure, the blackberry weakens and renders it porous, but also produces "new hybrid architectures," and in the meantime helpfully yields a "steady supply of jam."

Another example of the productive relationship between hard and soft architectures is the scaffold and building presented in "Doubt and the History of Scaffolding." The scaffold recalls a history of military uses ("from *scalado*, to storm by mounting a wall by ladders"), but it also promises an "architecture of happiness [that] would rehearse a desanctification of time, which is itself only a scaffolding" (162). Temporary and vertiginous, the scaffold "rhythmically expresses the vulnerability of the surface by subtracting solidity from form to make something temporarily animate" (164). Like the blackberry, then, the scaffold renders "animate" the hard surface of the building it leans against and opens to creative refashioning. "Its topography," Robertson says, "cathects with the desire to release identity and dissolve into material, which is the style of resistance we prefer" (165). At the end of the essay is this striking passage:

> Scaffolding substitutes for a site. By compression or condensation it transforms an atmosphere to a condition of access which is also a screen. This idea is easily inflated towards the surreal or the homeopathic, but it is based on observation. When at night we hear the scaffolding rustle, then look up to watch it sway, we feel voyeuristic longing. In darkness the scaffolding is foliage. Sometimes swinging on special leafy scaffolds we feel compelled to loose our little slipper. (166)

The scaffold that initially serves as a "condition of access" to the building which props it up turns into soft "foliage" and takes on a life of its own, and suddenly what seemed to be a construction site or military zone begins to turn into a Watteau pastoral. Instead of the worker's sabot there is the little slipper, loosened in an act that rewrites (recycles) the original act of sabotage. And while the scene refers to the "surreal" (the exteriorizing of an interior landscape), and the "homeopathic" (the micro-gesture), it also points to a collective militancy on the "*scalado*" in the implied refusal to work. Swinging on the scaffold, "we," who as workers are supposed to defer enjoyment, engage in a scandalous display of it.

Yet a poetry that plays with plentitude while referencing the political seems counterintuitive. Easy enough to play textual games, but deadly hard to address the *need* that seems to follow naturally from human physiology and the scarcity of resources, both of which appear to ground the narrative of lack in a simple realism. In "Playing House," a piece devoted to the history of shacks, Robertson challenges the realism of need. It is a form of belief, she says, and comments that "politics are collective experiments in belief": "When the shack dweller lays in supplies, she is composing a politics" (180). This is an important move on Robertson's part, because it introduces agency at a level where determinism seems to prevail and to render self-evident the necessity of work: we work to live. Robertson's work on shacks, however, introduces a question mark into this apparent truism. Thoreau's shack, for instance, includes not only kitchen utensils and rudimentary furnishings but "*a japanned lamp*" (180). Another list of shack provisionings amusingly includes "*a medieval visored helmet and axe*" along with two hand grenades (180) – and who is to say that such items are not "needed" in the context of that shack? "It is the task of the shack," Robertson says, "to minimize this distance [from hearth to field], in the service of an image of natural liberty" (179) – just as Value Village minimizes the reserve required for creative production. The shack's "catalogue of necessity" (181) suggests a variable measure of need and hence the negotiability of the distance of each shack dweller from "natural liberty." By contrast, the narrative of lack infinitizes that distance, because it is actually based on desire rather than need.

Robertson concludes this piece with descriptions of three shacks, each of which offers a different fable of human sociality. Rousseau's shack initiates the narrative of lack: it is the source of envy (and hence desire) for those still consigned to the open air and thus represents the beginning of social conflict and competition. Alberti's shack is a metaphysical one. Because it is structured with reference to the living habits of an immanent subject – a subject who is the absent cause of the shack – it suggests an "allegory of origin." As Robertson remarks dryly, "We wonder if there exists a body the shack could not imagine" (183). The third kind of shack is that of Vitruvius, which comes about through the "sociality of speech" (183) and the campfire gathering. Participants of this imaginary group disperse to create each a different kind of dwelling, some digging caves, and others making nests of "mud and wattles." From these early shacks, better huts come to be produced by imitation of the best features of each. "We find in Vitruvius a social generosity lacking in the republican myth of the shack," Robertson writes:

here mimetic building is not the guarded site of security, but a form of engaging speech. In the long series of the Vitruvian shack, mimesis constitutes a creatural social pleasure, a collective communicative agency, contrary to Rousseau's figuration of mimetic art as lack. At the threshold of the Vitruvian shack, architecture's choral function knits the commons. (184)

Through the window of the shack, then, we get a glimpse of what could be a new commons:

The shack is the pliant site that adds to our ideas new tropes, gestures learned from neighbours, creatures, moot economies, landscape, and the vigour of our own language in recombination. We wish to re-imagine the city through the image of the Vitruvian shack. Here citizens inflect shelter with their transient and urgent vernaculars, which include the mimetic lexicons of technology in the service of the *frisson* of insecurity. Here insecurity figures, not as terror, but as erotic collective being. We love shacks because they pose impossible questions. How can we change what we need? How can we fearlessly acknowledge weakness as an animate and constructive content of collectivity? The city is the shack inside out. It choreographs the delicious series of our transience. This is the future. (184–85)

In these questions, Robertson's commons converges with that of Mouré. Porosity, fragility, transience and weakness are the transvalued values in the work of both poets. To go back to Nancy's question, the task at hand is how to imagine a politics that is not based on self-sufficiency. On the cover of *O Cidadán* is Lani Maestro's tent city, a marvellous installation artwork consisting of square, see-through gauze tents (delicate, porous structures) held up by cords (bonds, ties). In a catalogue essay on this work, Caroline Forché writes that in the "motility" of this installation and others of Maestro's, the "agencement of tents, leaf piles, bedclothes, pages of ocean, cyclones of words, and swirls of hair, the 'disappeared' are called into presence – ethically, responsibly called – and so in entering these installations and the awakenings to consciousness they occasion, one is always accompanied" (11). I would like to imagine these charged spaces of Maestro's in juxtaposition, for a moment, with Mouré's points of "accueil" and Robertson's shacks and scaffolds. On one hand, the image brings to mind the worst sufferings of the world in the flimsy shelters of the homeless, the refugee, or the very, very poor; on the other, it gives visionary form to a network of porous, animate structures, tied to the earth with cords. These structures keep nothing in or out; rather, their function is to relate and separate, to articulate space and time into habitude.

Notes

1. I am indebted to Robin Blaser's "Mind Canaries" for this distinction between the arts, which present the world as form, and technology, which treats the world as raw matter or as an obstacle to be overcome: "Technology is neither an image nor a vision of the world: it is not an image because its aim is not to represent or reproduce reality; it is not a vision because it does not conceive the world as shape but as something more or less malleable to the human will" (22).

2. "En effet, si on néglige ce terrain, [le débat sur les valeurs], il sera occupé par M. George W. Bush, les télévangélistes et leurs suppôts puritains comme aux Etats-Unis, ou par les populismes fascisants comme en Europe" (Dufour, 14).

3. Gift logic is by no means a new or passing concept in contemporary poetics. See, for instance, Steve McCaffery's remarks on the Kwakiutl potlatch in "Writing as a General Economy" in *North of Intention* (1986) and Pauline Butling's "bpNichol and a Gift Economy: The Play of a Value and the Value of Play" in *Writing in Our Time* (2005). I am also indebted to Jérôme Bindé's distinction between a "logic of transmission" and one of exchange in his "Toward an Ethics of the Future": "It is no longer a question of the logic of reciprocity whereby anything given presupposes something to be returned, but a logic of transmission which gives the donor a particular place in the historical community. . . . The commutative logic of distributive justice is therefore replaced by a transitive logic. It is no longer a question of 'giving in order to receive,' but giving because one has already received" (69).

4. Consider, by way of an extreme and unveiled example of such nihilism, the mercantilism of Louis XIV, the aim of which was to conduct economic warfare on neighbouring nations to the point of destroying them. France, of course, was to be completely self-sufficient (Lyotard, 188–91). A more recent example of such nihilism might be the American fundamentalists, influential in the George W. Bush administration, who await the destruction of the world with the imminent return of Christ.

5. See Lingis, particularly chapter 19, "Importance, Urgency, Immediacy." For instance: "What has to be done, overriding our wants, is determined by the intrinsic importance of what is in danger and the intrinsic importance of what needs us in order to exist. The good in question may be our own survival or welfare. Nourishment, shelter, unpolluted water and air have to be secured. Our homes have to be protected against electrical fires; the city has to be protected against floods. But realities outside us also present themselves as having to be spared, protected, or promoted. This becomes the more clear in the measure that we come to know them. Although we may dismantle ancient temples and sell the parts for our own enrichment, the more we know those temples the more evident it is that to subordinate their existence to our private wealth is to denature them" (172).

6. The occupation and "democratization" of Iraq exemplifies the collision of incompossible political systems. The premise of democracy, as the western nations idealize it, is equality of persons. But Shia law, favoured by some factions in Iraq, is based on the inequality of women. In "Degrees of Not Knowing," Rory Stewart argues that the complexity of Iraqi society is little understood, and the western assumption that "the vast majority of Iraqis want . . . the equal treatment of all Iraqis regardless of sex, religion and so forth" has not been supported by recent election results which showed that "the majority of Iraqis voted for parties which did not favour such things" (10).

7. By "tolerable identity" I mean an identity that supposes a dignified life that is its own end, rather than an identity that instrumentalizes the other. For a phenomenological description of face-to-face encounters with strangers, see Lingis: "We can turn away from faces as we can turn away from the surfaces of things; we can push them aside, strike them with words and with blows. We

have the power to render a body incompetent and defenceless, we can corner an animal. . . . To recognize the sensitivity and susceptibility of another is to catch sight of these possibilities and to feel tempted by them. Then the one exposed to my eyes and purposes turns and faces me. In the contact the torment of another afflicts me as an appeal, the pleasure of the other presses upon me with the urgency of a demand" (132).

8. See also Mouré's reference to Aristides de Sousa Mendes, a Portuguese consul-general who issued three thousand visas to refugees during the Nazi era in defiance of official instructions (98).

9. I am indebted to Steve McCaffery for pointing out this passage in Augustine's *On the Trinity*, in a talk delivered at the Kootenay School of Writing, 12 May 2005. Augustine argues that the mind loves the "form" of the exchange with the other, and in the relevant passage, "form" has a Platonic sense as the generic of which particular instances are the species. The learner is "eager for knowledge" because he loves "that form [which] touches the mind that knows and thinks; it reveals the beauty of minds that have been brought together in fellowship by listening to and answering questions through signs that are known. And this form enkindles him with zeal, who is looking indeed for something he does not know, but who beholds and loves the form that he does know, to which the unknown thing belongs" (Augustine, 44).

In the contemporary philosophies Mouré cites, primordial sociality, rather than Platonic-Christian form, orients us toward others. What is intriguing about Augustine's thoughts on the encounter with otherness, however, is his figuration of the foreign as the *possibility* of meaning, rather than noise or the absence of meaning, as well as his notion that this possibility incites us to love. I do think, though, that my use of Augustine goes against the grain of his writing. It would take another essay to argue the extent to which love of the foreign might take us out of ourselves, rather than inward to the mind's contemplation of itself as pure Platonic form. Augustine's solution to variousness is ultimately the unity of God, the source of generic meaning, and it is the love of God that really informs the love of learning and love of otherness.

10. See Lyotard's much fuller description of capital as lack (inhibition, reserve) in *Libidinal Economy*. Lyotard argues as well that credit money includes a speculative use that is mercantilist – which is to say that capital is not just a self-reproducing system of expenditure and return (lack in circulation) but also a "looting" through speculation (227).

11. See Hannah Arendt on Walter Benjamin's historiography, in her introduction to *Illuminations*, especially the section "The Pearl Diver" (38–51). For Benjamin, Arendt says, the past was not authoritative but "citable," and the historian's relationship to it was comparable to that of the pearl diver or collector.

12. I do not claim that Mouré is a source for Robertson on this point, although the two are friends and readers of each other's work. I do see parallels between their respective strategies, however, and I find the passage in *O Cidadán* helpful in explicating a relationship that is tense, oppositional and productive without requiring the sublimation of terms associated with dialectics.

Works Cited

Arendt, Hannah. Introduction to *Illuminations*, by Walter Benjamin. Ed. Hannah Arendt. Trans. Harry Zohn. 1969. New York: Schocken Books, 1978.

Bindé, Jérôme. "Toward an Ethics of the Future." *Public Culture* 12, no. 1 (Winter 2000): 51–72.

Blaser, Robin. "Mind Canaries." In *Christos Dikeakos,* 17–36. Vancouver: Vancouver Art Gallery, 1986.

Butling, Pauline. "bpNichol and a Gift Economy: The Play of a Value and the Value of Play." In *Writing in Our Time: Canada's Radical Poetries in English (1957–2003),* by Pauline Butling and Susan Rudy. Waterloo, ON: Wilfrid Laurier University Press, 2005.

Dufour, Dany-Robert. "De la réduction des têtes au changement des corps." *Le Monde diplomatique*, April 2005.

Lingis, Alphonso. *The Imperative*. Bloomington and Indianapolis: Indiana University Press, 1998.

Lyotard, Jean-François. *Libidinal Economy*. Trans. Iain Hamilton Grant. Bloomington and Indianapolis: Indiana University Press, 1993.

McCaffery, Steve. "Writing as a General Economy." In *North of Intention: Critical Writings 1973–1986,* 201–21. New York: Roof Books; Toronto: Nightwood Editions, 1986.

Mouré, Erin. *O Cidadán.* Toronto: House of Anansi, 2002.

Nancy, Jean-Luc. *The Sense of the World.* Trans. Jeffrey S. Librett. Minneapolis, MN: University of Minnesota Press, 1997.

Robertson, Lisa. *Occasional Work and Seven Walks from the Office for Soft Architecture.* Astoria, OR: Clear Cut Press, 2003.

———. *The Weather.* Vancouver: New Star Books, 2001.

Stewart, Rory. "Degrees of Not Knowing." *The London Review of Books* 27, no. 7 (31 March 2005): 9–11.

O YES

Caroline Bergvall & Erín Moure

Dear Erin, dear Erin Mouré, dear Erín Moure,
dear Eirin Moure, dear EM,

I wasn't sure by which name to address you, so just to make
sure, I thought I'd greet you in all the ones I know for you.
I should say, the ones I know for your work. The more your work
as a poet and as a translator proliferates, the more your names do
too. Certainly you seem happy to take Pessoa up where he left off.
Of course, I could keep it simple and address you as a friend but
this defeats the public epistolary exchange we have agreed on at
my initial request. Since then, I've been travelling, I've been working, I've been sick with the flu and we're now just a short week
away from the already extended deadline, so I'm not even sure that
you'll have time to read this, let alone play its game, prior to publication. Still, having set up the artifice, and at the risk of it turning rather sadly (not to say typically) into a monologue, I mean to
fulfill it.

[It's a week since I sent you this by email. You wrote back more
or less immediately that it had reached you at the airport just as
you were boarding a plane to Toronto. This morning, April 10,
we've spoken on the phone. You're back in New Brunswick and I
am here in the spring sun of New York. You say you've started a
response. You also have some specific comments. As you talk, I
write some of them down. We agree that I will slip some of these
in my letter.]

Yet here I am, nearly immediately stumped as to what to call
you. It makes me wonder what a name provokes in you. You don't
seem to use it as a pseudonym. The names are misspellings rather
than complete hide-outs. Could one suppose that other kinds of
written work might also start to generate function-specific names,
or is it just poetic work that creates the spell? Would you rename

your name for an article, for an essay, or even for a public talk, for instance? Would you show up in a new name or are your names only written: re-spelt not mispronounced. I remember how you used to complain about the way editors would forget or displace the accent in your name. You certainly sorted this one out.

The more I see how you manipulate your name/s, the more I imagine that it must be once you've written it that you name yourself in the work. Or perhaps it'd be better to say that the work names you in it, unfolds an accent for you, points you to it, once the writing is done [**you say, as the writing is doing**]. As such, your writing has stopped being anticipated by your (social) name, writing in the name of what your name stands for (one imagines some kind of sustainable/straitjacketed reputation). Then there's the female gendering of your social name. This lends an additional and familiar ring to the mobility with which you approach it. Yet even though "Eirin" sounds like the name of a young, impetuous Icelandic fisherman or an Old Norse balladeer, I don't really think that taking on naming as a synecdoche of literary gender persona is a prime issue for you here. I may well be wrong. At any rate, it's not so much your social-authorial name that you're trying to live up to, writing one more book in the name of "Erin Mouré," but rather, each new spelling signs each new work off. Each new spelling is a signature in the narrative and structural, rather than the performative, sense [**you say, yes, it is definitely not only performative, it's good to point this out**].

So far, I haven't even opened the books! It is enough just to be thinking about the traffic on your covers. Knowing you and your work, of course, there's more to it. In fact, not just more, but a madness of names. Inside the work, within the pages, name after name, not yours this time, others' names. *O Cidadán* notably is a an affirmative jungle of names. The whole trilogy, starting with *Search Procedures* and following on with *A Frame of the Book*, revels in naming, but *O Cidadán* makes a feat of it. Nearly every page is a pretext to activate a name, to discuss an attributive process, "(Lorcan or Lispectoral)" (75).

At every level of the trajectory from the text to the book, names are spelt out, written down, quotes are attributed, there are epigraphs, not just one, but two, but three. *O Cidadán* opens with a dedication to no fewer than six poets/artists: "Phyllis Webb," "Robin Blaser," "Jorge Semprún," "Agnès Varda," "Yaguine Koita," "Fodé Tounkara." On the same page, three quotes are attributed to "Joseba

Arregi," "Fernando Vallespín," and "Lisa Robertson." [**You say, Yaguine Koita and Fodé Tounkara are not artists as such. Well, we could call them artists. They were two young African men, teenagers really, who in August 1999 hid in the wheel-wells of a Sabena plane on its way from Guinea to Brussels. Such a journey is impossible to survive, and they froze to death and tumbled out when the plane landed. In their pockets, they had stuffed letters addressed to "Excellent Sirs, members and responsibles of Europe," which were a plea to Europe to help Africa free itself from poverty, hunger, disease, and war. What arrived in Europe was their writing transported by their bodies. They were writers. They had used their bodies as an envelope to their writing.**] These tributes are broad, multidirectional. Later on, poems will emerge from named quotes, sentences will scurry with yet other names, "José Saramago" (whom you quote in Spanish from the *El País* newspaper), "Grosz" (Elizabeth never named), "Michael Palmer," names punctuate the pages, direct the writing, act as nodes to the textual threads, "De Sousa Mendes, Portuguese consul in 1940," confirm the reading, "Aurelius A," "Lyn Hejinian," names are chain reactions, "Cixous reads Clarice Lispector," "Derrida citing Levinas," ". . . said reb Armel. (E Jabès)," footnotes carry them on, some initials are decipherable when used as shorthand for a previously named name, "CL," others are not, their identity withheld yet functioning in the way literary or diaristic conventions often do on naming privacy: they initial it: "LK," "D," "Emma M." As it turns out, the initials get elucidated at the end of the book: "Liz Kirby."

It closes with a final page of acknowledgments. It lists some thirty-odd books, many written by contemporary philosophers. Then it lists the authors of "fleeting citations." You are fastidious about your sources. And the page that follows that one is another extensive page of thanks to sponsors, editors, friends, facilitators. The process of acknowledgment, with its blend of learning and influence, is explicit, excessively clear in the entire framing of the work. At every turn this writing makes visible its contact with others' work. An international and public availability of names. O cidadán! A plurilingual, pluricultural participation.

Of course, naming as an act of affiliation has a long and established literary tradition. It is a fundamental part of the paratexts that have historically surrounded and defined literature. Medieval texts, Norse sagas, even classical texts had complex and ritualized ways of dedicating their works, of asking for protection, of claiming literary lineage as much as social patronage. Closer to us, Ginsberg's long and fascinating pages of dedication are but a reminder of traditions of naming one finds in Sanskrit and Tibetan literatures. In a profound sense, it is a literary gesture, an act of literature.

In your work names don't only signal its exteriority, its cultural reach; they and the quotes they sign for also provide a structuring device. Everywhere in the book, names signal the anteriority of reading in the contiguity of writing. More than this, they provoke writing. They don't just frame the work, they are the work. This is poetry as an intellectual and investigative form of writing-knowledge, a highly specialized game, which is exemplified and confirmed by the kinds of names you quote. Here is poetry's flirtation with, or attempted assimilation to, philosophy. You mention "reading's gesture," you meditate on the philosophical "trait" or "mark" or "trace" of reading, your philosophers are masters of reading, they play language at its own palimpsestic game, they read to write, all of them, Derrida, Nancy, Levinas, Butler . . . and so do you.

Naming is an exchange and an acknowledgment of this. Here, poetry is perceived as a fluid yet critical process of exchange, one that formalizes acts of reading. Acts of reading are seen through the lens of thinking and the lens of a renewed sense of activism. Reading is inherently a practice of exchange, of responsiveness. It is radically communal. **[You say, YES!]** On closing the volume you write: "this book is a reading practice in a community of others." In effect, your poetry not only accepts itself as transit, and necessarily transitory, a critical landing station for names and texts, but it is as though such a transit can provide for a workable social practice of cultural resistance.

Am I far wrong? You assimilate poetic work with civic work **[you say, I want to believe it can be, must be]**. *O Cidadán* opens with this in mind: "To intersect a word: citizen." Certainly the extent to which one is free to manipulate ("intersect") one's culture's language and archives is always a question of democratic measure. In this sense, to write what one reads and how one reads can be seen as a point of civic responsibility. This remains especially true within the flux and reflux of political in/tolerance and the flux and reflux of gender socializations. Books were always hidden, or burnt. Reading is quickly precarious.

O Cidadán announces that it must meditate on texts and on

acts of reading in order to ask what citizenship might mean today, tomorrow. This is its declared role as poetry: to embody what it reads. To write how and what it reads. Quoting Jean-Luc Nancy, "the readings we can give each other, and the world, are the world, the 'sense to come'" (68). Reading gives body. "Reading's relation to the body is intelligibility's demeure" (70). I wonder whether this highly specialized and ventriloquized role for poetry can carry off a renewed sense of civic behaviour. (I'm not sure that I agree with this point; is specialism necessarily ventriloqual? I'm thinking of Said's institutional intellectual, feeding off Gramsci, the role of the specialist as ahistoric and recuperable by power. I don't know that this applies for a poetic universe which is stretched so far from any centre of power. I'd need to think it over.) [**You say, I agree with you, this has to be watched. Yet I don't feel there is anything in me that would qualify me as a specialist. I work outside fixed institutional frameworks and defend the idea that thinking can take place in interstices. You say, I don't like the word margins, for it cannot dislodge from the notion of a centre. Interstices are webs of thinking through and alongside each other, tugging and influencing. I'm just a node in a network . . . when various nodes flash, movement occurs, and the nodes themselves are altered structurally, but I don't direct anything or accept direction . . . I can transfer, shudder, enact, reverberate, blend . . .].**

Then I wonder whether there has ever been anything more important for modern poetry (and philosophy) to do than to unpack the ghosts of the past. These are, are these, the traces of your poetry's past: "georgette," "woman," "girl," "bodies," "o cidadán," "labial tendency." Your text's borders are its lesbian ghosts. Is its future called "O"?

Indeed, so it is that within your scrupulous practice of reading, you write a dream of love. While writing what you read, reading becomes a practice of responsiveness and of interdependency. It harnesses for poetry an unlikely kind of civic fantasy. Unlikely because girls, bodies, georgettes were never, could never be citizens as long as they were/are girls, georgettes. Yet reading in your work is that which attempts to trace and decode the lingering "policed sexuality" of citizenship, its unquestioned territorialities. Inevitably this pushes against the symbolic law of any normative sexuality. The civic is necessarily to an extent normative. Did it ever really care for poetry? I start to wonder whether this is not why there is such a mixed crowd of quoted texts and of names in this recent

work: each historicized, gendered, sexuated body-space, as pro-
posed in your various readings, is multitude, must be construed
and poeticized as lived multitude, both temporal and to-come, in
today's complex ways of considering citizenship. Each challenge
by social singularity, in its generosity and in its love, contains a
seed of tomorrow's collectivity, tomorrow's hoped-for modes of
citizenship, and modes of poetry, "O Georgette" (97), "O girls my
countries" (44).

I tell you what, though. That O in your title! That O in your
pages! How confusing, how marvellous. Here we have this
deconstructive poetic practice, cool and spatial, vaguely utopian
yet intellectually restless, and it gives itself over to the most
profoundly lyrical sign of them all. So what is O? The ancient,
centred exclamation that signals poetry, an interjection, an emotive point of address, a lament, a complaint. It is insistent refrain,
nearly song, nearing ballad. O is the old reminder of poetry's
musicality. It pulls your text towards this history. What is it doing
opening, punctuating so writerly a work? What is it doing framing
the self-conscious intellectuality of your poetic environment, where
poetry is a way of creating a textual body-space, which redefines
the emotional terrains it has occupied rather than mimicking or
emulating them?

Perhaps O is in fact there to confirm the obvious and to point
to an underlying rhythm. In addition to O, the book is punctuated
by the near-homophonic and very antithetical "or": "a scar or want"
(37), "or rigour" (36), "Afix or hesitate" (32), "or test archaeology
(32), "or coil" (16), "or insistence a trail" (17). From O to or. The
fact that O inevitably harks back to the poet's voice (you're careful,
you look for poetic anatomy not subjectivity, you call it her "lungs")
might be there exactly to remind us that the poet reads not just to
announce but to create shared body-spaces, amorous bodies, voiced
tracings.

Your text's desire for O is always a risk, feminine, politically
lesbian, therefore ghosted, doubly marked by singularity and likely
cultural cancellation. Markedly, pointedly, the historical examples
that are in your book point not only to sexuation, but more generally
to dehumanization, state law, or state terror applied to singular
bodies. Citizenship as poetic testimony is predicated on remembrance. In this sense, your text names names because it must "catalogue" the "Harms." Semprún, García Lorca, Marc Bloch . . .
If sharing one's readings is a practice of love, is it thus that O is the

desire that bleeds the courage to sing into the structural bones of scholarliness? Is that its civic address, its love, "O reader" (98)? Is the lyrical emphasis, the poeticized gesture of O a call, a confirmation of physical longing and of collective remembrance? Does it function as the rhythmical residue of some fantasized, physical "poetry"? Does it rescue poetic acts from oblivion? Does it rescue poetry itself from cultural disenfranchisement, does it manage to do this through fantasies of feminine address? Do you think poetry needs rescuing?

It's late now. I've had to let it go this last few days but I know from Nate you might get to see him this week. So I send this as it is, unfinished, incomplete, a sketch of thoughts and enthusiasm. If there's time, have a look to see if you can respond to any of this. I wanted to talk about your bilingualism, your switch from French to Spanish [**you say, I didn't switch, I amplified!**]. The bilingualism included in your title [**you say, it's actually just Galician, straight Galician . . . but I like what you've written about it, the way it becomes bilingual when a reader comes to it in English. As if the context of publishing a text primarily in English but with a non-English title in an anglo press makes it bilingual. Especially with the problematics around the very title of the book, and around insisting on entering the word "the citizen" at all. Galician *is* hard to see at first. It's a small language. A critic whom I usually find to be quite a good reader, actually accused me in a review of inventing Galician!** . . . *We continue talking about contexts for languages and how very small, minoritarian languages such as Galician (later, I wonder about Norwegian), spoken by a bare few millions, always have to struggle to find new structures, you say, passages, to speak into or they simply die. We talk about carrying languages in the body, in the mouth*]. I also wanted to talk about your use of a poetic bilingualism in relation to sexuality but this will have to be understood. I hope this finds you well!

Love, Caroline

10 April 2005

Dearest, queridísima Caroline,

What can I say in response to such a marvellous text? A text that mixes the acts of speaking, of hearing, of seeing, with the act of naming. To name. *Nomear* . . . this Galician verb (and sometimes there are things that only think themselves in Galician) so close to my own name . . . "a moure," the (girl) moure . . . and with its u flipped back into an n, again: nomear. A word that also contains "en amor." That dream of love of which you write is present in these conjunctions, these elaborations from a word.

And the significance of the O, this O which in a book of poems in English is ever an English O, for the reader comes to it in English. I see it now in your text, it's the letter without angles or anguishes . . . it pleases me that you see in this letter the female and lesbian body, when in Galician it is simply the definite article, masculine singular, the universal O of the *universO* that I insist I will inhabit as citizen, citizenne. An "O" is a "I" with air, an "I" (can you see it?) in blossom . . . is also an open eye, ready . . .

As I wrote *O Cidadán* I was thinking that the act of inhabitation can occur in language as well as in a place. To me English needed, and needs, words, word-acts, efforts, from other idioms, ours is so wounded, and the wounds are self-inflicted (given political speech we can hear on the radio every day that has just worsened since 9/11 . . . though *O Cidadán*'s writing predates 9/11). The borders, the frontiers of a language are also and must be open to what Manuel Rivas calls "clandestine passages." What I can offer English as a language in the title of this book is an encounter with Galician, with *galego*, with foreignness, with my eternal status as foreigner in English, with a linguistic reverberation that is not fully absorbable. (Though, as I said, to try to absorb it, one reader/critic claimed I invented Galician! That's one way out of a dilemma . . .).

And all this commotion and readability-lability, of course, when English should be my mother tongue! We talked of this, I told you my mother tongue is silence, and you called English, then, my *first language*. For I remember when I did not understand it, when what people were uttering was curious to me only, as they seemed to respond to each other as if the noises had significance outside of timbre and articulation, but I did not identify their noises as "words," I had no word for "word." (Did I ever say that when I was really little I could also not tell the difference between people and flowers? Well, never mind . . .)

Flúido. Lúdico. Lido. Leda. Illícita. Citada.
Fluid. Ludic. Read. Happy. Illicit. Cited.

Looking at that line of words generated from sounds, I realize I see letters as drawings, drawings of sounds more than meanings or senses (meanings of course attach themselves to sounds), and my name, too, this name I bear, a drawing of sounds, a name so often badly pronounced, with so many varieties and vanities, *variedades e vaidades*. But the border of a name is not a straight line. And has no final point either, except perhaps death, but no, death ends the organism only, and the name endures. The name of a dead person is still that person's name . . .

And me, I am thinking all this in Galician (and translating it now for you into English), in *galego*. The artist Orlan changed her appearance, the aspect of her own face, with surgeries. I changed my face by learning Galician, which puts different sounds into my mouth, that are pronounced in other areas of the mouth, and pronouncing words in this idiom changed the physiognomy of my face, of my body even, of my shoulders, my ribs, it changed my body so much that it also changed my manner of being and inhabiting English.

Flúido. Lúdico. Lido. Leda. Illícita. Citada. Cidadá. Citizen, because I can speak, because speaking itself alters the face, because *how can we* know, *until we have faces.*

And yes we have this responsibility, toward the civis. Of inventing ourselves faces. And yes we have an *eu*, an I, solely when we open ourselves to foreignness. O.

Will it change society? Society is, our societies are, already *revoltada*, upside down, in crisis. Society never ceases changing, and this, for the worst, unfortunately, at the moment. Perhaps these conversations we have with each other, these readings, can break the fall a little. If they could, another movement might be possible. Another flash. Trajet. Our faces might change because of the way we can enter speaking, or because of what we find it possible to hear. And for this, we need a plurality of idioms. And the multiplication of borders and porosities. Poetry as enactment, not consolation. It's this that I expect, await. And that we don't consume hope as we consume petroleum. There's not much of it left, after all.

Thanks for your text, Caroline, graciñas! . . . hoping that mine in some way responds to yours,

Erín

AN EXCHANGE ON TRANSLATION

Chris Daniels & Erín Moure

An open letter to Erin Mouré concerning, among other things, Sheep's Vigil by a Fervent Person, *her "transelation" of* O Guardador dos Rebanhos *by Alberto Caeiro (Fernando Pessoa).*

Erin querida,

When it comes to what I do, I have very little to write. Occasionally, usually in a classroom, which means *very* occasionally, for I'm almost never in a classroom, someone will ask me the right question, and then I find that I can talk. ("Eu sou uma pergunta," wrote Clarice Lispector, that sphingian writer, so dear to us.) The right question is: "What role does translation play in your life?" The question is usually phrased somewhat differently (*but, why do you do this?*). To some, this question seems naïve and its answer painfully obvious.

But I can't conceive of a life without poetry, especially poetry written in the Portuguese language; and the translation of poetry is, for all intents and purposes, my only creative activity. It is also, as I try to practice it, a political act.

Politics is the art of wielding and managing power over others. When I translate, I exert considerable power: like it or not, my English version is going to be received as an accurate, mechanical reproduction of a poem in Portuguese. It doesn't matter that we know this to be patently ridiculous, a sheer impossibility, for this is the way most people read translations.

I know that my translating is a null compared to the minuscule power wielded by a city council member, even, but there's nothing else I do that I care very much about besides translating, and I

177

have to live with myself. So a certain ethics has to be present at all times, and the easiest way to express that ethics is: *I will not translate a poem that does not demand it of me.*

. . .

I have asked myself that naïve question, and hope that what follows is at least part of a possible answer. I will also ask you and the readers of *The Gig* to forgive me if, in attempting to provide a possible answer and simultaneously trying to turn toward another question asked by your *Sheep's Vigil* ("What is a trans*e*lation?"), I speak almost entirely about myself.

. . .

Two definitions of the verb *to translate*, from the *OED*:

– To change in form, appearance, or substance; to transmute; to transform, alter.
– To transport with the strength of some feeling; to enrapture, entrance.

The other definitions don't interest me.

. . .

Translation is an act of friendship, as I'm sure you know from your experience of producing those remarkable translations of the Galician Chus Pato and the Chilean Andrés Ajens, who have surely become your friends, as the living poets I have translated have become mine. In my experience, the more difficult the work involved, the closer such cross-cultural friendships tend to be.

Translation fights cultural narcissism. When I surrender to another poet's work I am of necessity possessed by that poet's mind and culture. If I translate without learning as much as I possibly can about the entire culture of the poet I'm translating, without coming to care deeply for that culture, then I am not being translated, and there is simply no point in translating unless I myself am translated in the process. When I, a translator-poet, surrender to the work of another, I cannot help but hear the voice of Echo. Translation is never a solitary activity. When I open to the world and all its many peoples, I can be translated. When I hear Echo's voice, I am agape with what the Greeks called Agapé.

It's given that a great translation has to be "incorrect" when it needs to be so, and that only bad translations take no risk of language commensurate with the risk taken by the work being translated. But in your "trans*e*lation," the shepherd's crook of Alberto

Caeiro is translated into a pen in your hand and his sheep are translated into your cat in a time-loose Everyplace provisionally named "Toronto" in which you may or may not have lived in the past. You don't walk through fields or along dirt roads, but ride a bike over asphalt streets. The creeks of the Alentejo are translated into paved roads; all that is left of them is the sound you imagine them to make. Yourself translated into yourself – *after* Caeiro, a fervent man invented by another fervent man; you press your ear to manhole covers and carefully/caringly listen to that which whispers and gasps beneath the most mundane of all visible trappings of Western culture. This is so far beyond ordinary acts of translation. Your transelation goes so far beyond the usual decorous notions of literary transmission that it makes me laugh out loud. Temporality and scientism are demolished in a refusal to adhere to the differences between *ser, estar* and *haver*. Such creative imagining enriches Pessoa's poetry even more than it enriches ours.

. . .

Such creative imagining nourishes revolution in my heart.

Each and every citizen of my country so arrogantly named "America" knows, to a certain extent, that the edifices of our pre-eminence, privilege, wealth, and power float upon a slurry made of the triturated bones of countless human beings whose brief lives were and are mercilessly shortened, by murder or by exploitation, their names stripped from them, for the benefit of a few males of European ancestry, their families and their lackeys of every creed, gender, and percentage of epidermal melanin. Our rulers are guilty of centuries of theft and murder on an unimaginable scale. We see irrefutable evidence of this in front of us, every minute of every day. Too many of us choose ignorance, or we pretend that we have eradicated racism, prejudice and the unjust exploitation of our fellow humans. That choice and that pretension make us accomplices. Something very similar can be said about citizens of every country with a ruling class, and which country does not?

There are many ways to resist complicity, and I strive to make use of them all, whenever I can, in any combination. When I march in a demonstration, I add my voice and my body to a multifarious crowd insisting on decency in the world. When I read C. L. R. James, I'm struggling to understand serious Marxist thought and to see clearly the racism shovelled into me by the culture in which I grew up. When I read a book like your *O Cidadán*, I'm wowed and filled with enjoyment and pleasure as I continue my struggle to understand the sexism and homophobia that I (like nearly everyone else) was taught as a child.

I struggle to see clearly how gender, race, and class are "subject-positions" that function to keep us on edge, scared and apart. The struggle takes place among the finely-interlocking segments of my personality, and I doubt that this struggle can be won by me. I will never stop fighting to see clearly.

. . .

I could say more about certain particulars of your transelation, about how it works with and against Pessoa's original, but anybody who can read Spanish can understand Portuguese. Anybody can look at the original, or at Edwin Honig's translation, and compare it to *Sheep's Vigil*.

. . .

Do you remember, when you were reading/talking at the Poetry Center at San Francisco State University, and I embarrassed you, just a little, by stating that *Sheep's Vigil* is the ideal English version of *O Guardador dos Rebanhos*? I meant it then, and I still believe it.

For reasons having to do with the death of my little sister, before your fervent vigilance became known to me, I couldn't see the beautiful sense of humor in Caeiro. Thank you for showing me.

And thank you for your coinage, "transelation," which is the ideal term for what we strive to do. I am translated by your transelation, and all of your work is a great inspiration, something to which I will always aspire as a writer, a reader and a translator whose greatest desire is to be translated by the work at hand.

Um abraço do amigo todo traduzido,

Chris

6 May 2005, Montreal

Dear Chris,

Since reading your wonderful letter to me of course I've wanted to respond, to nod, wave at you from across the still porous but uptight border between our countries. And add my plea for translation to yours, my own musings on translation beside yours. Part of the beauty of engaging in translation being this reach through shared places of endeavour, and surprise.

But "shared endeavour" doesn't mean the "translation presumes shared codes," as I read in some other text – the presumption that what culturally inhabits one language can find its equivalent in the next. We know this to be false or, at best, patchily true. We have to bend our own idiom to let the other one enter, to make space for it. Or we risk bending the other to inhabit the dream (nightmare) that mastery exists in our own idiom, and that the curtailment of surprise means mastery.

It is not translation but translation's *audience* who has too often been trained to presume shared codes, perhaps even, as you say, equivalency. Translation itself, as we know, does not presume. It enacts or activates certain levels of language at the expense of others, it renders present certain histories and abolishes others that underpin the texts it draws from. For there is no equivalency, or "so little." There are echoes, absorbencies, unfoldings, resistances, stains, mirrors, mirages, saults.

In the translating I did last winter of Chus Pato's *Charenton*: in places her Galician verb tenses move between past, present and future as she describes a single incident; this verbal ambivalence evokes a synchronic shifting that also exists in the medieval literature, in the cantigas. Pato provokes it further. But to translate all these shifts of tense is just to sound bad in English for our verbal histories are not equivalent. So I left some of her tenses, let them ruffle and collide, then smoothed others. To create a similar disruptive tension and mild cacophony, I needed less. I needed to listen, not impose my language though. Each text demands something different, and always something more, of its translator. No presumption is possible.

We both know that translation cannot work in justice if it is presumption and the casting of equivalencies. Its job is to infiltrate, as an uptake factor that opens the blood vessels, not one that closes them. To do this, it sometimes has to create what looks like ruin in its own, beloved, "target" tongue.

It looks like "ruin" to the audience only when the audience will admit no more than what we already know, what presents solace to us, not challenge.

My work as a translator is to allow the language and works which inhabit me in an idiom not English, and which have already bent, changed, ruined the presumptions of my first language (which I do not call my mother tongue, for silence is my mother tongue, I remember silence before I could speak) and opened me to difference and to articulations impossible to me before I could speak it. Galician, for example, so similar to your Portuguese, Chris, that we can celebrate together: Galician changes not just the ear, but the physiognomy of the face. The face, that locus of Levinasian thought – is changed because Galician is spoken in a different part of the mouth than is English. From my new face, joy, anguish enter differently. Food enters differently. The ear is altered. The eye. The sense of taste and smell are altered.

And when I speak my own language, English, with this new face, people tell me I have an accent.

How to enact for the reader in a book-sized package the magnificence of such alteration! No solace. But: exposure. Self-exposure. The exposure of being-to-the-other that is what we call "self." For there is no self otherwise.

As Robert Majzels said last year in Guelph, Ontario: "Finally, through translation we gain the loss of self. We are freed from the limitations of that illusory stable reading self. We see ourselves as part of a matrix of force lines intersecting in the text. The addition of a translator into the relationship author–text–readers breaks the duality of self and other. The author, translator, and reader are no longer clearly delineated entities meeting in the text. They are effects of the text. That is why we are shaken when we read. We feel a shudder. That's our subjectivity shifting. That feeling of the ground moving under our feet is what we call the sublime."*

So translation is not about the "other" or the "self." It is about the opening, ever opening. It is "about" all of us. It is about reading, which is script as act, script-ure as incorporated act.

_____

*"What is lost and what is gained in translation," copy furnished by the author, given as a talk in Guelph, Ontario, autumn 2004.

And thus, as you say, it is opposed to the major current in the politics of our time, the language of which is about closure and exclusion and the dis-ease of borders.

Abraços para ti, amigo na tradución e na vida, e na revolução.

e

P.S. Robert Majzels also said to me: "Raising Levinas I think is particularly apropos about translation. His discussion of justice. And the phrase in the Sanhedrin tractate of the Talmud: Who knows the 71 languages of the nations? Only she can sit in judgment, serve on the court, judge issues of life and death. Ergo without translation in the world, no justice is possible." I would like to end with that, with Robert's voice, as the third translator. The third translator is always the word "justice." But a different justice than that we have as yet known.

ARTICULATE/PUNCTUATE: TRACKING AN OBSESSION WITH COLLABORATIVE PERFORMANCE

a. rawlings

Why does sound poetry please me. Reinvestment in the basic tools of language? Exploration of literary quality of sound production? Examining language for its structure and material, in addition to or in lieu of semantics?

Where do I begin. With sound?

How do I form meaning from sound. How do I name? Can a comma signify an inhale. Could I assign each alphabet letter a different sound, then try to re-pronounce words according to their re-ordered/re-assigned sounds. . . .

Again: the base material: sound?!

I experiment with sound production of the mouth of the body . . . ! I create a language of the mouth! I repeat sound to remember it! I teach it to others or they teach sound to me. . . . We organize the sounds to name.

We add movement, gesture; we name this communication; we name this communication speechmusicdance.

Articulate. Bilabial nasal sonorants buzz. Labiodental fricatives flick through teeth and lip. Sound exciting, exiting body: pleasure. Punctuate.

Please: when I slants to We. A map of collaborative performance.

2002: "Identity a Poem" by Gertrude Stein is a poem about human nature, identity, and a little dog. It is simply that, much more than that, that. Its simple, dense layers beg reading, re-reading, re-reading, reading. I e-meet Katherine Parrish through the UbuWeb listserv. I meet Katherine in person. I want to perform with Katherine, so I adapt "Identity a Poem" for two voices, and we read at the Lexiconjury Reading Series. Issues of public discourse, relationships, and communal identity play prominent roles in the work Katherine and I perform together.

February 2003: Katherine brings to the table "Switching," by Juliana Spahr. We adapt it for two voices. "Switching" is a quickly read, straightforward call-and-response adaptation, with an infectious refrain of "How to put one leg on one's shoulder and then the other leg stretched out or twined around the other person." We switch at the Lexiconjury Reading Series and at Jacquie Jacobs' art exhibition opening.

November 2003: Carole Maso refers to *Rupture, Verge, and Precipice* as an essay; I classify it as a long poem. Katherine and I adapt excerpts to perform as prologue for a digital poetics lecture we present to an Intro to Contemporary Literature course taught by Marcus Boon at York University. We punctuate the performance with moments of disruption (daydream drift, missing pages); we draw comparison to audience's experience surfing websites, reading books. We raise questions of similarity between digital and print text. We disrupt for pleasure.

July 2004: Margaret Christakos and I perform her long poem "Orphans Fan the Flames" for Scream on a High Note, accompanied by improvised piano, trumpet, and guitar. We speed-read, text biting at the heels of text. Text urges, purges: "Fix us. / Asphyxiate the other."

July 2004: I read "RUSH (a long way from H)" by Caroline Bergvall for pleasure. Frequently. I adapt it for Scream on a High Note, performed by Margaret Christakos, Peter McPhee, John Sobol, and me. "RUSH" explores the sights, sounds, intoxicants, and confusion of a trance hall. Adapting for four voices is a pleasurable challenge. I adapt for pleasure.

February 2005: Rachel Zolf invites me to join Sandra Alland, Margaret Christakos, and Katherine Parrish for a polyvocal performance of excerpts from *Masque*. Our rehearsal is recorded for high-school review. We perform at the Lexiconjury Reading Series.

May 2005: Jill Hartman and I improvise her moth poem from *A Painted Elephant* for a taping of *Heart of a Poet*. Pleasure in synchronous moments.

September 2005: I complete work on the text for my long poem *Wide slumber for lepidopterists.* I turn my attention to performance strategies. I've read excepts in a straightforward manner for four years; while the readings are a pleasure to give, the language much fun to slip off tongue, I'm eager to match performance with text. I puzzle at creating a sound-poetry-flushed version of the text. Working title: *Wide slumber for sound.* Katherine Parrish and I give a prototype reading from *Wide slumber for sound* at the Art Bar Poetry Series.

October 2005: Ciara Adams and I record two minutes from *Wide slumber.*

April 2006: Ciara, Alexis Milligan, and I spend ten hours creating and rehearsing a three-minute sound poem, performed at the Coach House Books launch of *Wide slumber for lepidopterists.* We focus on structured improvisation of "a hoosh a ha" (pp. 7–10) and "xxx y zzz" (pp. 40–41) sequences. Pleasure of full-body sounding, of repetition.

April 2006: Jill Hartman and I perform a fifteen-minute excerpt combining *Wide slumber* and her response text *sfurle* for the *NoD/ dANDelion* magazine launch in Calgary. Pleasure in listening to another's voice, in witnessing another listen and respond.

July 2006: Ciara Adams, Lori-Nancy Kalamanski, and I spend fourteen hours creating and developing a ten-minute performance of *Wide slumber* for the Scream Literary Festival. Conor Green provides feedback throughout our process, shaping the final outcome.

August 2006: Ciara Adams, Conor Green, and I perform a shortened version of our work-in-progress for Scream in the Square. Conor's male voice and beatboxing add different texture to performance.

September 2006: Jason Christie, Conor Green, and I perform a thirty-minute version of *Wide slumber* for Toronto's first Nuit Blanche. Our performance occurs at 1 a.m., part of Margaret Christakos's night-long celebration of experimental and experiential text. We use personal lighting devices as pseudo-microphones that light insides of mouths when speaking; a green umbrella draped in mosquito netting to create a cocooned Bride of the Withering Summer; humour; and improvised dance. Coffee tables include copies of the book, which attendees leaf through, as well as bottles of expired cicadas, monarchs, and honeybees.

September 2006: I spend a two-week residency with sixty students at Northview Heights Secondary School. Near the end of our adventure, we indulge in a morning on poetry in performance, a topic that tumbles easily into sound poetry. We breathe impassioned noise into our English classroom. Students sound with abandon, collapsing in giggle fits and exclamations of shock and confusion over our pre-semantics.

November 2006: Harbourfront Centre's Hatch: Emerging Performance Projects series awards our ad-hoc collective, dubbed Theatre Commutiny, a week-long development residency in their Studio Theatre. The commutiny comprises Amanda Brugel and Mika Collins working with me, Conor Green as director, Geoff Bouckley as lighting designer, Richard Windeyer as sound composer, and Susanna Hood as guest choreographer. We spend a fevered week examining and experimenting with performance strategies for adapting *Wide slumber* from page to stage. We present our creation in two forty-five-minute performances. Though a dizzying experience, we're left with the impression that there's so much more we can explore given time and resources. Pleasure in pleasure.

What's next: After Hatch, I took a weekend-long sound and movement workshop lead by Susanna Hood. It's ignited my imagination, and I'm eager to continue exploring the intersections of text, movement, and sound.

FIVE POEMS

Lise Downe

The Influence of Complete Darkness

In the dusk of a November evening
somewhere in the mid-seventeenth century
nothing is concealed or conveyed.
There is, simply
a concentration of sunflowers.

As the world turns, they turn
from pathos to persuasion
guided by the radiant light.

Two fresh puddles insert themselves
and are read as a dark ellipse.
Nothing hinders them from soaking through.

Perhaps a fish detects them before disappearing
its far-off murmur a mutter now
sounding something like the inscription
on a Japanese fan by Totoki Baigai:

"Outside the city walls there's an odd fish.
I don't know its name."

Perish the Thought

Alas, there is always the temptation
to think of what we speak
to reconfigure the haphazard assembly
into self-standing objects
enhanced so cleverly to halt
then hasten us into
the neighbourhood of a pine tree.

What real flowers flock there, are
flocking there so close to the ground?

We speak of what's given.
A calling.
Climate and soil.
Crisp and delicate fretwork
keeping vigilant watch along the frontiers.
Yet this is what happens.

And when it does, we tend to think
that if we keep repeating, loudly
in spite of the precarious wobble
that all will be well.
Decipherment easy.

In a sense this is written deliberately.
The leaves our senses urge, unfurling
to rustle, to swallow and stand one's ground
once shaking the tree.

We can relax then and credit the material
witness who has come back

        From where?

as if in a daze, knowing
when to bow and when to beckon
then dying shortly after learning to say "cup."

The View from Here

If not under acres of canvas and hide
    then bruised and dizzy.

If not suffering what some
distortion might suggest
cracking and dividing
    then the world grows older.

One attends to all of this
and one recovers
all those failures that render us into eclipse
into the meaning of meantime
high noon under hollow trees
what with
and clothed with
one short word of explanation.

All our lost mobility
obscures the silent horseshoe
the crucible, the vapour
gathering
and the hounds that pursue it
along the cliff's entanglements
                                out and into.

Fields of blue-stem grasses
hover seemingly
like the horseshoe under cover of darkness.
All part of the matter
of hours that furnish
us under what roof
and which stars.

Conundrum

Nobody, she said, but *nobody*
could have foreseen the day
of irreducible, irretrievable
hats, hats, hats.
Perhaps from the footprints
rather than their true colours
one might have detected a mingling
of more than texture and embroidery.

But now the tiles and pots have vanished.
Clues intensified by perpetual states of erosion.
All invented to aid the eye
through elements of wind.
And gravity.

And yet we always find below the profusion
of leaves and berries
here, in these unlit and seldom-visited spaces
how different the sanctuary is
when tending to the task of continuing afternoon.

Utterly absorbed, meticulous even
undergoing the vagaries of time
and time's again turn of the handle
where whole scenes change
reflecting each whim of a passing hour.

These tracks in the grass
(for instance)
coming or going?

It's all conjecture. Neither here nor there
has anything to do with the bend
or the number of bays that remain unaltered.
Only that just such excursions, such
milestones, open the aisles and gladly
welcome a stranger to their shores.

Turning the tide of travel
toward something less complicated.

A ring of maidenhair ferns.
Even fresher sprigs of mint.

The first pleasant surprise encountered
en route to what every schoolgirl knows
giving entry to spacious dioramas
with nary a sense of clutter.

Testimonial

If that word you passed was wildflower
for either of two reasons
the strain might extend our reach beyond
the familiar field of impressions
and might suggest
if only in a flattened form
an image of proliferation.

Sometimes in the
if
the whim graspeth thee
it may recall the muddy delta's
intake of air
the silting and mouthing of the word for water
taking to a boat to row
upon row
upon row
until we deposit some new expression
for the partially open
mother-of-pearl.

And if by some incredible chance
the unsettling provides
between the tides
a blossoming from tiny pencils

initially confined to small areas
but gradually covering the entire surface
then in our minds this long-delayed birthday
cashes in on more than a bank of flowers
and the invention of balloons

and toys with secrets of orientation
weight and measure
the mention of tender
slow liquid almost verbatim
the ringing of bells
and their – you
iris then.

Completely.

KAREN MAC CORMACK
AMONG THE PAGANS

Gerald L. Bruns

"Are you acquainted with Vienna?" Felix inquired.

"Vienna," said the doctor, "the bed into which the common people climb, docile with toil, and out of which the nobility fling themselves, ferocious with dignity – I do, but not so well but that I remember some of it still. I remember young Austrian boys going to school, flocks of quail they were, sitting out their recess in different spots in the sun, rosy-cheeked, bright-eyed, with damp rosy mouths, smelling of the herd childhood, facts of history glimmering in their minds like sunlight, soon to be lost, soon to be forgotten, degraded into proof. Youth is cause, effect is age; so with the thickening of the neck we get data."

– Djuna Barnes, *Nightwood* (15–16)

On several occasions Karen Mac Cormack has said that her poetic career began with the reading, at age sixteen, of Djuna Barnes's *Nightwood*, a novel published by Faber and Faber, under T. S. Eliot's imprimatur, in 1936. *Nightwood* is a work whose prose (like Doctor Matthew O'Connor's glorious talk, cited here in the epigraph) disengages itself from the grammar of consecutive discourse, including especially the logical progressions of narrative. *Nightwood* does not fail at these things, but it interrupts them. Barnes had difficulty getting her book published, revising it several times in order to give it the semblance of Aristotelian virtues that novels – even avant-garde ones – were (and are) still expected to possess. *Ulysses* and *Mrs. Dalloway* are, for all their formal innovations, arguably more integrated than *Nightwood*, with its peculiar, edgy, often sarcastic voice that prefers wild commentary to mere story-telling:

She did not smile, though the moment he spoke, she placed him. She closed her eyes, and Felix, who had been looking into them intently because of their mysterious and shocking blue, found himself seeing them still faintly clear and timeless behind the lids – the long unqualified range in the iris of wild beasts who have not tamed the focus down to meet the human eye.

194

The woman who presents herself to the spectator as a "picture" forever arranged, is for the contemplative mind the chiefest danger. Sometimes one meets a woman who is beast turning human. Such a person's every movement will reduce to an image of a forgotten experience; a mirage of an eternal wedding cast on the racial memory; as insupportable a joy as would be the vision of an eland coming down an aisle of trees, chapleted with orange blossoms and bridal veil, a hoof raised in the economy of fear, stepping in the trepidation of flesh that will become myth; as the unicorn is neither man nor beast deprived, but human hunger pressing its breast to its prey.

Such a woman is the infected, carrier of the past: before her the structure of our head and jaws ache – we feel that we could eat her, she who is eaten death returning, for only then do we put our face close to the blood on the lips of our forefathers. (36)

One can imagine Henry James admiring this passage, but also puzzling over "a woman who is beast turning human," a metamorphosis that reverses Ovid in a way that a Surrealist might envy. Her "every movement will reduce to an image of a forgotten experience." It's hard to picture what "an image of a forgotten experience" might look like. I wouldn't have imagined "a mirage of an eternal wedding cast on the racial memory" (the reference, neither the first nor last, is to Felix's Jewishness) complete with an eland (a species of antelope) in a bridal procession, with "a hoof raised in the economy of fear," as if the marriage ceremony resolved into a sacrificial one. The third paragraph in the citation is one of my favourites in all of modern literature. If you ask, how do these sentences hang together (adding up to a portrait of a lady we would do well to avoid but never do: "we feel we could eat her, she who is eaten death returning"), it takes some time to answer. One could begin by putting the question to Gertrude Stein, who was perhaps the first to explore the ways words could be made to form dissonant yet self-contained portraits:

A LITTLE CALLED PAULINE

A little called anything shows shudders.

Come and say what prints all day. A whole few watermelon. There is no pope.

No cut in pennies and little dressing and choose wide soles and little spats really little spices.

A little lace makes boils. This is not true.

Gracious of gracious and a stamp a blue green white bow a blue green lean, lean on the top.

If it is absurd then it is leadish and nearly set in where there is a tight head.

A peaceful life to arise her, noon and moon and moon. A letter a cold sleeve a blanket a shaving house and nearly the best and regular window.

Nearer in fairy sea, nearer and farther, show white has lime in sight, show a stitch of ten. Count, count more so that thicker and thicker is leaning.

I hope she has her cow. Bidding a wedding, widening received treading, little leading, mention nothing.

Cough out cough out in the leather and really feather it is not for.

Please could, please could, jam it not plus more sit in when. (324)

I think that the kinship between Djuna Barnes and Gertrude Stein is intimate and complementary. Provisionally one could say that Barnes remains within the horizon of the predicate – subjects, verbs and objects doing their work of mediation, however digressively and to whatever many strange purposes. Her reticulated prose retains the form if not always the content of what philosophers call "aboutness," whereas parataxis – the defeat of wholeness and hierarchies of every sort – is internal to Stein's sentences, which interrupt the discursive operations that integrate small things into large. Gertrude Stein's is an insubordinate poetics of the little and the discrete ("a little piece a little piece please" [337]), and this applies to her words and phrases as well as to the world of dainty Pauline, with her "blue green white bow." Djuna Barnes's meanwhile is a poetics of the long, slow amplification of particulars, as in the medieval (or is it gothic?) tapestry that the narrator weaves as a gloss on Felix's gripping encounter with Robin Vote's animal-iris eyes.

Karen Mac Cormack's *Quill Driver* (1989) is a text that seems to me to split the differences (and explore the family resemblances) between Barnes and Stein, and in the bargain it opens up a conceptual context that helps us to experience certain kinds of writing that are, even now, more familiar than understood. Here, for example, is the first paragraph (if paragraph is the word) of Mac Cormack's "Reunion the Reproduction":

Further alive. Perhaps when the heart stops beating the tiredness leaves. There are questions but not obvious ones, any other yellow centre. The furor she caused in Italy, buying daisies for a non-funereal purpose. Two women equally shocked. She told me other colours, occasionally the light would fail. Despite assorted revolutions we order our lives past, present, future, to apply to what is ongoing out of the tempest. If we line these up there's still the one, two, three of it but not Van Gogh. (31)

"Reunion the Reproduction" contains twenty-two such paragraphs of varying length. Like the writings of Barnes and Stein, it lays transparency to rest but not intelligibility. The task of the reader is (among other things) to understand how such self-interrupting sentences are connected, or at least to experience the ways in which the passage does not just break down into mere slivers. (Nonlinearity is not mere dispersal or diffusion.) Close reading in Mac Cormack's case reveals many small internal coherences such as references to death, colour, correctness, order (and, by implication, anarchy) – we narrate our lives according to Aristotle's rules, but what if we did so according to Van Gogh's, colour and texture trumping continuity and point? As philosophers of complex systems have explained, chaos is paradoxically a condition of orderly arrangements. Foreigners and the weather refuse to act predictably, but if we follow the two carefully as they proceed we will see patterns develop, even if no reason (or future) can be assigned to them. Rationality is not rule-governed behaviour but the ability to negotiate turbulence (an ability Aristotle called *phronesis*, or practical reason). The coastline of California has a form that fractalists can explore in detail, but it duplicates nothing but itself. A world of random particles can only be described by reproducing it piece by piece. Death to universals.

Karen Mac Cormack's *Quill Driver* situates itself within complexities of this sort. For example, I read Mac Cormack's work as an ongoing exploration of Jean-François Lyotard's anarchic conception of the phrase.[1] *Phrase* is the French term for sentence as well as our term for grammatical relations beneath the level of a complete thought, but Lyotard takes it to be the (indefinable) basic unit of language on the hither side of every conceivable grammar, logic, genre or norm of discourse. Those things are some of the "phrase regimens" that phrases make possible, but none of these regimes can say what a phrase is. There is no *metaphrase*. To be sure, a phrase implies a saying of something to someone about something (the "phrase universe"), but nothing can be said about a phrase in general except that it is capable of linking up with other phrases, and there are multiple and heterogeneous forms of linkages, some of them syntactical (subject-verb-object), some logical (*if-then*), some propositional (*s* is *p*), some hermeneutical (this *as* that), and some narrative (this *then* that), but Lyotard's point is that there are (indefinitely) more forms of enchainment than those we learn to use in school (reasoning, describing, questioning, narrating). Phrasing is not systematic construction. We inhabit a universe of phrases that are rhizomatically proliferating and tangling like crabgrass. There is no first or final phrase:

The paradox of the last phrase (or of the last silence), which is also the paradox of the series, should give *x* not the vertigo of what cannot be phrased (which is also called the fear of death), but rather the irrefutable conviction that phrasing is endless. For a phrase to be the last one, another one is needed to declare it, and it is then not the last one. At least, the paradox should give *x* both this vertigo and this conviction. –Never mind that the last phrase is the last one that *x* says! –No, it is the last one that has *x* as its direct or "current" addressor. (*The Differend*, 11)

Lyotard's application in our present context lies in his conception of the pure negative freedom of phrasing: "To link is necessary, but how to link is not" (66). A link is a gap between phrases, which we fill willy-nilly with many things, including passage phrases, but without being able to close the gap. For example,

The phrase that expresses the passage operator employs the conjunction *and* (*and so forth, and so on*). This term signals a simple addition, the apposition of one term with the other, nothing more. Auerbach (1946: ch. 2 and 3) turns this into a characteristic of "modern" style, paratax, as opposed to classical syntax. Conjoined by *and*, phrases or events follow each other, but their succession does not obey a categorical order (*because; if, then; in order to; although . . .*). Joined to the preceding one by *and*, a phrase arises out of nothingness to link up with it. Paratax thus connotes the abyss of Not-Being which opens between phrases, it stresses the surprise that something begins when what is said is said. *And* is the conjunction that most allows the constitutive discontinuity (or oblivion) of time to threaten, while defying it through its equally constitutive continuity (or retention). . . . Instead of *and*, and assuring the same paratactic function, there can be a comma, or nothing. (66)

Paratax: the phrase of modernism. This is a crucial paragraph, if paragraph is the word, because it describes Lyotard's own poetics, which is to write, not books, but "notes," "fragments," "sketches," "rudiments," "lessons," "discussions" (these are the terms he applies to his writings). The point is to avoid "big talk." The structure of *The Differend*, for example, is segmental and performative rather than simply informational. In his vocabulary, his writing is a form of *paganism*. A pagan is someone who thinks, judges, acts and links phrases together *without criteria* (Lyotard, *Just Gaming*, 16). ("Pagan," from *pagus*: boundary, frontier or edge. A pagan is someone who traverses these things.) In Lyotard's sense, Gertrude Stein, Djuna Barnes and Karen Mac Cormack are pagan poets phrasing outside the limits of regimens favoured by logic, linguistics, Aristotelian poetics, structuralist poetics (among other formalisms), and most philosophies of language, not to mention current critical methods and numerous poetical schools, with their suspicion of opaque language. Writing is, as Lyotard says, *une affaire d'enchaînement de phrases* that leaves us open to complexity. It is the opposite of such phrasings as calculative reasoning or representational thinking, which are, in contrast to paganism, redeemed beforehand by their formal procedures, which simply give us what we want – framing rules, connecting ends and means, constructing models, forming concepts, putting things in their proper places, producing narratives. Pagans love category mistakes, or in other words are satirical with respect to forms of correctness.

Here is a portion of Karen Mac Cormack's "Sleep Is Incurable in Our Lifetime":

Serenity is unpopular, it distracts from the major ambushes of exterior concerns. Never a bugle boy. The manufacture of white gauze, its disposal after first time use. Then there was the birthday we went to tattoo you. A flesh wound. Deemed eligible, the bank account provides a sense of style (so might a fedora in turbulence). It's become more than six months ago I referred to another sequence of daring. Do men blink more often than women? Certain reflexes seem to count as memory in nerve, muscle and example: the cat looks up to a drawing of its counterpart losing feathers. A title doesn't confer talent conveyed. Calvados from a snifter late into what they also knew last century. First sip. Not implant but tenacious hamstrings. Complaint of content – its lack thereof or from. An elegant suppleness should be consumed relatively young. Orgasms aren't oblique on the morning of, or in the night. Sex is precision. "No local passengers carried between stations marked A." It's froth on the inside that's dangerous. Whist, the silent card game. . . . The dead don't borrow from us as we do from them. How different is brooch from broach. The cat rolls on flowers but doesn't crush the print, as in cotton, not a description of the auto-erotic. In that chair this conversation, a utilizable not employable table. How tender in twelve? Supplant this with the word *terse*, or focus on all the visible points simultaneously. Light doesn't blister itself but the epidermis becomes disorganised. Pallor, sometimes misconstrued as a manifestation of *missing*. (*Quill Driver*, 18)

This poem continues for another several sentences before breaking off – Mac Cormack's poems stop but do not end. Like Dr. O'Connor's monologues, each of her poems is cumulative rather than conclusive and could still be unfolding somewhere in a parallel universe. What is compelling about "Sleep Is Incurable in Our Lifetime" are the subtle, fragmentary interactions between one phrase and another. There is a kind of echo principle at work, not so much at the level of sound (but by all means keep your ears open) as at the level of

reference, perception, and concept: phrasing here is a kind of thinking (without criteria) – thinking that proceeds by the proliferation of phrases rather than by some linear principle of internal
necessity (phrases do not add up to statements, except under severe
coercion). I'm not sure why serenity is unpopular, but I know
serene people are less shaken by "ambushes of exterior concerns"
than I am, and maybe serenity is just another form of supercilious-
ness. Coincidentally just the other day I was listening to the
Andrews Sisters sing their great World War II hit, *Boogie Woogie
Bugle Boy (of Company B)*. A bugle boy is certainly a source of
external ambushes, as for example at 5:00 a.m. Meanwhile bandages
made of gauze had *better* be discarded "after first time use." Amateur
tattoo artists are apt to cause a "flesh wounds" requiring, etc. "Do
men blink more often than women?" It depends on who we think
is more reflexive in "nerve, muscle and example." Talent trumps
pedigree, except in the hierarchies of academic life. "First sip" is of
"Calvados [a splendid cognac] from a snifter late." "Orgasms aren't
oblique" because "Sex is precision." "Sex is precision" is at once
erotic counsel, an elegant piece of graffiti, and a philosophical
theory. "Not implant but tenacious hamstrings" may be for all I
know a source of sexual precision. A tenacious hamstring sounds
erotic to me. Implants are for the young.

Players only love you when they're playing: a traditional hermeneutical way to respond to pagan poetry is to appropriate a phrase
rather than to try to decipher its intention – this means that one
makes the phrase one's own by taking it now this way, now that,
the way the ancient rabbis used to read scriptural verses: not consecutively, but by linking them with verses from other (sometimes
distant) parts of the Bible, finding echoes in words and even parts
of words. So reading becomes itself *une affaire d'enchaînement de
phrases*, reweaving texts into new networks of phrasing. "An elegant
suppleness should be consumed relatively young": such consumption could apply here equally well to cognac or to sex, although if
so the line is apt to make an old man scowl. I'm sure Mac Cormack
didn't have this reading in mind. Hermeneutics says that the rule
of reading to be followed is that of charity, or the invention of
truth conditions – reading does not decipher but improvises sup-
porting language (or contexts) that enables the phrase in question
to come out true. For some phrases this is easy: "Whist, the silent
card game," fulfills the conditions of a true statement for the
same reasons that "Chess, the silent board game" would. Likewise

"The dead don't borrow from us as we do from them": an *aperçu* worthy of *The Tatler*. "'No local passengers carried between stations marked A'" is true just as a rule is true if enforced and obeyed; anyhow the phrase is a citation, which technically cannot be false ("British intelligence reported that 'Iraq has weapons of mass destruction'" is a true statement about false intelligence, and also, therefore, a classic piece of official rhetoric).

But Mac Cormack eludes even the most charitable hermeneutics. Most of her phrases play with truth conditions, multiplying rather than just fulfilling them: "Light doesn't blister itself but the epidermis becomes disorganised. Pallor, sometimes misconstrued as a manifestation of *missing*." My counsel is to construe these sentences lightly, keeping to one's breast thoughts of sunburn and anemia, allowing the phrases to percolate their nuances, since the super-formation of nuances is pretty much the poetics at work here. Appropriation, after all, is a form of regimentation, settling what is mobile into place – an execution of nuances in both the formal and the lethal sense. As Lyotard says (in a section of *The Differend* devoted interestingly to Gertrude Stein's phrases), "A phrase is not mysterious, it is clear. It says what it means to say. No 'subject' receives it, in order to interpret it. Just as no 'subject' makes it (in order to say something). It calls forth its addressor and addressee, and they come take their places in its universe" (67). This is good anthropological advice: the idea is to learn how to inhabit the milieu of this strange language until one feels at home – Clifford Geertz calls it "becoming real," feeling the purpose and pleasure of the Balinese cockfight, no longer having to justify it. Explanations have to come to an end somewhere. The point is to change oneself so as to experience the thing as it is. And if you keep changing, so will the poem. Think of reading as a practice of musical accompaniment.

Pagan poetry is frequently the work of great comic writers, owing perhaps to the anarchy of it: unregimented phrases are usually (and unusually) funny:

Furniture isn't everything. Did Eve enjoy the first orgasm¿ Accompaniment ends in isolation from the event. Then dovetail. Percussion in the anteroom to conger the doctors. ["conger"? Conger is a species of eel. "Congeries" are aggregates of heterogeneous elements, so "conger" used as a verb would mean "to gather together." But one can also imagine percussion in the anteroom *conjuring* doctors – conceivably a more efficient way of getting to see them than we presently have.] A bale of direct contraries. (*Quill Driver*,15)

Which is most interesting. From tricycle to try sexual. [Could someone be quadrisexual? Perhaps a quadropedophile.] (23)

Inheritance is the cleaning process our forebears foreswore, occupied as they were, in each other's esteem. Not that society is polite, it is rude to those who don't agree with its particular modes of savagery. I don't wear pearls. All those articles of torture. A man once slept in a room with a cow's head suspended by transparent fishing line above the mattress on the floor. Hopefully height is not crucial as I don't want to lie. There's the biography minus the kittens. Why was the amethyst thought to prevent intoxication? (37)

Reconstruct the spiral stare. (39)

Who invented the first commercial weed killer? (53)

Of course, in a certain sense it is a distortion to cite these lines out of their contexts, for doing so subverts their resistance to interpretation, because in context each phrase works as an interruption (a shift from one context or register to another) – "Who invented the first commercial weed killer?" is, all by itself, without complication, but as situated it pops like a gun:

An aberration in the earth's crust, for example. Who invented the first commercial weed killer? Recitals. Written in front of you not as a door but a latch, now lift it. (53)

Interruption: we tend to be bothered by interruptions, but they are crucial to sociability, as is brevity, which interruption makes possible. Recall Maurice Blanchot:

I wonder if we have reflected enough upon the various significations of this pause that alone permits speech to be constituted as conversation, and even as speech. We end up by confining someone who speaks without pause. (Let us recall Hitler's terrible monologues. And every head of state participates in the same violence of this *dictare*, the repetition of an imperious monologue, when he enjoys the power of being the only one to speak and, rejoicing in the possession of his high solitary word, imposes it without restraint as a superior and supreme speech upon others.) (75)

One wonders what Blanchot would make of Dr. O'Connor's monologues, those oratorios of purple gusto:

. . . but the interruption was quite useless. Once the doctor had his audience – and he got his audience by the simple device of pronouncing at the top of his voice (at such moments as irritable and possessive as a maddened woman's) some of the more boggish and biting of the shorter early Saxon verbs – nothing could stop him. (Barnes, 14)

II

Gertrude Stein and Djuna Barnes have distinctive voices. Karen Mac Cormack is polyvocal, ranging from an avocal or neutral voice in which "no one speaks" to complex heterophonies culled from the histories of languages and the writings of ancestors, as well as the idiomatic expressions of old and new forms of popular culture.

At the avocal boundary, *Quirks & Quillets* (1991) – tricks and quibbles, quirks of fate and how we evade them – is made of forty "sentences," each one occupying its own page (so that an experience of white space is part of the experience of the poem):

> The untried decibel of seamless hose
> unhurried sentence its adjectives the chosen
> ladder geological manoeuvre or landing
> strip spangles the same man connected
> *paillettes* cramp the page's reproduction not
> ours or the level's pinafore before piano
> trudging words ahead of their names an
> algebra of what is scene momentous
> underneath. (9)

Here the challenge would be to know how to read this poem aloud – where (or whether) to introduce pauses that would shape the sentence rhythmically if not semantically. (Karen Mac Cormack reads the pieces in this volume fairly rapidly in a cadence that avoids any hint of prosody: no pausing for emphases, so the poem ceases to be made of lines.)[2] The semantics of this particular "sentence" lies in "its adjectives" ("trudging words ahead of their names" like "seamless hose," "unhurried sentence," "geological manoeuvre," "landing strip," "the same man," "connected *paillettes*"). The poem contains only one transitive verb, "cramp," and possibly not even that, since a "cramp" is more often felt as a noun. ("Scene," to be sure, implies "seen.") In truth *Quirks & Quillets* is not, strictly speaking, made of sentences, but of proliferations of phrases within loose, unpunctuated periods. Proliferation here is an event of complexity, an anarchic defeat of unity, structure, closure and point (but not, curiously, of an internal play):

> Foregoing impartial likeness threads drop
> where the thermometer left off it only
> matters to someone else that the door is
> closed upon leaving for now the
> proliferation of exits is grief enough arms in

> these leaves drying an open solitude in
> increments the belief that there's paint on
> walls paintings patching anomalies or
> marbles in the mouth a fast-growing
> background attention span in the form of
> everyday objects of a given culture basting
> corrects this sink is full. (47)

Notice that the phrases here all make a kind of sense – "Foregoing impartial likeness," "threads drop where the thermometer left off," "it only matters to someone else that the door is closed upon leaving," "for now the proliferation of exits is grief enough," "arms in these leaves [read it as a verb] an open solitude in increments," "the belief that there's paint on walls," "paintings patching anomalies," "marbles in the mouth," "a fast-growing background," "attention span in the form of everyday objects of a given culture," "basting corrects [dehydration]," "this sink is full." The poem appropriates the semantic ingredients that go into sentences – the readymade *enchaînements* that make possible everyday speech (about "everyday objects of a given culture"). The phrases of *Quirks & Quillets* are not poetical, but they are tricky and evasive (no pinning them down). The point is that each one (almost each one) is recognizable: these are phrases that, but for a twist here and there, we ourselves might have used.

After all, where do phrases come from? From our various discursive environments, which Karen Mac Cormack seeks to reconstruct and explore by investigating several centuries of linguistic usage as well as the idioms of contemporary popular culture. Her poetry is, among other things, an archaeology of language, as the title of *Quirks & Quillets* suggests – it takes a good deal of searching among dictionaries to find the word *quillet*: thanks to Shakespeare it is still occasionally cited as an archaism. The point is that phrases, whether contemporary or archaic, are *found objects*. They are not products or creations – they cannot be traced back to an origin. Phrases are, in Heidegger's lingo, "at hand": they have an equipmental rather than objective mode of being – that is, we don't hold them up for inspection but rather put them into play, which is what Lyotard means by phrasing or enchainment. What Karen Mac Cormack does is alter the field of play by citing (and rephrasing) texts from both past and present.

Recall the concept of poetic diction. This was, in the eighteenth century, a circle drawn around our vocabulary that excluded certain words as flatly unpoetic: *duck, toe, fart, potato, intestine* – make your own list. Modernism did not reject the idea of poetic diction, but it enlarged the circle so that its centre would be everywhere and its circumference inaccessible: hence "etherized upon a table." The purpose of much of Karen Mac Cormack's recent work has been to develop new forms of poetic diction out of found texts. In *Fit to Print* (1998), written in collaboration with Alan Halsey, the found texts are newspaper items – news stories, advertisements, notices, but also forms of layout that make the page the basic unit of verse:

OUT ON THE EMANCI-PATIO

roots dangler lowdown upstart	fermi down and roar
drawback cocksure live	to-die-for
oral stroller	recovery in times of duress
aggregates anoint conundrum	loans abstrusity
balanced marshiest oasis	hard-to-get comparison
two-times tagalong	early in a burden
outsourcing deliverables	as if a mistake could "improve"
virtual courseware	to encash outdo
sharpshooter's clone	day-to-day tread
estop "Hurricane buys site"	subject crop weedy
now inhale finalize	greetings uncouple prefer (35)

A note explains that the title of this poem was originally a typo in the Toronto *Globe and Mail*, and that "Hurricane buys site" was a "headline for a *Globe & Mail* article stating that Hurricane Hydrocarbons Ltd. wins right to become major oil producer in Kazakhstan in 1996" (61). Likewise Mac Cormack's *At Issue* (2001) is, she says, "a series of poems most of which (but not all) utilize the vocabulary and spelling found in magazines of a diverse nature" – *Vogue*, for example, and others even more strictly "geared to a female readership" (9):

AT ISSUE III

Putting shape into getting without perfect in a culture that doesn't think, pumps up, the two traits go at the face of rate themselves, cropped by impasse, express your monochromatics from within, discover it blushes, reduce the signs to surface, sharing space in a new high-tech fabric, the pale face extra – prevent every day year after year, retreat returns by filling out advance notice, since seeing is oxygen more supple, sways, just take graceful, tilt feature-controls are big, stable rattles accept different speeds sing, sprawl-moguls seized a story, raking in celebrity, heat-activated genre, hands full turned, loops removable gusseted, postpone television, revelations, introspection, an assemblage not incidentally imposed, crossover success, so many boxes yet smashes toward toward. . . . (17)

Two points: The exhibition of found texts is a form of satire – the phrases of the text are jumbled in a way that exposes (and so defeats) their rhetorical purpose ("express your monochromatics from within"). *At Issue* is, among other things, an essay on cultural narcissism (culling its language from publications like *Self*). But perhaps the formal point is more interesting. By appropriating her vocabulary and spelling from found texts, Karen Mac Cormack accomplishes two (paradoxically competing) things: (1) in the spirit of modernism, she enlarges the field of poetic diction to include the language of everyday life (whatever its virtues or comedy). However, at the same time, (2) in the spirit of traditional poetic diction (as well as in the spirit of such writing communities as Oulipo or the "chance operations" of John Cage and Jackson Mac Low) she subjects her writing to a system of arbitrary constraints (no phrases allowed that don't appear in *Self*). Recourse to source texts or found language is a poetics that subjects the writing subject to an objective language (or linguistic field). It is a poetics of finitude that combines the openness of chance with the confinement of originary stipulations: no saying what has not, in some sense, already been said, but doing so without repetition – imagine citations taking the form not of quotations but of collage. The idea seems to be to find a new form of originality, one that is more rhetorical than romantic because it is a form of writing that interrupts and recomposes what has already been written and not a form of creation *ex nihilo*. As I said earlier, language is not internal to the writing subject but is an environment of phrases capable of open-ended redistributions. The crucial point is that these environments are local rather than global: one writes from the standpoint of inhabitation within discursive communities. Certainly one can make fun of the idiom of *Vogue* and *Self*, but the appropriation of these idioms is also a form of redemption, because now one experiences their peculiar comedy, richness, and even utopian potential.

John Cage perfected the form of the found text after having invented the mesostic by "writing through" modernist texts like *Finnegans Wake*, using Joyce's name as the spine along which his (Joyce's) text is reassembled:

wroth with twone nathandJoe
A
Malt
jhEm
Shen
pftJschute
sOlid man
that the humptYhillhead of humself
is at the knoCkout
in thE park (137)

Writing *through* found texts is, as Cage argued, a way of escaping the confinements of subjectivity, in which confinement means repetition, self-imitation, the articulations of style, identity and tradition, and where escape means bringing oneself arbitrarily under the discipline of the environment of another's language in which one is (anthropologically) free to explore, expand, and rearrange. Here the transfer of composition is from a Chomskyan linguistic competence, in which the subject is able to produce an infinite number of original sentences from the deep structure of linguistic rules, to the pragmatic discourse that appropriates and renews what is given in the discourse that constitutes a social and cultural world. A poetics of the lively surface of historical particulars replaces a structuralist poetics of innate rules and conventions that mechanically reproduce a history of universal forms.

Found texts are archaeological artifacts. Mac Cormack didn't find her texts by accident. *Implexures* (2003) is an exploration of her ancestry, which evidently goes back to Elizabethan times (when the word "implexure," meaning fold or folding, was still, if only rarely, in use). The poem is in part a series of "historical letters" made of heterogeneous voices from many sources and periods – "To absorb a history of family through the centuries requires a forebear's attention to facts and no fear of paper" (10). The voices (and years) cannot always (and never easily) be identified or distinguished from one another – "'Language as primary environment' applied to re-reading letters (one's own and others) the decades interleaved on every surface to blur and redefine the living in & of perception's architecture" (44–45) – except perhaps for the (italicized) letters home from a modern young woman travelling to places like Mexico, Italy, Greece, and Turkey:

I enjoy traveling solo. There are problems, but they are not insurmountable. The Italian and Greek men are totally perplexed by single women going around the world & it seems to unnerve them that there are so many. (53)

But mostly the language is incremental in its phrasing, as if a collage (or perhaps "implexions": entanglements, interweavings, interfolds) were being constructed from ancestral fragments:

Form at certain taverns never documentary during their scramble. To the west spell jeopardy and drop to lower ground rasp's running with a lantern. Later through the front door, down the hall and out again, coach, frills adhere to it. Horn of boxwood and in existence a diary usually is a provoking document. Hovered very much to the fore and exasperating. Consent withheld and why? Every record drawn a blank and so impossible to forgive her being a Perfect Lady. Drifting coming on to the answering mountain made a picture. Into three editions and many infidelities (the former begot missiles). An independent line . . . freedom of outlook (not one but two bribes of peerage failed) and then the Repeal of the Salt Tax. Meanwhile, diligent in her Latin and "very new-fangled of my Italian," she didn't object to his taking a sprogue now and then. A "nip" appeared in the pit and he was then alone. Trappings beyond perennial drain, the dusk, in his chair, but no marker or tablet, it being December what flowers could there have been? (19)

Again: a portrait of a lady – but as in Gertrude Stein's portraits the subject here is integrated into her environment, and so the collage is of a time and place and not simply of a subject, meaning that the references are local and temporal, embedded in lost contexts, and thus outside the glossing capabilities of modern readers – and most libraries, although industrial-strength research will turn up some interesting connections: "sprogue," for example, is hard to find anywhere except in *Finnegans Wake*: "A strangely striking part of speech for the hottest worked word of ur sprogue" (507.19). Every dictionary I know of rejects it. The context in Mac Cormack's poem suggests that it could mean "a drink now and then," but Joyce's context makes it more likely a word for language (*sprog* is Danish for language, so *ur sprogue* would be something like *Ursprache*). *Sprogue* is also probably a Joycean pun (sprog, brogue). Diligent polyglots won't mind a pun now and then, or a gyre and gimble in the wabe, nor will Space Rogues (or "sprogues," as they call themselves). Sprogue is a common surname, evidently origi-nally Cornish, but it is more interesting as a phantom noun – a found word that eludes lexicography. (Karen Mac Cormack tells me that the word means "jaunt," or an aimless stroll.)

Speaking of dictionaries, one section of *Implexures* is called "DEVELOPMENTAL DICTIONARY (from 1967 to circa 1982)." It is a text in two parts. Part Two consists of what looks like a random series of words:

contiguity induction chimerical inimical didactic vicissitude pithy maxim aphorism portentously sedition sedulous irascible specious plausible esoteric contrite intellect intellectual faculty usurp sagacious discernment artifice contrivance negate glaucous rapacious respite retrieve vituperative obsequious euphemism ascribe disparate acumen ingenuous expunge intrinsic tacit cogent denote acquisition peripatetic ebullient anomalous pullulating extraneous jejune hyperborean abstruse incondite tantalum acronychal erudite tautophony (59)

Mostly familiar words, perhaps used less commonly than others – appearing, I would guess, more often in writing than in speech. Some you'd not think to use ("incondite tantalum acronychal"), and you'd want to consult a dictionary before deploying a number of others. And that appears to be the point of their appearance in *Implexures*. Part one of "Developmental Dictionary" is a list (three-and-a-half pages in length) of definitions, synonyms or instances of the words in part two. So in reading one applies the following to the first five words of the series –

> contact, proximity
> prologue, introduction,
> production (of facts) to prove
> general statement
> of fanciful conception
> hostile
> meant to instruct (56)

– and these to the last five:

> ill constructed, crude, unpolished
> rare white metallic element
> highly resistant to heat &
> action of acids
> happening at nightfall
> learnèd
> repetition of same sound (59)

"Developmental Dictionary" is an archaeological document – as is, when one considers it, any dictionary, especially one that supplies the meanings of words with a history, allowing one to dig up old uses or to discover that words are protean, owing to their multiple and heterogeneous etymologies: "induction" is not just one word but several, depending on the context. In the Elizabethan theater, it means "prologue, introduction." It is also, of course, a term of art in logic and the foundation of the empirical sciences. And it is also how one gets into a Hall of Fame (or, worse luck, into the military). As a good archaeologist, Karen Mac Cormack gives us the Middle English meaning of "specious" ("of good appearance" [56]), and in the bargain alludes to its proximity to the next word in the series, "plausible" ("seemingly reasonable or probable" [56]), which "specious" in our current use of the word must be: a baldly incoherent explanation, incredible from the start, would not be "specious." Plausibility is a condition of deception.

Just so, the words in part two of "Developmental Dictionary" do not make up a *random* series but are internally connected – phonetically, morphemically, semantically: "induction" is an instance of "contiguity"; "inimical" echoes "chimerical," and so, more subtly, does "didactic" (the series is an example of "tautophony"). Maxims are pithy, and so, being maxims, are aphorisms. "Obsequious" is a reversal of "vituperative." And without doubt the series grows more "abstruse" or "erudite" (recondite but by no means "incondite") as it draws to a close. "Acronychal" – "happening at nightfall" – concerns the rising or setting of stars, as opposed to their rising or setting at sunrise (which is "cosmical"). The *OED*'s entry is worth a moment of your time (you'll be hard pressed to find the word anywhere else). While in the neighborhood, consult "acrophony."

Poetry as an archeology of language brings new life to the now tired concept of "open form." The idea is to recover and explore different linguistic environments, whether ancient or modern, high or low, lost or forgotten. Let me conclude by citing *Vanity Release* (2003), in which Mac Cormack appropriates a number of unique vocabularies. She begins with "a statement re: 'sourced' poems in *VANITY RELEASE*":

I have become increasingly intrigued by late 19th and early 20th century shorthand dictionaries and manuals (and most recently a mid-20th-century typewriting manual), in addition to phrase books for travellers through the 20th century.

The choice of word lists, sentences to learn by, and the exercises in these respective manuals reflect not only the ongoing changes in North American English for this period, but also shifts in educational, business, and technological terminology. To engage with these terms in a context of contemporary investigational poetic practice is one way to meaningfully perplex what is so easily taken for granted technologically, linguistically, and socially in our own times. (5)

"*UP*," my favourite poem in the volume, takes its words and phrases from *Universal Phonography*, H. M. Pernin © 1886, Sixth Edition, 1893. Phonography, literally "sound-writing," is a form of stenography invented in 1837 by Isaac Pitman. "*UP*" begins:

Phonography dispenses with useless letters by recording the *sounds* of words only. In practice you should endeavor to forget the ordinary spelling of words, and think only of the sounds of which they are composed. Remember always to write *what you hear* and not *what you see*. Accuracy is the first essential . . . "Make haste slowly."

Sz sh zh, j ch, are horizontal curves traced from left to the manner indicated on page 36 facing the right. The sound of x is a combination of the sounds k s

Get the doctor a cup of black tea. Harry feared the boat would veer to the left. A red leaf fell at the foot of the oak. (31)

The first "stanza" gives us the basic rule of phonography, which is to forget the phonetic alphabet and to replace it with minor strokes of the pen or pencil, as indicated in "stanza" two: the sounds "sh" and "zh" are written as curves like the lower right quarter of a new moon. The first sentence of the third stanza would be written as follows:

— · |(′ | ′ — | ′/ ′ — ·\′( )(˙ —| .

However, what matters in Mac Cormack's archeology is not simply the recovery of the forgotten text but the recuperation of its peculiar idiom – namely, the pedagogical *sound* of the late nineteenth-century office manual:

The majority of business houses prefer their correspondence type-written, it being not only more legible than ordinary longhand, but also much more rapidly executed. Comparatively few people are really good spellers, a fact due in a great measure to the absurd construction of the language and partly to early neglect of this important branch of education. The stenographer who would keep abreast of the times should also be acquainted with the shorthand literature in general. *The word* us *has been inadvertently omitted from the Lord's Prayer.* (36)

The "absurd construction of the language" indeed. It turns out that what Karen Mac Cormack's poetic research recovers from these manuals is the struggle between the rationalization of the world, the programs of efficiency, control, and split-second reproduction on our which modernity depends, and the essential paganism of language – the sheer excess and unmanageability of a language not really made for literacy, legibility, or the various technologies of word-processing. The attempt to streamline human speech, including the manufacture of buzzwords, acronyms, soundbites, not to mention email and who knows how many new forms of digital shorthand, fails because, as *Vanity Release* shows, streamlining produces its own special forms of comic materiality, as in the penultimate poem in *Vanity Release*, "WE-23."[3] The source-text for this poem is a typing manual, *Gregg Typing, Book One: General Typing*, 191 Series © 1965 by the McGraw-Hill Company of Canada, Ltd., filled with finger exercises, helpful hints, moral encouragement, cautionary notes, and useful examples for the eager secretary.

> BODY centered opposite the *J* key, a hand-span from the machine

> She fed us egg salads. Ed fed us eggs.
> Fred sells red jugs; red jars are free.
> Ask Dr. Grass. Dr. Grass leads us all.

> This book has many "clinics."

> area dear drag flu gush gulf hire huge
> idea jugs lark kill read self side drug

> *Errors should not alarm you; instead, they should guide you.*

> Control Hyphen, Q, and ? keys
> Can you keep your elbows still?
> sofa soap sock soak son sod sox sow
> side of the center

> STRESS: Continuity

> *Watch* for it. Get set. (41)

The poem continues for several pages, concluding with what is surely the twentieth century's most important advice: "REMEMBER: Don't give in to the temptation to look up!" (57).

Notes

1. See Steve McCaffery's "Temporality and the New Sentence: Phrase Propulsion in the Writing of Karen Mac Cormack," esp. pp. 154–57.

2. See Marjorie Perloff, "After Free Verse: The New Nonlinear Poetries," which includes a discussion of Mac Cormack's poem "Multi-Mentional."

3. The last line of the poem explains the title: "in *we 23* the *23* is typed by the same fingers, in the same sequence, as the word *we*" (57).

Works Cited

Barnes, Djuna. *Nightwood: The Original Version and Related Drafts.* Ed. Cheryl J. Plumb. Normal, IL: Dalkey Archive Press, 1995.

Blanchot, Maurice. "Interruption, as on a Riemann Surface." In *The Infinite Conversation,* trans. Susan Hanson, 75–79. Minneapolis, MN: University of Minnesota Press, 1993.

Cage, John. *Empty Words: Writings '73–'78.* Middletown, CT: Wesleyan University Press, 1979.

Lyotard, Jean-François. *The Differend: Phrases in Dispute.* Trans. Georges van den Abbeele. Minneapolis, MN: University of Minnesota Press, 1988.

—— and Jean-Loup Thébaud. *Just Gaming.* Trans. Wlad Godzich. Minneapolis, MN: University of Minnesota Press, 1985.

McCaffery, Steve. "Temporality and the New Sentence: Phrase Propulsion in the Writing of Karen Mac Cormack." In *Prior to Meaning: The Protosemantic and Poetics,* 149–60. Evanston, IL: Northwestern University Press, 2001.

Mac Cormack, Karen. *At Issue.* Toronto: Coach House Books, 2001.

——. *Implexures.* Sheffield, U.K.: West House Books; Tucson: Chax Press, 2003.

——. *Quill Driver.* London, ON: Nightwood Editions, 1989.

——. *Quirks & Quillets.* Tucson, AZ: Chax Press, 1991.

——. *Vanity Release.* La Laguna, Tenerife: Zasterle Press, 2003.

—— and Alan Halsey. *Fit to Print.* Sheffield, U.K.: West House Books and Toronto: Coach House Books, 1998.

Perloff, Marjorie. "After Free Verse: The New Nonlinear Poetries." In *Poetry On and Off the Page: Essays for Emergent Occasions,* 141–67. Evanston, IL: Northwestern University Press, 1998.

Stein, Gertrude. *Writings 1903–1932.* New York: Library of America, 1998.

RESPONSES TO & FOR
KAREN MAC CORMACK

Alan Halsey

These pieces were composed in response to four books by Karen Mac Cormack; the responses are direct in that they were written during the first readings of the books at the time of publication. They are here collected together, and the source texts specified, for the first time. They are views and not reviews: records of the act of reading, the pleasures of new acquaintance and the unfolding of unexpected relations and unforeseen alignments in a reader's mind.

Sequel Drift for the Nineties
& Karen Mac Cormack

Re *Quill Driver* (1989)

Giving up trying will never be the same as trying not to again: more forms you and yew, dear Io, than the night a thief comes in to at last end era conclusion to some young thoughts. A point of view is a kind of (ad)vantage on a land where old money will forever let the rope clause out. Overheard instinct word overhead, *ex*claim, all the verbs lend hands when the point of opacity appears to be a glass in somebody's direction. An estimate was all the esteem age demanded. Satisfactory production levels down the line then rules across the board but if memory serves for the time being truth looks white as the nerve to bare witness. Albion snowman shaken on the peaks, the odd volute turned up when volume was required to eke out windy rationale for security and art's sake, for a leisure centre whose natural sport by expanding circumference everywhere annotates the spheres. To be addressed in the words you stand up in or upon, any pretext.

Notes, Queries & Exhibits
for Karen Mac Cormack

Re *Quirks & Quillets* (1991)

1.1 Ho(we)ver.

1.2 Endanger & engender.

1.3 Relic lyric.

2.   Let's call this the eighteenth century
     with strings attached, so that our mark
     of looking is back, both ways.

3.   Whatever interprets the sense interrupts.
     Where there's a way there's willpower,
     where there's a will there's a wishing-well.
     Doing in perception does dot eyes
     or at least eyes dote, doors open
     and the doing in itself just does.
     By miracle America's in creases.
     By the way there's a wall but no reason why.

4.   As if World could abide when Word were abed.

5.1 As an impasse impulse, threaded, threw.

5.2 Watch the news tip the glass
     over titular act again over.

5.3 Force ever and for severance ever.

An Alphabet for Karen

Re *Marine Snow* (1995)

A colony is no more a kernel than pronounced command.
Beauty when a culture's a passport's a quality of syntax.
Cerecloth since sincere yet loath to be part.
Dover was to a beach as a cliff's condition.
Early when employed and easy for each could be either.
Fid of origin unknown pinning topmast to faith.
Graze where gold may significantly ground in a garden.
Homeland and then some even if somatic and the same.
Imperative to reinstate implacable Latin.
Jewelled as a day and night watch dualistic.
Kaput's the capital city of an alphabet's heartland.
Lucid tries a line on for size.
Miles more than memory is minuted by flicker and flux.
Nouns a motor noise in the ear ticks a notice over.
Once was an overdue opening for others often.
Presence plays across a stage in private pieces.
Quiet or enough and too middling.
Ripples when a sound through papers in quest.
Spinning so far as the top's been soldered to its north and south.
Ten times as many lorries as a transport policy.
Utterly unchanged by the utmost repetition.
Verbatim on the one side and verboten on the other.
Women in an alphabet wanting double you.
Xerox of zero on the rocks.
You of your years become a sort of a story.
Z seldom seen though in size but neither bruises nor begins.

At Sixes and Sevens

Re *Vanity Release* (2003)

I knew spring would be late
when December went missing
and now I can't sit still
for favour minutes. Did you
see that rhyme fly right past
my head? Rapidly as figures
fingers may write so time
me sometime – draw a map of
any city with your
eyes tight shut or else sleep by
proxy. Some valuable
things are available
but not all available
things are etc.
A blind man taps in past
tense spat. Disc loss may follow
disclosure but not in
any Peking order
discolours. Did you see
that rhyme, a real cutter, hit
the spread-sheet? It knocked the
bottle over the beetle
was in now the beetle's out.

AN INTERVIEW WITH
KAREN MAC CORMACK

Stephen Cain

SC: You have recently published the collaborative project, *Fit to Print*, with British poet Alan Halsey. How did this collaboration come about, and how did it work?

KMC: *Fit to Print* is my first finished, published collaboration. (Steve McCaffery and I now have two incomplete collaborative works, both titled "From a Middle." The first was abandoned more than ten years ago, the more recent one we began in June 1999.) *Fit to Print* was already underway when I decided to reread Alan Halsey's *Reasonable Distance* at the end of December 1995. I wrote a poem as a response to it (though not in the double column format that dominates *FTP*) and sent it to Alan, whose own response (poem) to the then-recently published *Marine Snow* crossed the Atlantic at the same time (January of 1996). I then sent him the existing *FTP* poems along with a description of the project and he responded to those, at which point we realized a collaboration was in effect. (I should mention that I first met Alan in England in 1989 when he came to a reading of Steve's and mine in Oxford. Prior to that I'd written to him [after reading some of his work in *Writing* magazine earlier in the 1980s] so a correspondence was already in place.)

    FTP's format on the page intentionally refers to that most daily of reading materials – the newspaper. However, the poems themselves, while displaying a concern with and for daily events (and these range from earthquakes to conditions of weather), do not adopt a "transit" theory of meaning. Together we approached the newspaper format as a way of fusing issues of mass culture with a non-traditional writing practice. The newspaper column produces unexpected ruptures that the reader learns to negotiate. Our intention was to apply this achieved negotiation to a writing that departs from the "habit" of a conventional language.

Most of *FTP* was written on either side of the Atlantic and the poems were sent sometimes singly to and fro, sometimes in batches. (Alan was still living in Hay-on-Wye in Wales and we were both amazed that on average our letters took three days to arrive in either direction! Alan bought his first computer while *FTP* was in the works [his initial *FTP* poems were done on a word processor].) Alan did visit Steve and myself when we were living in California in 1997 and that was the only time we discussed the work face to face and wrote some of it in the same locale. I don't recall either one of us suggesting changes to one another's poems and the collaborative process was an arm's length one.

FTP was eventually considered "complete" by summer of 1997. The order is more or less chronological. I'd hoped to tackle as many aspects of the newspaper as possible (but the Sports section defeated me, so I was delighted when Alan dealt with that so effectively!).

SC: How do you feel the process of *Fit to Print* affected your own writing? Would you work with other poets in the future?

KMC: The collaboration's effect on my own writing is more difficult to express. To have another writer as intensely involved in the same project yet whose work responds to that project differently (and because of that makes one see one's own in a new way) impelled me to test limits more strenuously than ever. By limits I mean the parameters of the project (not all the poems in *FTP* took the form of the newspaper's double column), and my own "risk taking" insofar as what could work seemed to escalate. That experience has contributed immensely to my subsequent writing.

As for working with other poets (or visual artists or videographers or anyone else!), Steve and I haven't abandoned our second attempt at "From a Middle," and I'd welcome the opportunity to collaborate in other situations.

SC: Can you talk about your new project, *At Issue*, which is in some ways a continuation of your exploration of print media initiated in *Fit to Print*?

KMC: I decided that I wanted to continue working with a form of mass culture (*At Issue* began while I was still working on *Fit to Print* – I write slowly and my projects often overlap). In *At Issue* I

examine the format and contents of the magazine instead of those of
the newspaper. The interruptions and syntactical dis-arrangements
in *At Issue* reflect the experience of reading that format (within
what is certainly a critical agenda on my part).

At Issue is a series of poems utilizing the vocabulary and spelling
found in magazines of a diverse nature. (An interesting if frightening
fact is that there are fewer typos in *Vogue* than in most scholarly
books published in North America!) To counter *Vogue* I have also
been writing through *Self* (a health/fitness magazine also geared to
female readership). As other alternatives I've considered a science
journal (perhaps *Scientific American*), a news magazine, and perhaps
a computer-oriented journal. Originally the project was to incorporate four (monthly) magazines at a year's worth of issues, one
issue per poem. Having gone through nine issues of American and
British *Vogue* (at time of writing I'm working on the tenth) and
four of *Self* I think that those two magazines will provide the right
amount of material and that *At Issue* will either become a chapbook
or a section in another book.

SC: You hold both British and Canadian citizenship, and have
lived in several countries including Zambia and the United States.
Do you feel that geography – or movement between various locales –
has played any part in the development of your aesthetic, or how
you view borders (either textual or political)?

KMC: Most of my life has been lived in an "elsewhere." I have
access to three citizenships, having been born in what is now
Zambia to British/Canadian parents, who lived there only briefly
before embarking on what for me became a trans-Atlantic upbring-
ing (I was less than a year old when they returned from Zambia to
England). Subsequently, from 1974 to 1982 I lived for varying
periods in Mexico, Greece, Italy and the U.S. and there again (in
California) in 1989 and 1997. Perhaps more revealingly, between
1989 and 1995 my books were published outside of Canada, even
if poems of mine continued to appear in Canadian journals. Then
Marine Snow was published here and the collaboration with Alan
Halsey, *Fit to Print*. (The chapbook *Multiplex* with work by Ron
Silliman and myself [not a collaboration] appeared in October
1998 through Wild Honey Press in Ireland.)

I don't identify with geography in terms of a sense of "place"
being core to my creativity. Certainly the fact I've lived in many

different places (as well as travelling extensively) has contributed to my perception of how and in what ways and degrees "difference" manifests culturally, politically, personally. I don't think that travelling per se has played any part in how I view textual borders.

SC: How does gender play out in your writing, and in your view of innovative writing in general? While the appearance of – and your inclusion in – such anthologies as *Out of Everywhere* and *Moving Borders* suggest that much of today's radical poetry is being produced by women you have also noted the disparity in the ratio of women to men appearing in anthologies both past and contemporary.

KMC: The anthologies *Out of Everywhere* and *Moving Borders* (the first published by Reality Street Editions in the U.K., the second by Talisman in the U.S.) both "prove" that women are innovative practitioners. I'm keenly aware of the fact that in many English-speaking countries male innovative writers still outnumber women in terms of published work. Certainly there have been discrepancies in past anthologies in both directions (indeed, in gatherings of conventional poetry women might sometimes outnumber men!).

Gender is certainly part of my writing (there are differences between women and men and in the way they express themselves creatively or otherwise), and sometimes I deliberately draw attention to this. I've also drawn attention to the fact of difference between languages (for example, the existence of gendered nouns, even in Old English).

For me to discover innovative work (writing, visual art, film, video) is a pleasure and if a woman is the artist that adds to my pleasure, but it's not a prerequisite for enjoyment. Nor does the enjoyment diminish if the artist is a man.

SC: As well as expressing an interest in the nuances and potentialities of language your poetry also exhibits a keen awareness of the page, and how the placement of words alter and/or generate meaning. What are your thoughts on the relation between typography and poetry?

KMC: I've been fortunate to have worked mostly with publishers/designers who invited and encouraged my participation in the publishing process of each of my books. I've learned from each one of them. *Straw Cupid* was probably the book I was most actively involved in in terms of design. Maureen Cochrane and I went through every decision and worked through every layout problem together on what was my second publication. But when Chax Press decided to publish *Quirks & Quillets* (as a trade publication) I wanted Charles Alexander to "surprise" me. (Chax Press's hand-made, limited editions are extraordinary.) The proofs were sent to me but beyond that I had no idea what the book would look like (though I encouraged Cynthia Miller to do an original drawing for the cover and I'm delighted with her response to that work. She's also responsible for the artwork on the cover of *The Tongue Moves Talk*). Texts are always affected by typography, but I'm not a designer, I'm a writer whose projects sometimes require new (for me) ways of thinking about typography and making a text work "on the page." (My methods for achieving this aren't necessarily the most expedient, as I learned after the fact about *Fit to Print*!)

SC: How would you characterize the development of your writing from your first work, *Nothing by Mouth*, to the most recent?

KMC: My early work was an exploration of altering the way we perceive the day-to-day, while allowing "language" to be shown as an entity itself (rather than a transparent vastness through which to "see" our world). This led to an investigation of "sentence effects," particularly the integration of poetic line with prose period. (This was not to enact a conciliatory synthesis of the two genres, but to delineate their radical sympathies and contradictions, i.e., not to write a prose poem, but to reclaim an exploratory usefulness from the sentence, in order to extend the poetic form to more challenging/ rewarding modes of readership.) So what began in *Quill Driver* (1989) as a propositional language, becomes in *Marine Snow* (1995) a fusion of propositional language with stanzaic configurations (in order to explore phenomenological and social implications in per-ception, when the latter is mediated through the orthodox and the errant trajectories of language, writing and space). *Quirks & Quillets* (1991) explores a similar state of mediation but utilizes a different momentum by suppressing the period in favour of a series of brief, intense phrasal continua. For the most part, the writing deliberately avoids punctuation so that grammatical patterns can shift in both their functions and effects. The intention was not to produce an "abstract" or non-referential text, but to reveal how meaning emerges in the sites of its production.

The Tongue Moves Talk (1997) explores the perceptions, mis-conceptions and current role of the social concept of the "carrier." The poems deliberately repudiate any of the "reader comforts" of familiarity and habituality of normative language. *The Tongue Moves Talk* establishes a deliberate resistance, structured upon patterns that offer a rigorous positioning of their linguistic materiality.

SC: How do the somewhat aphoristic statements in your poetry function? (Ex. "Beauty is a cultural decision." [*MS*]; "Sex is its own conclusion for those who haven't noticed." [*TMT*]; or, "Take away the page and leave the writing." [*QD*].) While they are often taken up as the most quotable, or the "actual" expressions of your personal thoughts regarding writing and/or philosophy, are they always intended to be so? Are they perhaps stylistic "red herrings" for those readers who tend to gravitate toward any sense of stability in decentred texts?

KMC: The "somewhat aphoristic statements" that recur become part of the exploration of meaning. "Beauty is a cultural decision" is followed by "All hollow." There's a shift in "Sex is its own con-clusion for those who haven't noticed." (A reader can infer that certain people haven't noticed that sex is its own conclusion and/or that that conclusion is only for people who haven't noticed . . .) "Take away the page and leave the writing" might refer to a computer screen and/or it could also imply that writing exists independently of paper. I'm particularly inclined to alignments that disrupt/destabilize conditioned (or conventional) combinatory meanings and some of these are more (or less) aphoristic, for example, "Begin with four quarters a round-edged coin" is less aphoristic than "Don't covet the past it belongs where it is over" (both from *Quill Driver*).

"Meaning" and the weather both change. Why an insistence on the static as a given, in what is anything but a stable environment? Meaning is at once precise for the moment and shifting over time. Consider slang, for example. "Gay" meant something very differ-ent for the Victorians than it does for us: a "gay" woman was a prostitute. "Queer" as in "odd" was in relatively recent usage, if not in North America then in other English-speaking countries. The titles of two of my books both came from slang: *Quill Driver* means "writer" (at least eighteenth century, possibly older), and *Quirks & Quillets* ("tricks and devices") was in use in the sixteenth century. "Bread," as in "out of bread," formerly meant out of work, slightly different from its 1960s meaning (the roots are over two hundred years old). "Pig" referred to a police officer as early as 1811, but who's to guess that "tickle text" refers to a parson?

SC: Gertrude Stein appears to be a major influence on your writing, but what other figures, either modern or contemporary, do you view as influential or inspiring? What about LANGUAGE writing? In the "Toronto Since Then" issue of *Open Letter* (8:8, 1994), Victor Coleman characterized you (and Steve McCaffery) as standing "a lonely watch" over the "paucity of language-centered poetry in Toronto." Is this a fair assessment: do you consider yourself a LANGUAGE poet, does the aesthetic itself require a geographic community (whether that be Vancouver or Buffalo) to be considered a viable force in the literary community (national or international), and has Toronto changed "since then"?

KMC: As to the question regarding L=A=N=G=U=A=G=E poets and poetry, and my position therein: upper case/equal sign "L" writing encouraged me to recognize and confront my own habits and formulae – to move on and grow, and I regarded "L" writing as more contemporarily vital than anything else I'd encountered when I came to it in 1982. (As an aside, I read Bataille's *Death and Sensuality* two years before reading any "L" writing.) But it was through L=A=N=G=U=A=G=E writing that I went on to read the work of such modernist poets as Mina Loy and William Empson. Though they are usually overshadowed by the more luminous Joyce, Stein, and my "favourite" Djuna Barnes (whose *Nightwood* I read early, when I was sixteen), their texts for me are of considerable importance. Indeed, I would say that the writing of all of the above-mentioned has influenced my own, though not necessarily in an immediately apparent way. I would also add to the list the French writer Francis Ponge and the Austrian Robert Musil.

I don't think a writer's "position" should require a sharing of "confidences," explication of "codes," divulging of "experiments" made on the way to completed works; in short an "explanation," which may or may not benefit those interested. The act of writing is simultaneously intensely personal and historically collective (whether or not the writer is aware of prior works of shared or similar concerns and explorations). This act is separated from the reading of text-on-page through time, and the further removed one is (in time) the more general the context. (Hence our perception of those "decades," "eras," and "movements" of our own century [and the many preceding] culminates in such blanket terms as "modernism," "neo-classicism," and "romanticism.") Thus L=A=N=G=U=A=G=E writing became LANGUAGE writing becomes language writing . . . I'm not an upper case/equal sign practitioner but the effect on my work is evident.

Certainly Toronto's poetry condition (yes, that's deliberate) has changed since Victor Coleman's 1994 "Toronto Since Then," and geographic communities usually prove to be unstable. Whether or not any version of language writing would ever be considered a "viable force" in any literary context isn't the point as far as I'm concerned. If texts survive because readers continue to find them rewarding in new contexts then that's viable.

SC: You have objected to the term "experimental" in discussing the writing of, for example, Stein, preferring the term "innovative." What is the problem with "experimental," how does "innovative" differ, and where do terms such as "avant-garde" or even "normative writing" fit in your understanding?

KMC: Even today we live with the troubling term "avant-garde,"a word so familiar that it's used without giving the meaning much thought. Most of the writers I know want no part of the "garde" even in some distant future, so being slotted into the "avant-garde" makes for an uncomfortable mis/fit. Others accept this term as a badge or indicator of their work being outside of the norm. Some prefer (and embrace) the soubriquet "experimental," if anything even more misleading, or as the late B. S. Johnson so aptly put it:

I object to the word experimental being applied to my own work. Certainly I make experiments, but the unsuccessful ones are quietly hidden away and what I choose to publish is in my terms successful: that is, it has been the best way I could find of solving particular writing problems. Where I depart from convention, it is because the convention has failed, is inadequate for what I have to say. The relevant questions are surely whether each device works or not, whether it achieves what it set out to achieve, and how less good were the alternatives.

Elsewhere, John Cage has written:

The word experimental is apt, providing it is understood not as descriptive of an act to be later judged in terms of success and failure, but simply as an act the outcome of which is not known.

If a writer, or any other artist for that matter, applies the term "experimental" to an unknown result in a public context then how can one suspend evaluation? If the various and numerous acts the outcome of which "is not known," were to be combined with an absence-of-evaluation then the recurring result would frequently be one of mediocrity (at best). Without experimentation no "new" results would be forthcoming, but I concur with Johnson that one's unsuccessful experiments should remain privately hidden away.

So we arrive at "formally innovative" or even "formally investigative" as alternatives to the outmoded or inappropriate terms still applied to writing practices regarded as variously "new" today. At this point "innovative" seems just as much a label of convenience as any other but it signals a more positive (for me) sense of departure from "normative writing."

First published in Queen Street Quarterly 3, no. 4 (Winter 2000).

KAREN MAC CORMACK'S
IMPLEXURES:
AN IMPLICATED READING

John Hall

a.

On the back cover of *Implexures* Cole Swensen's endorsement describes the text's structure as "poly-biographic." This term seems to have emerged when a name was needed for a participatory method devised for compiling a history of medical sonography through the medium of an internet discussion list. Initially the instigators of the project had used the term "poly-autobiography" but had changed this because the historical archive was proving to be "both biographical and autobiographical." The aim was to create a history of a group activity through equal contributions of individual members of the group without conventional editing or univocal narration. Terry J. DuBose, apparently the author of the term, comments: "The primary problem anticipated will be the differences in individuals' writing styles, and a possibly confused organization" ("Polybiography").

b.

The Great North Road was intended by Cecil Rhodes to run up through Africa from Cape Town as a symbol and means of economic and political colonizing of an entire continent. It passes through two territories that for a while bore inflected variants of his family name and that were, for a few decades, administered by the company he developed. In the more northerly of these, now called Zambia – its name coined as an adaptation of the name of a river rather than of a hero of an infiltrating people – it runs up through Lusaka, through Kabwe, and then, six kilometres north of Kapiri Mposhi, takes an easterly turn and divides off from the main road to the copper belt.

This is map, not memory. It is someone else's mnemonic, not mine, though an earlier version of "me" did travel those roads, and these names sounded through my early childhood and in later family storytelling. I was born in Kabwe at a time when it was known to white English speakers as Broken Hill, named after a mining town in Australia. I was born there because there were no hospital facilities in Mkushi, where my family was living because of my father's posting. Mkushi is just off the Great North Road after its easterly turn.

Karen Mac Cormack was born some years later in a town on the southwest of the copper belt called Luanshya. She was to spend very little time in the country. She seems pleased, in biographical notes, to name it as her birthplace, and to speak of her two passports, one Canadian, the other British.

According to the "World Factfile" on the CIA website, English is the official language of Zambia to this day. The site lists the "major vernaculars" as Bemba, Kaonda, Lozi, Lunda, Luvale, Nyanja, Tonga, with "about 70 other indigenous languages." Employment in the mines at Luanshya attracted speakers of many of these tongues, though I believe that Bemba is the main one of the area. My mother learned Bemba and Nyanja. I could speak only one language and that was English. I left Zambia when I was just thirteen.

c.

Many countries are mentioned by name in *Implexures*. Zambia is not one of them. Nor is Canada. The following are: Malta, Ceylon, Sudan (the Anwar dam), Ireland, Saint Lucia, Mexico, the Isle of Man, England, Scotland, Greece (Naxos, Athens), Sardinia, Tenerife, Lanzerote, the United States of America (Boston, San Francisco, New York), Italy (many parts), Portugal (Porto), Turkey (Istanbul), South Africa (Cape Town).

These places relate to different aspects of this family biography, and therefore to different times – some to more than one. They seem to derive from archives, from parental nomadism, from the travellings of a western (young) adult ("This is the faraway those living in a cold climate vacation to" [24]), from replayings of family memory in talk and letters.

The list above could be resequenced to show which of the countries had once been under British rule, which ones operated officially or significantly through the English language, which of the rest are fully receptive to English through tourism. The CIA "World Factfile" has English last in its list of languages in use in Sudan but adds that "a program of 'Arabization' is in process." Under Article 8 of the Irish Constitution, "The Irish language as the national language is the first official language" and "The English language is recognized as a second official language."[1]

I think the name Canada is carefully avoided at one point in *Implexures* through the less political "North America" (60). And here is another avoidance – more telling, for my purpose:

Is this even vaguely similar to the disenchantment with the touchstone (now estranged from), that country so forming and formative whose language I live in? (44)

I take that country so mentioned to be England and the bracketed phrase to be full of ambivalence. A touchstone was used to test the quality and genuineness of metal alloys. Is this estrangement a loss of faith in this device for testing good faith? Is it a metaphor for the country as a whole set of values? For a language? Is it (also) a nostalgia, a pain at the loss of a means of returning home? The silence of "Canada" is very loud and sounds like the refusal of any *here* as privileged place of return, of "I," of "home."

Movement as a *place* itself so no motion is homeless. (28)

d.

In the abstract of his essay on "polybiography," DuBose defines the term as "the history by many of the many events." I prefer to be less certain about where the *poly* leans in *Implexures*. Yes indeed, the voices of many, sequenced or layered through. But *many* can have, as any sociologist of language could tell you, one collective voice, a plural homoglossia; or different voices that together harmonize their differences in the making of a unified and coherent *topic* or chant. *Poly* is not necessarily *hetero*, especially where genealogy is at stake. Isn't genealogy usually a discourse of the *same*, a search for or recitation of *homology*?

DuBose chooses to slip in "events" where etymology would suggest "lives," on the assumption that a biography is the writing of a set of *events* that constitute a life. At one point in *Implexures* Mac Cormack also adopts the word in a way that treats events as inseparable from "experience":[2]

(Chronology is the death of us.) *When* we experience an event is only important to the individual whereas *if* and with what results the experience has occurred is of concern to a collective. The family goes in so many directions as to render the singular forever invalid. (35)

I find this a significant but troublesome passage. The "if" status of an experience is particularly troubling, marking uncertainty in the form of a "whether." "If" here is a phenomenological condition – closely related, I think, to that epistemological modality of uncertainty that Keats called "negative capability." How do you experience not experiencing? This can also get close to an elaborated practice of vicariousness, in particular of proxy experience by way of identification with the experiences of selected others, family in particular. Time includes what hasn't happened: the missing events also need their chronology.

The passage is one of many aphoristic wisdoms that double as commentaries on the purpose and method of *Implexures*, and that consequently provide an immediate means of testing the proposition from the surrounding text. The poet has just listed a sequence of strong visual memories: "The sunrise in Naxos, the sunsets in Mexico . . . the rainbows at Bolton Abbey." Memory and writing of memory can bring these together into a simultaneous set, into a single (sequenced) sentence. Chronology is usually taken to imply a listing of events in the order in which they occurred. But *when* is not the same as putting into line, as the book's opening epigraph makes clear. As demonstrated, memory can jump between *whens*, absorbing them into the *now* of its own inescapable present tense. *Implexures* is full of *time writing*, and of deliberately writing across time; is much taken with different methods for this task. *Implexures* indeed is in large measure a *chronology*, a discourse of and on time.

The passage quoted above assumes that chronology and a relation of individual and collective can be spoken of in the same breath, though not with the same article. It is "*the* individual" and "*a* collective," and there is an easy slide from "collective" to "family," though this time it is "*the* family."

Plurals in English grammar are imprecise, perhaps particularly in relation to personal pronouns. The death of "us." When "we" experience. I suspect that language historians of the future will be able to date – to chronologize – such usages, perhaps as "humanist first-person plural." And what of this other collective singular, "the family"? Is this the generic term that anthropologists use? Or is it the particular family whose biography is here being written, which is being narrated *as family*? It is certainly not, in this context, the ideological term often invoked in the phrase "family values." Is a family not a kind of singularity? Isn't a genealogy that is narrated from within the network of genetic affiliations it narrates always a singular perspective? These are *my* people? Blood is thicker than water.

Implexures is a writing of many lives, but not *any* lives. Most of the many are *already* in formation under a collective term, await-ing as it were a confirmatory writing. Some have even prepared that writing with a writing of their own. But it is a writing that does not want to claim any singularity of perspective, nor know-ingly to adopt the modes that might lead that way. Its chronology is a mixing of time. It is a polybiography in the sense that it con-tains many writings of a life or of lives, whoever provides them.

e.

Let me try a wavering distinction and pretend that there isn't a huge weight of past philosophy pressing up against it.

There is a writing driven by and towards an ontology, a dis-course on *being*. This writing wants to push around in being, in status, in posture – either the being of the implied utterer or of the objectified world which authenticates this same being as co-present and as witness. As I understand it, this kind of writing wants to be at once singular and universal. Ontological *method* (a writing is always a method, viewable also perhaps as genre) universalizes the singular, the particular. Typographically this can be represented as an oscillation between *being* and *Being*.

Any ontology that relies on writing is also, pragmatically, an utterance working in *interpersonal* modalities. It addresses some-one or knows that someone is overhearing. To mix grammar in there, there is no ontology without *person*, and because person is a grammatical set there is no person without the *other* persons of grammar.

Any genealogy that is also in part autobiographical is both an inquiry into and an act of specific ontology: this is who *I* am and this is how I know. It is I who speaks thus, with all these others lined up behind and around me, including all those others who are part of the temporal ensemble of my I-through-time and of those various sets to whom I can belong as "we."

And then – and here is a first distinction – there is a writing that knowingly operates in nets and modes of knowledge. It might well do so in a spirit of disputation, want not only to push statements and ideas around, but also to disturb vectors of knowledge, very much including those that are linguistic. There is an extreme form of this position in writing, and one with which I'd connect Karen Mac Cormack: any act of writing, even the purportedly ontological, intervenes in knowledge and finds its way into available patterns of intersubjectivity.[3] Within this position, for example, syntax is always also argument, at the levels of both grammar and discourse. The argument may well be *against* ontology, against any predication that seems to be sourced only in deictic utterance.

In two earlier Mac Cormack texts – *Fit to Print* (with Alan Halsey) and *At Issue* – the argument or program has been fully specified. On the back cover of *Fit to Print*, there is this:

Structured on patterns of meaning that foreground linguistic materiality, these poems negotiate the newspaper format to enact a fusion of mass culture with an innovative writing practice.

The author's foreword to *At Issue* includes this:

In *AT ISSUE* I examine the format and contents of the magazine instead of those of the newspaper, as Alan Halsey and I did in our collaboration *FIT TO PRINT*.

A poem is claimed back as a mode of expository writing. It can take the form of an "examination." Inevitably these specifications can act as rubrics (i.e., "directions for . . . conduct," *OED*) for readings of the body text. And an academic apparatus of bibliographies, lists of sources and references, reinforces this sense of cross-genre.[4]

I leave only slightly to one side an additional modal and generic question, that of *story*: knowledge modalities that rely on narrated networks of textual *persons* all *doing* things and having them *happen*. Here is Cole Swensen again, this time from an interview:

– but the "I" in a poem can only say: it's the third person that can "do" in a poem. I find that an interesting dichotomy: as soon as we get the first person in literature, we're reduced to speech, and in turn, speech becomes action, as in J. L. Austin's performative language. The spoken word is always an act. A primary act.

How the first person singular has troubled writing! First the first person can only "say" and not "do" and then it turns out that all saying is doing after all. What are these different kinds of acts? Once a *person* has got into a poem it may not make much difference whether it's first or third. There is, for a start, the difference between the "I" who speaks through that pronoun and the one who narrates the actions of herself as "I."[5]

What does a genealogy "do"? Is "we" both an augmentation of "I" and a way past it?

f.

I am going to attempt an extreme summary of the way the argument immediately above can apply to Karen Mac Cormack's writing.

The genealogical project of *Implexures* is at once ontological, epistemological and narratorial (being, knowing and storytelling). This folding together is the task of any genealogy that is *told* from within. Karen Mac Cormack is evidently conscious of recent proscriptions, within certain writing environments, against their convergence. The texts that are being "examined" are, in a sense, Karen Mac Cormack's "own." This could have produced a reneging on or a disavowal of the *methods* of her preceding books and I'd be surprised if some readers don't see it this way. As I see it, she knows and wants the difficulties. For one thing, I am suggesting that the book represents her own renegotiation with first-person pronouns (singular and plural), on terms. For another, she opens her units of composition up well beyond the sentences and lineation that had set her earlier compositional constraints.

g.

Cecil Rhodes' British South Africa Company secured, as part of its charter, mineral rights in the territory that was to become Zambia. Until 1924 this charter also required the company to provide administration. In 1924 this responsibility passed to the Colonial Office of the United Kingdom.

I was born in Zambia because my father was a "colonial servant." At first it was a job and then it was as though he had been called. In his case, and those of many of his friends, this did not mean that the call of Home ever quieted. The place he called Home was somewhere unknown to me. It turned out later that there was no specific locale for this Home. It was geographically dispersed across counties and I don't think was ever so simple as being nameable as a "country" (England-Scotland). Country, yes. A country, no. Cities were never part of the poetics of Home as I absorbed them. Nor are they a strong part of the poetics of *Implexures*.[6]

I was born away from Home. This just happens to be I.

Pick a childhood to look at. This doesn't have to be your own, but if it is, the strangeness of certain events may shift unexpectedly. The more central regions are established before questions reach those limits. (10)

And then there is a difference between being at home nowhere and of being sort of at home anywhere (or at least where English is spoken or where an English-speaking traveller or settler is expected).

h.

No home but in and through Language. The domestic place is marked off ahead with a personal pronoun, sets of interpersonal pronouns. Refusing these is to refuse to be at home in language in the very act of using it as refuse. Of course, languages are always leaving home, sometimes for good. It is that mode of language that is designed to operate away from home – what Basil Bernstein called the "elaborated code" – that can fold an expansionist exile back into all its routine operations.

The Tongue Moves Talk, Fit to Print, At Issue – poems made from the re-assembly of the already uttered, mostly of the already written, of the already re-assembled. *Someone* makes things out of words and because they are words this is already a kind of speaking. Even where procedures are strictly aleatoric there will even so be found the thrower of the dice, the deviser or acceptor of the procedures of chance. And these throws will be motivated, even if they are motivated to be unmotivated. Writing through. The author's name on the cover. Suppressing the *I* may just be not *saying* it (like taboos against naming God that are the opposite of denial).

So, three takes, which do not exclude each other.

i) At any one time, something moves a tongue or a hand to talk or write, or an already moving tongue or hand moves further talk or writing. Even if nothing *comes out*, the movement towards it is there, and to the extent that any such movement is discernible, *something comes out*. There is a potential for utterance from a marked place, a perturbation at a precise point and moment in the fields of language. This perturbation marks a witnessable place of desire, even if not yet either of speech or writing. Those are your lips that move, or that don't quite move. Those are your hands. Sometimes a holding back may be motivated by a counter-desire, the desire to avoid the double collusion of *I*. What happens *if* I don't speak? Is this experience of "if" not itself a kind of negative utterance, a speaking not-speaking?

This may be a motif (and motive?) in *Implexures*.

ii) The other take. Put it extremely: Language is a landfill site of the already spoken, the already written.

Perhaps "English" is on the way to being co-terminous with global late-capitalism.[7] Through what feats of trickster-ism can any speaker of English step out of this relentless drift?

iii) And at any one time, a third: neither the about-to-speak, the would-speak, nor the toxic detritus of the already expended. But the present participle, the in-use, engaged, occupied. This is not a difference between speech and writing that can fuel wars between their exponents, as between owls and nightingales, leaves and flowers. This is being caught up in the movements of the tongue moving talk, in the eddies and swirls of situated inter-desires. Where a tongue (hand) is moved, there is a social presence, a social performance, a motivated disturbance towards, within, or out of, language.

What is it to disturb the already uttered so as to disturb also this sense of social performance: to suppress the voiced or even implied *I*, to break up any syntax contaminated by its issue from a desiring (and perhaps intrusively dangerous?) mouth? To voice is to encourage (heart) breath rhythmically to disturb your larynx. This is not "the" body. It is yours.

i.

In the 14th century the English language replaced French "at the tables of the aristocracy." (66)

No doubt this has something to do with the fact that those same aristocrats had lost their Normandy estates and, by that, their privileged channel-crossing and identification with an over-there.

To what century will be ascribed the change that split "Made in English" off from "Made in England"?[8]

j.

In the forty-seven pages of poetic text of *The Tongue Moves Talk*, the following are the only instances of "I" or "me."

i) The title of the first poem is "I'm Big On Ladders" (11). This feels like citation rather than autobiography.

ii) In "Do You Know Who Your Employer Is?" (19), "(I would refer all terms to 'grafting.')" appears in brackets.

iii) In the double-columned piece "At Issue II" (37), just below the epigraph and, like the epigraph, in italics:

he this
        i that

Neither the "he" nor the lowercase "i" is placed in relation to a name.

iv) Included in the long prose periods of "At Issue III" (39) is: "furniture I can ride and left profile."

v) In "Deca," there are two instances: "I ran for the response was thrown so received where ushered ending up to leave" and "I examine 'to continue' a semblance of the other side all of unhinged deserves better" (43).

That's it.

Of course this is a very crude survey. It could be extended to take in also the uses of "you," of "we," and even the implied person of all the imperatives, a mood that may often be prominent where "I"s are being suppressed. Or even the exhalation of breath that forms an "ah" and in doing so marks the emotive place of utterance (13).

The examples in (iv) and (v) above are embedded in a syntax that is fairly typical of the books that precede *Implexures*. Pseudo-sentences seem to be composed out of existing phrases whose severance from prior sentences leaves jagged edges in their new syntactical home. For example, are there source sentences for "furniture I can ride and left profile"? And if so are there two or are there three?

Statements and predications are by no means fully suppressed even if the place (and motivated agency) of utterance is disguised. Who states? Who predicates? And then there are those intriguing devices of person avoidance, of avoiding attribution of knowledge: "it is," "there is" (see perhaps especially "Untitled," *TTMT* 20).

k.

The first striking instance of the first-person pronoun in the book of *Implexures* is in the dedication, that place where a text can become a gift, a consecration, an offering:

> *This ongoing text is dedicated with love*
> *to those (living and deceased) who form*
> *my community, creative and personal.*

Initially the dedicator avoids first person through a passive voice that neutralizes or abstracts agency. This abstraction ("is dedicated" rather than "I dedicate") may well underwrite a *performance* of dedication through its invocation of a beyond-personal. The third line, though, homes in on person exactly where singular and plural are expected to commingle: "my community." Here a "community" is in part a willed effect of textual activity, a made home, a putting into relationship, through text, of nameable persons, of pro-nameable persons. This is the other side, perhaps, of a deliberate distancing, through devices of linguistic disturbance, from the implied (the implicated) communality of an apparently common tongue.

l.

a
word
in
the
ear
of
another
word's
order

(*AI*, 11)

m.

The place names in *Implexures* do not pull unarchived memory back the way that they do, say, in Erin Mouré's earlier books.[9] Mouré sings a memory tune that is in her head. It is never over. The narrative will always have its commentary, whose form of words might itself become a memory, ripe itself for commentary and so on. Memory is unavoidable repetition. Commentary can be both testimony to this unavoidability and a means to escape it. In Mouré the folds are wrappings, can always be wrapped further or unwrapped. In Mouré memory may be recursive because Home is a present tense and a migrant skin – or a present tense that also surveys the other tenses. Memory is an interior, like Alberta, like that collectivity of organs that is a body felt as a within. And there are those passages and openings out and in, especially lips (labia). It is the way the *I* forms between the lips of the mouth. Out it comes, whatever its ironical turnings back and away.

In *Implexures* memory is a research project, an archive ("a referral to birth") of connected pasts and others.

To absorb a history of family through the centuries requires a forebear's attention to facts and no fear of paper. (10)

Or even to have (find) forebears whose lives will be archived, who expect to live in the fore-life of an archive, who are not feared by paper; whose houses have (had) libraries.

n.

I write this in the southwest of England (in Devon, a proper name that features in *Implexures*), at the rural edge of a country that gives its name to this language of expansion, drift, commerce, globalized fantasies, reorientations and explanations; and I read across gender, an ocean and political borders, but still I don't expect to have to translate. There may be all kinds of estrangement *within* this language position. There is certainly anger *without*. If the source is French, someone (Fiona Strachan, Barbara Godard, Marlene Wildman, Caroline Bergvall?) will have de-estranged aspects of the language for me (perhaps you could say that the better they have done it, the more effectively they move me between different modes of estrangement). In the language of Microsoft and the White House I pretend to attend to *cidadáns* of elsewhere.

What do I know about Canada? How does my ignorance of English-speaking Canada differ from my ignorance of French-speaking Canada?

I know that English is a powerful vehicle of privileged nomadism through time and place, and that it is an instrument of person, time and relation. Wasn't it an English-speaking Canadian man who coined the term "global village"? Where English is a first language there will still be entanglements of European genealogy (history read back from a genetic subject). Where English is an "official" language without being everyone's first language there will be other entanglements. As a reader I can be folded into the writing in English of a Canadian poet, can find myself implicated there. At the same time I am cautious. I read across gender, across borders, across an ocean, whose crossings and recrossings were, and still are, motivated, criss-crossed with waveforms that very much include the textual.

Where an instability between languages is within a text, and cannot, by virtue of its own internal linguistic textual crossings and recrossings, be put in the hands of a "translator," then I am reminded of the uncertainty of my place as reader, of my insecure rights to and within the elaborated code of an ideological world traveller.[10]

o.

In *Implexures* it is not only words and phrases that are folded into
each other; it is also those modes of discourse I have talked about
above. This may be why Karen Mac Cormack needs a prose line in
these "poems." There is a strong sense of cohering principles – the
narrative of genealogy and an enveloping *argument*.

I shall itemize nine obvious folds, though there are others, I am
sure, including that of a commentary that seems to oversee all the
folds and to produce a string of gnomic wisdoms. I do not include
in what follows the two exceptional sections: section 11 ("on reading
An Inland Ferry"), whose mode seems to be that of the "writing
through" familiar from some of Mac Cormack's earlier books; and
section 14, the "Developmental Dictionary" (lexical explanations
with the *explananda* held back until later).

i) Epigraphs. There is at least one epigraph at the head of all
except two of the numbered sections. These are either from
well known authorities (for example, Aphra Behn, Deleuze
and Guattari), pointing a forceful and suggestive interpreta-
tive line into the body text; or they are from figures who are
themselves part of the topic and texture of the body text (for
example, Susan Hicks Beach, Margaret Mac Cormack).

ii) A sequence of excerpts from letters or postcards (or a diary?
but I think these were *addressed*) represented in italics, dated
and placed, all from between 1974 and 1980. These are chatty,
excitable, belong to their time, and are always from an elsewhere (Castries, Saint Lucia, Jan, Feb 74; Naxos, Greece, May
76; Carrara, Italy, 77, 78, 79, 80; Athens, Greece, June 77;
San Francisco, USA, 75).[11]

iii) A variant on these, in the form of reminiscences from the
implied present of the writing, such for example as the whole
of section 15, a first-person anecdote that leads to the one-
line moral: "As for a blind date, well, that's how I met *I*" (60).

iv) A genealogical set of folds derived it seems both from paper
(and web, perhaps?) research and from visits and journeyings.
The family names that recur include Christian, Gregorie,
Curwen, Hicks Beach, Ward Thomas, Mac Cormack.

v) Aphoristic disquisitions (if this is not a contradiction in terms) on memory, time, archiving, journeyings, maps as mnemonics and scores (I am treating this one as including the little random chunks of "history" – not obviously related to the family chronicles – that probably represent another mode, related to the lexical enquiry, below (vii)). These can read like excerpts from a writer's – and/or reader's – notebook.

vi) Aphoristic disquisitions on grammatical and ontological person, and the extent to which a person is ever separable from a collective, dispersed across time and place.

vii) Glosses on a history of gendered nouns, drawing particularly, it would seem, on Jane Mills.

viii) Line drawings – just a few of these, including two scenes (Greece, Italy?) on the title page; the diagrammatic drawing of a fan; and two seed-like objects appearing just below the expression of a wish to suspend the use of lines.

ix) Black and white photographs (four, all except one given a whole page). One of them also appears on the cover. These aren't captioned but the copyright page connects them with the italicized correspondence from Carrara, thereby authenticating that address as *not fabricated*, and by extension also the others.

p.

This polybiography is also polymodal. If this is a problem, as DuBose thought it might be, it is obviously one relished by Karen Mac Cormack.

q.

The conventions of western genealogy, especially in its written modes, have been an important part of the superstructure of patrilinealism: male-line succession as the immortal extension of individual mortal, an I in a line of "I"s, constituting a "We" under the banner of family name. These conventions are in stark contrast with the lesbian countermove of Monique Wittig and Sande Zeig cited as an epigraph by Nicole Brossard in *Lovhers*: "Since the day when the lesbian people renounced the idea that it is absolutely necessary to die, no one has" (30).

I assume that all patrilineal cultures demand a privatization of biological acts of conception only to project on to the concealing screen repeated tales, texts, images and regalia of succession. Men whose stories assume succession have no visible pregnancy of their own to demonstrate incontestable consanguinity.

I know very little indeed about my mother's mother.

Karen Mac Cormack eschews diagrams of succession or any neat linear narratorial gathering. She wishes to suspend "the notion of lines, straight or otherwise" (67).[12] Her image is a fan, not a branch diagram (13). This is not a metaphor to be taken, I would say, too strictly. All the folds of a fan are joined both in folded sequence and also at their point of convergence. She does not provide the equivalent of these joins, this convergence. Her textual structure is nothing so mechanistic as this. Often the sources are no more than pronouns in her text and the connections are assumed rather than given. I find the way that the word "fold" as used in geology or in cooking more descriptive of her procedures.

r.

Let me read my way into section two, as an example of texture.

The section's title is the number, given as a word. Then, after a double space, there is an alternative heading: "historical letters 2," with the number given as a figure. This suggests that there will be two ways of counting these sections, that the two counts should be kept separate but that counting counts.

Immediately under this subheading, there are two epigraphs, italicized: "*Desire knows no time but the present. –* Aphra Behn"; and "*The present is always insatiable because it never exists. –* Charles Bernstein." Neither of these two authors is listed as a "source" in the section at the back bearing that heading. These two epigraphs, taken together, can be read in the form of a chiasmus: desire and insatiability forming one diagonal, the other the repetition of "the present." The first epigraph posits a present tense (and perhaps a presence) charged by desire; the other, a present tense doomed to attempt to consume itself into an existence that will never arrive *as present.* A theme has been declared: a desire for a present that tantalizes that very desire. These texts have been *found*, with a purpose. They may have been attracted there by a prior "meaning"; they may attract a meaning to come ("A promotion to meaning enlists words" [11]).

Let me call "meaning," for a moment, and in this context, nothing other than an insatiable desire for sense.

Next there is a three-line "paragraph" in the place where the introduction would be:

Within the orbit, a pick, a path and much tracasserie. At first, entangled leads to more so notches ride the space before the eyes. Enliven the odds. Reduce the party and its funds. Distinguish between examples.

The first (elliptical) sentence is perhaps a scene, an image. The definiteness of the definite article is rendered indefinite through lack of contextual detail. I don't know which "orbit" is meant here. The best claimant for "the" is perhaps the orbit of the earth. I don't think so. Something comes round. An orbit is not a straight line. And within "its" circle are a pick, a path and much bustling around. "Pick" next to "path" sounds like choosing, or the path might be being dug; but in either case why rush around? In the next sentence there is narrative: something happens that is to do with "entanglement." Then three phrases in a row, driven by imperatives, urgent, sensible in tone, but quite without a context.

Those epigraphs about desire are still there in my reading. *Entangled leads to more. Enliven. Clarify.* These sentences are folded into paragraphs in ways that disturb the status of each – of sentence, of paragraph.

Then there is a paragraph about having pneumonia in Mexico. This one seems to mediate a prior description ("Many descriptions of landscapes, city and town squares . . ."). This is a writing that is a reading – one from which deductions can be drawn, for the paragraph ends quite unexpectedly (at this stage anyway) with a wisdom: "Maps augment possibilities, shift decisions, and co-exist with timetables' fascination." This is as thematic as the epigraphs.

The final paragraph I shall comment upon is the one that leads up to the drawing of the fan.

For a Victorian not prudish on the page, having made mention, she remained discreet, disagreeing (it would seem) with a forebear's tenet that "few of one's secrets are worth keeping to oneself." Falling portraits woke her in the night but possibility of an intruding danger occurred only after her facts were re-positioned.

That we might view ourselves across the century in anything other than static form, introduce a working draft to clearer scrutiny, steal in the pen to library's likeness engrave . . . this is not a conversation nor a theme, it is a letter, another fold in a fan where the writer in this decade sees the angled history of a past decade's correspondent snapped shut.

As reader, I'll have to pick (up) – or not – who this *she* is, find a desire path through my reading. This will already be insatiable. I can't stop anyone in mid-flow to ask because this is writing. After my reading has orbited back through the whole book to this section I think I know. This is, in any case, writing about a writer. The previous paragraph was, I believe, an example of a writer folding her own earlier writings back in to a "present" text. In this case she folds in her readings of the writings of – almost certainly – a "forebear." I take the "repositioning of facts" to be what writers can do – in this case, write themselves into awareness of danger.

After the ellipsis there is an example, to be found throughout the book, of a folding in of reflection on the book's own methods. Perhaps this has already occurred with the wisdom about maps.

Enliven the odds. Distinguish between examples.

s.

28 August 2004

Dear Karen,

Ten months after acquiring *Implexures* (and having it inscribed) in Conway Hall in London, I have been reading it with care and real interest, not least because it is doing what I have been trying to work out how to do – that is, set in play, into an always refreshable presentness of a text, different pasts, including acts spread by memory of journeyings and archival record, to produce the charged pseudo-memory of genealogy and geographical reach.

I can see why two of the sections – the ones set out in a lineation that says "poetry" – are not called "historical letters," but not what the difference is between those others that are and those that aren't.

But the main impulse for this email is the discovery of another intersection between our own histories and genealogies (I mean in addition to being born in the same country while our parents were away from "home"; and in addition to the fact that we bump into each other – and each other's texts, perhaps – at events connected with poetry).

So, here is the intersection. A genealogical tic started up every time I read the name Christian. The more I came across it the more I thought I needed to check my own paternal family connections. This is what I found. My great-great-aunt, Frances Emily Hall, married, on 5th May 1855, Alfred Christian of Malta. Alfred was the son of Samuel Christian of Malta (banker) and Susanne Gregorie.

I assume that Alfred was "of Malta" on account of his father's banking activities. He certainly continued to play a part in the life of the Isle of Man.[13]

. . .

t.

My own genealogy converges with the one woven through *Implexures*, at the time and place of another convergence: of banking, naval activity, military/colonial administration, all related instruments of an act of colonization that belonged to European power conflicts of the late eighteenth and early nineteenth century.[14] The lure of Malta had nothing to do with settlement; everything to do with strategic control. I suspect that the nineteenth-century banks of Malta were from the start more than purely local facilities.

English is still an "official" language of Malta, along with Maltese.

These are troublesome notions of a collective. "Families" play out their parts, according to their "place," in the scripts of economic and political history, which do have their chronologies, of sorts.

Reduce the party and its funds.

u.

The epigraph to "At the Front," the final poem in *The Tongue Moves Talk*, is from Emmanuel Levinas and reads:

The chosen home is the very opposite of a root.

I finish my own reading by angling back into the text of *Implexures* another from the same author:

The I always has one responsibility more than all the others.

Notes

1. Embassy of Ireland, "Gaeilge," http://www.irelandemb.org/gaeilge.html.

2. I can't resist the etymologies of the two words, in this context. An "event" is something that comes out (*e* + *venire*) – I would add – anyway. It so happens. "Experience" is closely related both to "experiment" and to "peril." Its Latin verb source (*experiri*) can be translated as, "to try, to put to the test." For those at peril of the events that constitute their lives, in memory. I am grateful to both Paul Zeal and the *OED* for these etymologies.

3. "imagine / being / and not / knowing" – Tom Raworth, "The Conscience of a Conservative" (*Collected Poems,* 162).

4. Karen Mac Cormack is not alone among Canadian writers in her inclusion of a book list. Erin Mouré's Acknowledgment at the back of *O Cidadán* starts with this comment: "This book is a reading practice in a community of others. References abbreviated in the text and critical to the book's conception and movement, expand as follows: . . ." (141).

5. There are many games with this word in *Implexures.* I have myself tried out my thoughts on personal pronouns in a piece called "Missing persons: personal pronouns in performance writing" (Grammar for Performance Writers 3) in *Performance Research* 3, no. 1 (1998): 87–90.

6. I take city (Montreal, Toronto, Vancouver) to be implicit in the poetics of Nicole Brossard, Erin Mouré, Lisa Robertson . . .

7. "Half of all business deals are conducted in English. Two thirds of all scientific papers are written in English. Over 70% of all post/mail is written and addressed in English. Most international tourism, aviation and diplomacy is conducted in English" (Kryss Katsiavriades, http://www.krysstal.com/english.html).

8. I have just received from Stuart Mills a small white square folded card whose cover consists of four lines of capitalized (and squared off) red and blue text: "MADE IN / ENGLISH / MADE IN / ENGLISH" (Belper, U.K.: Aggie Weston, 2004).

9. For example, *WSW (West South West)* (Montreal: Véhicule Press, 1989) or *Sheepish Beauty, Civilian Love* (Montreal: Véhicule Press, 1992).

10. For example, Erin Mouré's *O Cidadán* (2002) and Caroline Bergvall's *Goan Atom: 1. jets-poupee* (Cambridge: rem press, 1999).

11. Elsewhere to where, though? See section c., above.

12. There is a wonderful ambiguity produced for me by that word "suspend"; if a line is suspended the chances are that it will straighten! It depends what it's made of.

13. From an email from John Hall to Karen Mac Cormack. "Frances Emily" has been corrected from "Emily Frances." Genealogical evidence indicates that my great great aunt married Karen Mac Cormack's great great great uncle. I have no idea how many people I could claim retrospectively as my "great great aunt." I know of Frances Emily only because in the archives available to me

the (patri-) line has not been suspended. Frances's sister, Eliza Jane, married a Chamberlain. One son was Basil Hall Chamberlain, a Japonologist credited with bringing haiku to the attention of the English-speaking world. Another was Houston Chamberlain, who left the English language behind him to become German and to develop theories of race that were to win him the admiration of Adolf Hitler.

14. "The British colonisation period began in 1800. It is thereafter that Maltese banking history really starts in a pure institutional sense" ("The Banking History of Malta," http://www.bankinghistory.de/Bulletin/ EABH-web/www%201-2001/New%20Research%20-%20John%20A.%20 Consiglio.htm). This notion of instrumentality works in both directions. Colonization was an "instrument" that aided military activity and banking and was, most certainly, a method of and framework for administration.

Works Cited

Brossard, Nicole. *Lovhers.* Trans. Barbara Godard. Montreal: Guernica Editions, 1987.

DuBose, Terry J. "Polybiography of Diagnostic Medical Sonography." http:// www.obgyn.net/us/us.asp?page=/us/feature/polybiography.

Mac Cormack, Karen. *At Issue.* Toronto: Coach House Books, 2001. (Cited as *AI.*)

——. *Implexures.* Sheffield, U.K.: West House Books; Tucson, AZ: Chax Press, 2003. (Cited as *I.*)

——. *The Tongue Moves Talk.* Sheffield, U.K.: West House Books; Tucson, AZ: Chax Press, 1997. (Cited as *TTMT.*)

—— and Alan Halsey. *Fit to Print.* Sheffield, U.K.: West House Books; Toronto: Coach House Books, 1998.

Mouré, Erin. *O Cidadán.* Toronto: House of Anansi, 2002.

Raworth, Tom. *Collected Poems.* Manchester: Carcanet, 2003.

Swenson, Cole. "Interview with Cole Swenson." By Jon Thompson. *Free Verse* 5 (Winter 2003). http://english.chass.ncsu.edu/freeverse/Archives/Winter _2003/interviews/C_Swensen.html.

Afterword

A reader's first point of contact with a body of writing remains important long after they've developed in other directions. In the early 1990s, while doing an M.A. at the University of Toronto, I stumbled upon British avant-garde poetry via Donald Davie's writings on Roy Fisher and J. H. Prynne. Next came American Language Poetry, courtesy of Marjorie Perloff's *Radical Artifice*. Although I was born and educated in Canada, my discovery of the experimental poetry of this country came some time after I'd started to parse those initial entry-points. My introduction came in the form of an elegant, rather mysterious purple journal on the racks of a Halifax newsstand: issue 12 of *Raddle Moon* – a strange find indeed, nestled among journals like *Descant* and *Fiddlehead*. The magazine's balance between the "local" (Vancouver; Canada; the English language; poetry) and a wider, internationalist, cross-arts perspective was exemplary within a poetry culture often closely tied to cultural nationalism – in part because of the agendas of public arts-funding agencies in Canada. When I began *The Gig* in 1998, *Raddle Moon* was a constant reference-point – and often a useful heads-up about authors worth seeking out for submissions.

Raddle Moon and other West Coast magazines like *Writing* (and later *W*) were important among other things for drawing attention to a wide range of women's experimental poetries in Canada, and this also proved one important thread in the weave of *The Gig*. *The Gig*'s back-pages included a wide range of work by Canadian women writers: glass-shard lyrics by Catriona Strang and Deanna Ferguson, Lise Downe's prismatic riddling, the haunting aporias of Lissa Wolsak's *pen chants*, Lisa Robertson's *The Weather* with its alphabetized, antiphonal text-blocks, extracts from a. rawlings' *wide slumber for lepidopterists* (surely a text whose origins lie in a delirious typographical confusion of entomology and etymology?), Erin Mouré's mindbending workings from Chus Pato, Christine Stewart's textual forestry, rare glimpses of Susan Clark's self-consuming artefacts, Karen Mac Cormack's startling turn (with *Implexures*) from taut postmodern lyric to polybiographical collage. . . . But *The Gig* is primarily a poetry magazine, and I felt that these authors' work, and the interconnections between them, deserved to be explored more carefully through a collection of critical essays, especially since, while a few of these authors have been widely read and written about, many others have received scant critical attention to date. This book attempts to serve as an introduction to the work of these writers, or (in the case of the more familiar names) give a fresh slant on their work; the perspective is deliberately internationalist, drawing on the many readers these poets have found both inside and outside Canada.

As an account of women's experimental poetries in Canada, this book is inevitably a very partial one. (I toyed with adding extra qualifications and semantic restrictions in its subtitle, but it began to seem impossibly unwieldy.) It seemed, in any case, more valuable to provide in-depth accounts of a smaller number of authors than to try to include everyone who might deserve mention. For the most part *Antiphonies* deals with authors who emerged in the 1980s and 1990s, rather than an earlier generation of writers such as Sharon Thesen, Daphne Marlatt, and Maxine Gadd; it also largely omits authors primarily identified with performance poetry or visual poetry. One omission needs special mention: when this book was being planned, *Verdure* magazine had just published a valuable Nicole Brossard special issue; her work was omitted from this book simply to avoid duplicated effort. Other omissions were simply the result of circumstance, when essays failed to materialize or (in two cases) were turned down. It's worth mentioning that the original plans for this book included pieces on Alice Burdick, Margaret Christakos, Lise Downe, Dorothy Trujillo Lusk, a. rawlings, Christine Stewart and Catriona Strang. There is some representation of most of these authors here, but I had hoped for much more.

This book was many years in the making. For much of that time it was simply "the Canadian women's poetry book" – the title is the result of my coming across the word "antiphonic" in Christine Stewart's piece here at the same time I was reading *The Antiphon,* by one of Karen Mac Cormack's touchstones, Djuna Barnes. I would like to thank all the poets and critics involved in this book for their advice, encouragement, and above all patience as it came together; and also all of The Gig's supporters and subscribers. Aside from the poets and authors themselves, Pete Smith and Aaron Vidaver have been essential West Coast contacts over the years, suggesting poets to read and in many cases mailing me hard-to-obtain small-press publications. Special thanks to whoever it was – I've lost his name now, alas – who visited Halifax in the 1990s and (after our chance encounter over a copy of *A Various Art* at Dalhousie's Killam Library) put a pile of Tsunami publications and issues of *Writing* and *West Coast Line* in my hands. And an enormous thank-you to my parents Tom and Marla for essential, timely financial assistance and moral support: this book wouldn't exist without them.

Lastly, I wish to dedicate this book to the memory of the late Nancy Shaw.

Nate Dorward

CONTRIBUTORS

Tom Beckett is the author of *Unprotected Texts: Selected Poems 1978–2006* (Meritage Press) and the curator of e-x-c-h-a-n-g-e-v-a-l-u-e-s (willtoexchange .blogspot.com). He lives and works in Kent, Ohio.

Caroline Bergvall is a poet and writer based in London. Her latest collection of poetic and performance pieces is *FIG* (Salt, 2005). She has developed audioworks, visual textwork, net-based pieces, live and sited performances, both in Europe and in North America. Her critical work is concerned with mixed-media writings and multilingual poetics. Recipient of an AHRC Fellowship, Southampton University, UK (2007–10).

Gerald L. Bruns is the William P. and Hazel B. White Professor Emeritus at the University of Notre Dame. His most recent book is *On the Anarchy of Poetry and Philosophy: A Guide for the Unruly* (Fordham University Press, 2006).

Edward Byrne works at the Trade Union Research Bureau in Vancouver, and is associated with the Kootenay School of Writing. His poetry includes *Aporia* (Fissure/Point Blank) and *Beautiful Lies* (published serially: *Raddle Moon, Sprang Texts, W*, FORM). Current projects: *Sonnets: Louise Labé*, reviews for *The Rain* (www.rainreview.com).

Stephen Cain teaches modern and avant-garde literature in the School of Arts and Letters, York University. He is the author of four poetry collections (most recently *American Standard/Canada Dry*) and co-author, with Tim Conley, of the *Encyclopedia of Fictional and Fantastic Languages* (Greenwood, 2006).

Susan Clark lives in Vancouver and is on the board of the Kootenay School of Writing. She was editor of *Raddle Moon,* and is the author of *as lit x: the syntax of adoration* (Friends of Runcible Mountain), *Believing in the World: A Reference Work* (Tsunami), and a number of hitherto uncollected/unpublished texts.

Chris Daniels, the godless, anti-capitalist son of language-arts maestro David Daniels, was born in New York in 1956. He dropped out of high school and never went to college. He lives and works in the San Francisco Bay Area. A committed translator, he is working on a gigantic anthology of Lusophone poetry. The first volume of his translations of the poetry of two of Fernando Pessoa's heteronyms has just been published by Shearsman.

Lise Downe's books include *A Velvet Increase of Curiosity* (ECW, 1993), *The Soft Signature* (Coach House, 1997) and *The Soft Signature* (Coach House, 2002). She lives in Toronto.

John Hall's most recent collection is *Couldn't You? (Shearsman). Else Here: Selected Poems* was published by Etruscan Books in 1999, and a "brief textual adventure" called *Apricot Pages* came out from Reality Street in 2005. In recent years he has been busy as an essayist. He has worked for many years at Dartington College of Arts.

Alan Halsey's books include *Marginalien* (Five Seasons, 2005), which collects his poetry, prose and graphics 1988–2004, and *Not Everything Remotely* (Salt, 2006), a selected poems. *Quaoar* (West House 2006) records in poetry and graphics his journey to the twelfth planet with Ralph Hawkins and Kelvin Corcoran. West House has recently published *The Last Hunting of the Lizopard*, a collaboration with David Annwn.

Born in Leduc, Alberta, **Reg Johanson** lives in East Vancouver, B.C. *Courage, My Love* (Line Books, 2006) brings together works that have appeared over the last decade. Critical work has appeared or is forthcoming in *XCP: Cross Cultural Poetics, West Coast Line, The Rain Review, Parser* and recomposition.net. A former member of the Kootenay School of Writing collective and co-director of the Pacific Institute for Language and Literacy Studies, Johanson teaches comp and lit at Capilano College.

Peter Larkin works as Philosophy & Literature librarian at Warwick University. From 1988–2002 he ran Prest Roots Press, with its commitment to affordable fine press work. Among his books are *Enclosures* (1983), *Pastoral Advert* (1989), *Scarce Norm Scarcer Mean* (1992), *Seek Source Bid Sink* (1995), *Three Conformities of Forest* (1997), *Landscape with Figures Afield* (1998) and *Parallels Plantations Apart* (1998) A collection of ten years' work, *Terrain Seed Scarcity*, was published by Salt in 2001. Since then he has published *Slights Agreeing Trees* (2002), a chapbook-threesome from The Gig, *Sprout Near Severing Close, What the Surfaces Enclave of Wang Wei*, and *Rings Resting the Circuit* (2004), and *Leaves of Field* (2006).

Born in Luanshya, Zambia in 1956, **Karen Mac Cormack** is the author of thirteen books of poetry, including *Nothing by Mouth, Quill Driver, Quirks & Quillets, At Issue* and *Vanity Release*. Volume 1 of *Implexures* was published by Chax/West House in 2003 and the full text is forthcoming from the same source in 2008. She is an advisor to the North American Centre for Interdisciplinary Poetics, and an advisory editor to the Centre Interdisciplinaire de Poétique Appliquée, Université de Liège, Belgium. Of dual British/Canadian citizenship, she currently lives in the USA and teaches at SUNY-Buffalo.

Erin Mouré (Erín Moure) is a Montreal poet and translator. Recent books include *O Cidadán, Little Theatres* and *O Cadoiro. Sheep's Vigil by a Fervent Person* (2001) is a translation from the Portuguese of Alberto Caeiro/Fernando Pessoa. She has also translated, with Robert Majzels, Nicole Brossard's *Installations, Museum of Bone and Water* and *Notebook of Roses and Civilization*. Her translation of Galician poet Chus Pato's *Charenton* just came out from Shearsman (UK) and BuschekBooks (Canada). She is currently translating Pato's *Hordas de Escritura* and is working on a new book of poetry, *O Resplandor*, with Elisa Sampedrín, and on a long collaborative work with Oana Avasilichioaei.

Miriam Nichols teaches contemporary literature and theory at the University College of the Fraser Valley. Her recent publications include editions of Robin Blaser's *The Fire: Collected Essays* and *The Holy Forest: Collected Poems*. She is currently writing a book about the New American poetry.

Peter O'Leary lives in Berwyn, Illinois. His most recent book is *Depth Theology* (University of Georgia); as Ronald Johnson's literary executor, he recently reissued *Radi os* (Flood Editions). He teaches at the School of the Art Institute of Chicago.

a.rawlings is a poet and multidisciplinary artist who lives in Toronto. Her first book, *Wide slumber for lepidopterists* (Coach House, 2006), was featured in the *Globe & Mail*'s top 100 books of 2006 and received an Alcuin Award for Design; it was translated from page to stage for Harbourfront Centre's *Hatch: Emerging Performance Projects in Toronto*. angela co-edited *Shift & Switch: New Canadian Poetry* (Mercury, 2005) with derek beaulieu and Jason Christie.

Susan M. Schultz's books of poetry include *And Then Something Happened* (Salt, 2004) and *Memory Cards & Adoption Papers* (Potes & Poets, 2001). Her book of essays, *A Poetics of Impasse in Modern and Contemporary American Poetry*, was published in 2005 by the University of Alabama Press. She edited *The Tribe of John: Ashbery and Contemporary Poetry* for Alabama in 1995. She teaches English at the University of Hawai'i-Manoa, and edits Tinfish Press out of her home in Kane'ohe on the island of O'ahu.

The poet and art critic **Nancy Shaw** is the author of *Scoptocratic* (ECW, 1993) and co-author with Catriona Strang of *Busted* (Coach House, 2001) and *Cold Trip* (Nomados, 2006). She passed away in April 2007, after several years' battle with cancer.

Pete Smith is a retired psychiatric nurse; born in England, he has lived in British Columbia since 1974. He writes: "The 'Out-Takes' are offered in the spirit of DF's contributions to poetics symposia in *Boundary 2* (26:1) & *Oblek* 12, i.e. obliquely & in not-prose. Many voices: no flags – tho' the last line is her imagined response to my piece. PS has chapbooks etc. with Wild Honey Press, Poetical Histories, & above/ground, & longish sequences on-line at *Great Works* & *Alterran Poetry Assemblage*."

Christine Anne Stewart is from Vancouver and currently writes, teaches and researches experimental poetry and poetics in the English and Film Department at the University of Alberta. Selected publications: *Pessoa's July: or the months of astonishments* (Nomados, 2006); *From Taxonomy* (West House, 2003); *Daddy Clean Head* (Lumpe Presse, 2000); "We Lunch Nevertheless Among Reinvention" (*Chicago Review* 51:4/52:1, Spring 2006).

Catriona Strang lives in Vancouver and homeschools her two children. She collaborated with the late Nancy Shaw for over ten years. Their last book, *Light Sweet Crude*, is forthcoming from Line Books.

Lissa Wolsak is a native of California but has lived for decades in Vancouver, B.C., where she works as a goldsmith and energy field therapist. She has authored *The Garcia Family Co-Mercy; An Heuristic Prolusion; Pen Chants or nth or 12 spirit-like impermanences;* certain ongoing ana of *A Defence of Being;* and *THRALL. Squeezed Light: Collected Works* is forthcoming from Station Hill and *Of Beings Alone* from Tinfish.

INDEX